In Green

LOUIS D. HALL

In
Green

Two Horses,
Two Strangers,
a Journey to the
End of the Land

DUCKWORTH

First published in the United Kingdom by Duckworth in 2025

Duckworth, an imprint of Duckworth Books Ltd
1 Golden Court, Richmond, TW9 1EU, United Kingdom
www.duckworthbooks.co.uk

© Louis D. Hall 2025
Diary entries © Kiki Ho 2025
Illustrations © Molly Beardall 2025
Map © Liam Roberts 2025

All rights reserved. No part of this publication may be reproduced, stored in a retrieval system, or transmitted, in any form or by any means electronic, mechanical, photocopying, recording or otherwise, without the prior permission of the publisher.

The right of Louis D. Hall to be identified as the Author of this Work has been asserted by him in accordance with the Copyright, Designs and Patents Act 1988.

A catalogue record for this book is available from the British Library

Typeset by PDQ Media

The authorised representative in the EEA is Easy Access System Europe, Mustamäe tee 50, 10621 Tallinn, Estonia.

Printed and bound in Great Britain by CPI Books

1 3 5 7 9 10 8 6 4 2

Hardback ISBN: 9781914613838
eISBN: 9781914613845

For Leo, Victoria and Siu

Contents

Map	viii
Author's Note	xi
Introduction	1
I Into the Mouth of the Wolf	7
II Death of the Dorado	107
III The Dark Sun	187
IV This House of Us	261
Afterword	287
Acknowledgements	290

The Route

- Cutón
- Fazai
- La Espina
- Ossès
- Lesaka
- Lannemezan
- Cape Finisterre
- Negreira
- Zestoa
- Larrun
- Louvie-Juzon

PYRENEES

FRANCE

SPAIN

E
LIGURIAN ALPS
Forte
Ceperana
APENNINES
les
Giovo Ligure
La Brigue
Lucignano
Siena
Trigance
ITALY
Torre del Greco

'When life itself seems lunatic, who knows where madness lies? Perhaps to be too practical is madness. To surrender dreams – this may be madness. Too much sanity may be madness – and maddest of all: to see life as it is, and not as it should be!'

from Don Quixote *by Miguel de Cervantes*

Author's Note

For tuition on how to prepare for a 2,000-mile journey by horse, do not use this book as your guide. I didn't know what I was doing. I still don't. See this text more as written proof that it can be done, and that to do so is utterly exhausting and consistently dangerous. Reason will not prevail.

For those interested in a more authoritative approach, look to the latter years of Don Quixote, the gentleman from La Mancha, as recorded by Miguel de Cervantes in 1605 and 1615. This is where your facts lie.

There were certain choices I made on this journey that were misguided and selfish. I would like to say sorry to the person I have hurt. I was blinded. I was wrong. This story has been written down not for me, nor for anyone else involved, but as evidence of the mysteries that lie in the heart of a horse and proof of the illusions that lie in ours.

Introduction

In the midst of blind ignorance, there was one moment of total lucidity. A bright flash of a dream in a dimly lit room. One year ago, I stumbled onto a path with a horse by my side and thought I could see what lay before me. In the vague but definite distance, I knew there was a destination that would bring me good. I just had to get there. That place was called Cape Finisterre, 'the end of the land'. But what I had in my mind is not the story that I have come to write down, nor were any answers found where I thought they would be. Time and words have a canny way of revealing what is real and what is not, laying bare the moments in between. I should have remembered the first rule of adventure: nothing is as it seems.

The writing of these III days has been difficult; capturing onto a page a time that once seemed like it should never end. On other occasions it has led me to discoveries that I hope never to forget: those who are gone can make us live the most; looking lost is the best way to make friends; wolves are on the rise; falling in love can be a danger to others; always travel with honey, it protects the wounds. While all things turn and change, and while wonder continues to die, the natural world cemented over, and as humans think more like machines, I must always remember that the horse stands still, shining in silence at the centre of all.

A car passes outside, rolling by. Seatbelts secure. The roof and the walls around me keep out the wind and the rain. The complete human experience – from our psychedelic joy to the craws of inner suffering – there's now a pill to mediate that too. If there is one thing that I wish now more than ever, it is for this ride to be unridden, this book unwritten, and to feel what I felt as if for the very first time. Over and over again.

Not knowing what will happen tomorrow. This I miss the most.

Growing up in Scotland, there were two ponies in the field. They looked miserable. One had no teeth, Eric, and the other was overweight and ferociously stubborn. His name was Chunky. My true understanding of the horse began much later, when I was eighteen years old. Along with two friends from school, Frank and Ido, I travelled to the eastern steppe of northern Mongolia in search of the Tsaatan tribe. I had read about them in a book. The best-made plans come from books.

The Tsaatans are said to be a unique people, famous for their curative powers and their lives spent with reindeer. The three of us were curious to see if their healing abilities were as real as the books claimed. Most of all, with school finished and a couple months of odd jobs behind us, we were ready for adventure. Any adventure.

We discovered that the tribe lived somewhere beyond the north-west of Lake Khövsgöl: 262 metres at its deepest, 85 miles long and 22 miles wide, this is the largest freshwater lake in Mongolia. After buying a fishing rod and four rough-looking ponies from a toothless farmer, we set off upon a track that wove between the edge of dense forest and the western banks of the open water. But our mission was short-lived. By day five our ponies had been stolen and we found ourselves completely stranded in a taiga gorge.

Horseless and now lost, we packed up the tents and retraced our steps, desperate to find a clue or a person that might lead us to answers. After a couple of hours, a fisherman and his five horses came round the bend. We told him what had happened. He hadn't seen anything on his travels, he assured us, neither thieves nor horses, but for the price of two of our Russian saddles we could ride with him. He was headed south.

Six days later we arrived at a village called Hatgal, situated at the southernmost point of the lake. From here we contacted the British embassy on the village phone and, upon hearing our story, a police van with seven officers was duly dispatched from the capital, Ulaanbaatar, 540 miles away. The posse arrived the next day and our ponies were soon returned. The thief was the toothless farmer's son.

Justly proud of his work, the policeman in charge of the investigation stood up inside the fishmonger's shack – the building commandeered for questioning – and chucked us all a Parliament cigarette from across the table. He then sat back down. His face became stern.

'It's not normal that foreign people ride these horses,' he said. 'They are wild. Sometimes tourists rent them, with a guide, but never do they own them.' He lit his cigarette with a match.

'Everyone in the village knows of your story now. To be safe, you need to leave at dark. You must beware and watch for thieves. Travel at night with your horses and they will not find you. Ride up the eastern side of the lake—'

'Bear country?' Frank interrupted.

'Yes, bear country,' he replied. 'You must go into the place these thieves will not. This is the only chance you have to not lose your horses. Maybe then you will find the Tsaatans.'

Taking the policeman's advice seriously, we headed east at twilight and became increasingly lost. Our compass refused to work and, between us, the only source of direction we had was a children's map of China, picked up by Frank at Beijing airport. We didn't eat for two days and on the third, when delirium had replaced hunger, we thought we spotted a reindeer walk ahead of us, past us, picking its way through the continuum of pine. Unsure what to believe, we all stood still. The mirage moved on, out of sight. With horses in tow, we pursued the animal as discreetly as we could, not wanting the thing to flee. The reindeer was real. It led us to a wide, open space of grass and yurts – and people. It was the Tsaatan tribe. Conveniently for us, they had decided to spend the summer months on the south-east side of the lake, where no one could find them.

We lived with the tribe for two weeks. Eager to earn our keep, we fished each day and shared everything we caught. The lake was heaving with Siberian taimen. We smoked the fish on lines that we tied to thin pine trees either side of our fire and found a raised-up rock to cook and eat upon at the cape of a headland. The tribe were convinced that the devil lived in the water. When they saw us swimming they took advantage of our impiety and handed us a net. We swam out and dropped it into the deep, implacable blue – more fish and more food.

The lake was so big that in the mornings, when the sun rose into an endless clear sky, the water underneath it would be shrouded in violet blackness on one shore while coppering in colour on the other. Every two days, one of us would ride four hours south to a small settlement that had a basic store. We would stock up on cigarettes, chocolate and drink.

We didn't speak the same language, but the Tsaatan devotion to the reindeer, our ability to fish and our shared appreciation for the horse allowed for words to become needless. That and a united adoration for vodka. For a fleeting time, the entire world was determined by fire, water and horses. The glistening shapes upon our faces as we watched the wind dye the embers through the night, the horses cropping the grass near us in the half-light. We did not ask the tribe to perform any magic nor prove their healing capabilities. Frank, Ido and I: we were living. Little rugged pieces of something bigger.

But the time came for us to leave. We made our way back to Hatgal and sold the horses to two men for more than we bought them for. The summer ended and reality returned. It was time to grow up and leave the lake behind, as memory.

Hardest of all was the feeling that something we had only just found was then so quickly and surely taken away. University was dreamless, Mongolia a different life. Battling with an intense unhappiness, I scraped a degree.

Unsure of where to go, I thought of horses. It seemed not much had changed in me during the last three years. Perhaps I had regressed. Now, though, at least I could do what I wanted. I read online about a stable in London, and a day later I took the train and found myself walking down a cobbled mews, just off Hyde Park. I looked around and saw only closed doors and shiny handles of converted garages, all stables once upon a time, the horse long since replaced by the car. But then I smelt it. That unforgettable scent of hay and horse shit intermingled with sweat. It made me smile. I stopped in the middle of the street. They were here somewhere, hidden within the metropolis. They must be. And then, there in front of me, an old cob emerged from behind a dark blue stable door. His name was Enigma. There were sixteen other horses inside, ready for their afternoon ride. I had found the extraordinary Ross Nye Stables.

The work was hard and the people wonderful. Kirsty, my boss, thought I was too skinny and would make extra lunch for me. Along with several mice, I lived alone in a studio flat the size of a shoebox and only trusted myself to cook soup, spinach, boiled eggs and porridge. It was bliss.

With the stagnancy of university over, I was desperate to make things happen. I fancied myself an actor and managed to get an agent; in the summer break I walked across the north coast of Spain and, later, with the encouragement of Kirsty and my colleagues, I rode a Highland pony down the UK for charity. I was anxious to not lose more time.

It was only with the horses that I felt a sense of real stillness. Clarity. Mucking out at the stable, grooming, tacking up, sweeping straw, riding along the park sand tracks on an animal that can take you anywhere. My mind would float away, far beyond the walled-up horizons of the city. I would go to made-up places, barren plains, blue and green valleys. A release from the restlessness; the pressure, the crippling anxiety, the failed auditions, the loneliness, the expectations, the comparisons, the ecstasies and setbacks of young living – the horse was my consolation, my door into the present. In my mind, I would always be riding to the end of the land.

I

Into the Mouth of the Wolf

'What he values is a task that, demanding of him all he has and is, absorbs and so releases him entirely.'
from The Living Mountain *by Nan Shepherd*

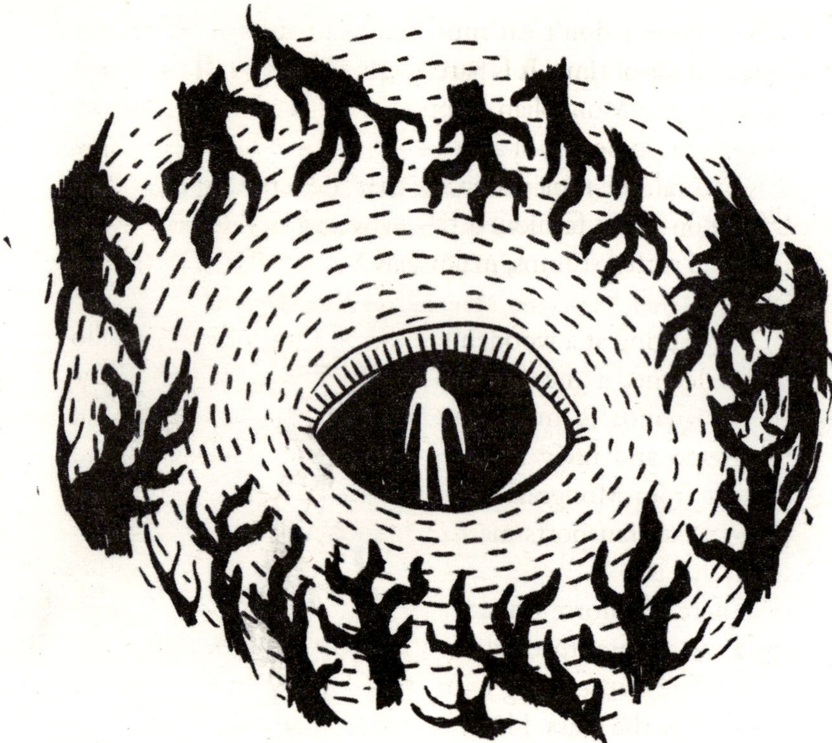

20 March 2022
Lucignano, Siena, Italy

When alone I don't eat much and can survive off tea for long periods of time. It is hard to get good tea in Italy. When riding in the Mongolian steppe we drank tea like it was an earth right, some sort of affirmation that what we were doing was natural. We took water from the lake and brought it to boil upon a fire fashioned from the taiga's debris of fallen pine and rotted stumps; making tea made us feel part of that land.

I am sitting at a wooden table in the grounds of Castello del Calcione, a medieval castle situated near the village of Lucignano: 50 miles south of Florence, 20 miles west of Arezzo and 1,667 miles from Scotland. Although even further from Mongolia, the strange-tasting tea that steams next to me transports me to wherever I want to go. In my head, that is.

There is a horse outside. His name is Sasha. If I stand up, I can see him through a window set deep into the stone wall of the outbuilding I am lodged in. His head is bowed as he crops the grass. I have only known him for three days. His mane is shaved to three inches long. It's a jet-black mohican.

My young host, Savia, is somewhere in the woods with her horses. A fire roars in front of me, the shadows of flames flickering on the stone tile floor, and there is a vast map of Europe hanging on the wall. The countries look like swelling bodies, forced together. Somehow, Sasha and I are going to journey across these bodies – all the way to Cape Finisterre, a rocky peninsula 49 miles west of Santiago de Compostela that juts out into the vast blue water. The last step of land before the Atlantic Ocean.

First, however, we need to reach the Alps. We will leave Castello del Calcione and travel north, up through Tuscany. As far as I can tell, the route seems simple enough. We will take it slow and ask people for food and shelter as we move. I aim to make sure we always have somewhere safe to sleep at least three days in advance of wherever we are.

And then my plans become blurred. Beyond Tuscany there is the ominous lacuna between Italy and France that goes by the name of Liguria. I have no idea what this will bring. Something cold, I imagine. How do you cross the Ligurian Alps with a horse? In late May of 218 BCE Hannibal crossed these mountains from west to east with 37 African elephants and 15,000 horses. Although still in dispute, it seems probable that he breached the frontier along the Col de la Traversette, 2,300 metres up. This route is too far north for what I need and will no doubt be covered in snow. Swapping elephants for mules, Napoleon followed suit in May 1800 CE, using the Great St Bernard Pass. This ancient route cuts up the Alps north-west to south-east, before arriving at the Italian Aosta Valley that borders France.

Yesterday, I got hold of an Italian priest and part-time tour guide local to the Aosta Valley to help me solve this Alpine puzzle. I'd tracked down his home phone number on an outdated mountaineering website.

Me: 'I think the St Bernard Pass is too far north... My plan is to head west. I am trying to reach the Atlantic Ocean.'

Priest-trekker: '*E che dire delle Alpi Liguri?* What about a route through the Ligurian Alps?'

Me: 'Yes, this is my problem. I don't have one.'

Priest-trekker: 'I know of a hiking route that I used many years ago, beginning near a town called Ceparana in the north-west Apennines, only ten kilometres from the sea—'

Me: 'The sea?'

Priest-trekker: 'Mar Ligure, the Ligurian Sea. The route is almost 500 kilometres long: Alta via dei Monti Liguri... it took me from Italy to France. But I believe that the paths have not been assisted in two years now and that the wolves have become brave. And if it snows, well... then it snows.'

Me: 'If it snows it snows?'

Priest-trekker: '*Sì. In bocca al lupo.*'

I have decided to take the priest-trekker's words seriously. I must find out more about the Alta via dei Monti Liguri – this may be the best way to cross the Alps into France. Hannibal's Col de la Traversette is unpassable, Napoleon's St Bernard Pass travels too far from the westerly line, and the third option is out of the question: the concrete road.

The fire rejects an ember onto the stone floor. Outside the sky is an undisturbed bluey grey. Temperate and vacant. It is a miracle that I am here. A week ago, I had no horse and this trip seemed dead on its knees. I had spent two months training stallions in a run-down palace north of Naples, in the promise that I would be lent a capable gelding for my troubles. That didn't work out. The proposed horse was produced on a Friday morning and by lunchtime the poor animal had an intravenous catheter pumping fluid into his unformed and dehydrated body. He was completely unfit. Of course, it was my mistake for taking the yard manager's word seriously. 'He will lead you to the end of the world,' the man had claimed, 'and back.' The yard manager was a Savoy prince, and the yard a palace, so I thought it impossible that someone like that might deceive me. Now I know differently.

I left the palace that night and travelled north in my Skoda hire car. I looked at four horses in five days – mostly recommendations from a young woman called Kiki. No horse was right. As the fifth day approached, I wondered how long this could go on for. Perhaps the broken gelding was a sign: there are limits. Money too, was going to run out at some point. Hire cars and hotels were not part of the budget. I started to panic. I was running out of options. I told myself that this is going to be it: if I can't find a suitable horse on the fifth day, then the journey is over. The ride is not meant to be.

The Skoda dragged me past the Emilia-Romagna town of Piacenza and then up a winding track. It scraped its belly on the rocks and then ground to a halt on a sand-coloured plateau. A clean, smart modern stables loomed ahead of me: 'BOSANA'. Bored horses were tied up to a wooden railing and there was an endless cacophony of brushing and touching and patting. My mood was low.

I got out of the car. The Apennine landscape demure and endless. The air cold.

Bravely, the owner presented two horses to me that she thought might be up to the task: a journey over remote mountains, through entangled cities, under sun and snow, in the heat and the cold. We are all warned to take a horse dealer's word with a pinch of salt, but I was so tired that I clung to what she said like a mosquito to blood. She could have told me that the horse had three legs and I would still have found a way to interpret it as something positive: one less shoe for the farrier, perhaps. But there was no need to worry. The young owner, Diana Origgi, was straight-talking and kind. She had a dreamer's mind, with an attitude that wanted to make things happen. I could barely believe my luck but, as far as I could tell, both horses she showed me were healthy. And better yet, the second one was very badly behaved. He had spirit.

'This one is called Czarchi Rogg,' she called out, as we watched him struggle to make a circle in the manège. He had a rough bay coat, strong haunches, a straight back and an unusually robust-looking torso. Diana whistled and Czarchi Rogg came to a stop. I went towards him. Warily, he watched me approach with dark marble eyes. As I got close, I showed him my hands and lowered my head. I looked up to see him looking at me, his ears pricked forwards.

Lightly, I placed my right hand against his jaw, feeling his wintry beard, and then pressed three fingers against his forehead. There was a white mark. His face was handsome. Growing impatient, his mohican head then jerked up like an angry teenager and his nostrils flared. His gentle eyes stirred.

'He is from Poland,' said Diana. 'This is why his chest is big.'

'What does Czarchi Rogg mean?'

'The Devil's Horn.'

We saddled up and rode out of the manège and up a winter-beaten Apennine hill.

'He is very strong,' remarked Diana, riding abreast of me. 'If there is one horse that will not stop, it is this. He is also the friend of Kiki's horse, though they do not know each other so well.'

I remember closing and opening my eyes and wishing that everything that Diana was saying was reliable and true. The lies told down in Naples were still so fresh in my mind. The prince grinning at me with mozzarella oozing from the corners of his mouth, repeating over and over that I must trust him. 'All will be well... all will be well.'

The wind against my body was getting colder, my limbs ached, and the late winter light was threading into evening. The mud-green hills burred.

*

It wasn't long before I changed his name to Sasha. It is no doubt sacrilege in certain equine circles, but there was absolutely no way that I was going to be riding 'The Devil's Horn' all the way to Cape Finisterre. But I've found a horse! I'm free. The world is turning once more.

Luck permitting, I will leave here with Sasha in a couple of days and travel north along a route called the Via Francigena, up through Tuscany. Then there are the Alps, and then France, the Pyrenees, and the north coast of Spain, where I aim to use pilgrim routes to guide us west. I have an appalling sense of direction and so I reckon that staying in view of the good-hearted public might keep us on track. And I love the idea of riding through a town or city with my horse. The journey should be around 2,000 miles long.

From what I have saved, I have enough money to keep me and Sasha afloat for about three months. But anything could happen. One fall, one vet bill could leave me high and dry. Keeping him full, keeping him sound and healthy, this will be my main concern.

I am nervous. Upon arriving at Castello del Calcione, a twisting sensation has begun to develop in my stomach, like I am about to be thrown down a trap door. I need more tea.

My saddle bags were made by a kind man called Ciro in the town of Torre del Greco, just outside of Naples. Ciro's little workshop was down an alley and lit by one single light that hung from the middle of the low ceiling. He was a bus driver by trade and took cash for his beautiful leatherwork. He had dusky eyebrows, like ebony, and his hands seemed more pelt than skin.

Together Ciro and I designed two motorbike-style saddle bags to be clipped on either flank of the saddle, two pocket-style bags to be draped over the front of the saddle and a final cylindrical bag that was to be attached behind me on the cantle. Everything was crafted using lightweight calfskin. For the saddle itself, Ciro modified a vintage Podium endurance model I had hastily bought when working at the palace, for a horse I would never ride. He lengthened the pommel at the front, raised the cantle at the rear and pushed forward and then softened the knee rolls so that it would fit me. His work was elegant and smart, and all the colours were matched in dark chocolate and brandy tan.

Ciro and I communicated very little. He gestured with his eyes, I nodded back, and, silently, he worked on. I found myself in so much peace sitting in the warm darkness of this man's workshop. For some reason, after being surrounded by people and things that I could no longer trust, Ciro made me feel calm. My mind would drift off and I'd think about how little I had learnt these last few years, from Mongolia to now. In my head I can vividly see the fury in the mother magpie's eyes after Ido climbed the tree and stole her chicks in hunger and how the silhouette of flames danced on the faces of horse thieves as they silently rode up to us in the night, hoping that we were asleep and unaware.

Recently, I have been seeing Ido more clearly than ever, as if he were with me, waiting around corners. His combed dark blond hair, his round, slouched shoulders. He stands with a curving grin that never shows his teeth. Despite the years gone by, I still have so much anger inside me at what happened when we returned to the UK. He broke what was made in Mongolia. Maybe this is why I am here, to rebuild it. I can never trust him again.

◆

The due date is an oncoming storm. Sleepless nights. I think of meeting Kiki. I think of when we first saw each other, four months ago now. It was a cold night in November. A figure walked towards me along the cobbles of Bathurst Mews, London. I was sweeping up the last of the loose strands of straw outside the stable I worked at. I leant on my broom to wait for the young woman to pass and then, out from the dark, she called my name. I immediately recognised her voice. So soothing and so sure. I then panicked as I realised we had planned to meet that evening and that she had come all the way from Amsterdam to do so.

In a mad rush to appear prepared, I put down the broom and led her to the nearby Victoria pub. It was here that she explained why it was she wanted to come on the journey with me. Aged thirty, her sister, her only sibling, had taken her own life.

'A few weeks after Siu passed, I was on a plane with my boyfriend,' said Kiki. We were sitting at a small round wooden table with a pint of Guinness and a half pint of Moretti.

'Somewhere over Spain, I looked out of the window and saw dark green mountains. I closed my eyes. In that moment, all I wanted was to be alone with a horse on those mountains. After some time my boyfriend turned to me and said, "I know someone who does that"... so that's when I contacted you.'

Together we made a plan that Kiki would join me once the journey had begun, after a fortnight or so, somewhere between Italy and France. That way I would have enough time to make some mistakes and get into the flow. But we were not quite sure exactly where and when and, indeed, how things would be once we met. I had no doubt, though, that this ride was meant for her – it was Kiki's means of finding that mountain. I thought to myself that if I could help her reach this place, or at least be a small part of that force, then this entire endeavour would be worth it. Our meeting filled me up with someone else's reasons.

Kiki left me at the pub and returned to her work, her houseboat and her boyfriend in Amsterdam. We remained in contact.

Where is she now? Will she even come? Somehow, I doubt it. She has probably found a renewed solace in her boyfriend and the city. As much as I would like one day to see her again, I know I must let it be. My time with the prince and what happened with Ido has taught me first-hand that nothing goes to plan; to put absolute faith in the plan is like sculpting in ice. Everything changes. It always will. Accepting this fact is my challenge – this is where faith belongs; faith in the unknown through faith in the letting go. Ice melts in the hands, and the shape of what you perceive constantly transforms. In my mind, there is always so much at stake. I wish I could just allow the water to flow freely between my fingers.

Perhaps meeting Kiki on that night in London was the only time I'd ever see her, but hearing her story has affected me. As has her voice. I have been approached by a young woman who has lost her only sibling, the closest thing to her in the entire world, and she wants to make a journey with a horse to further understand why it has all happened. Perhaps she wants to make a journey to find her sister. Kiki mentioned too that she wanted to raise money for a Dutch organisation that fights to destigmatise neurological divergencies.

Meanwhile I drink tea and write at this table hidden from the world, telling myself that I am on a mission to never see life as it is but only as it should be: I need to ride now, act now, use what I have. Live. There is no alternative. To ride, to explore, to uncover more life; to reach strangers, to feel danger and to learn; to find unknown places; to reveal the renewed way; to share this renewed way, this old, slow way, with man's patient, most forgiving and most loyal friend – the horse.

Who the hell do I think I am? I am a middle-class twenty-six-year-old man-child and I know no real loss. I have never been persecuted and I do not know what it is to struggle to live.

I think of the top of a mountain, any mountain, and imagine Kiki there, and her sister Siu. The horses crop the mountain grass, the world is drenched in green.

◆

I am unaware of a prescribed preparation programme for a ride across Europe, but I have spent the last couple of days walking with Sasha in the oak woods and riding him gently round Savia's homemade Palio track that sits on the south side of the castle. It is a round 339-metre racetrack covered in sand. Dating back to the early 1630s, the Palio race is held twice a year in Piazza del Campo, Siena. The seventeen districts of the city, *contrade*, compete against each other for their names and horses to be written down in history.

Cantering like a lunatic and raising my fist into the air, I scream back at the crowds of olive trees that surround me. I imagine myself doing a lap of victory: the first Scot in history to win the Palio di Siena. The branches of trees become hysterical women, blowing kisses at me in navy, jade and silver dresses. The looming cypresses form the confines of the piazza. One particularly severe tree takes the role of the Torre del Mangia. It's a good release of energy. Rooks circle the sky, observing the circus below.

Savia is a friend of a friend. Not knowing anyone else in this part of the world, I reached out to her as I sped north from Naples. She has been kind enough to let me stay in an outbuilding of the castle, in a room that overlooks the valley and down onto Sasha's paddock, a soft, tawny square space amongst an olive grove. As I parked the Skoda outside the castle walls, I was too tired and relieved to care what our meeting might be like. And then I saw her walk towards me in a pair of blood-orange jodhpurs and a wax jacket. She got closer. Her eyes were dark, her lips fine, her skin pale and her black hair thick and long past her shoulders, untied. She was tall. I hugged her and the pressure of her fingers on my back made me want to sink into the ground. No doubt she was just being polite, but the feel of her bones on my body made me want to explode with tears and kiss her at the same time. She is beautiful. Her irises are the colour of copper, and they demand attention; she is either seeing something you can't or looking at the very thing that's on your mind.

I don't think her mother likes me particularly. She is not a woman who takes kindly to fools.

For the past three nights I have jumped into a lake I found beyond the woods, in an attempt to shock me out of my restlessness. It is cold, but not cold enough it seems. The horse is my only true escape into the moment. Why can I not be present, *here*? Why can't I *know* it? I want the wind to pull me to the ground, the night to be starless and black so that I am forced to feel only the coarse roots underneath my feet and the barbed limbs of trees on my skin. I want to reach across the sheets of my bed and find someone next to me that I want. Savia, perhaps.

I want to want Savia.

0 miles, 0 days

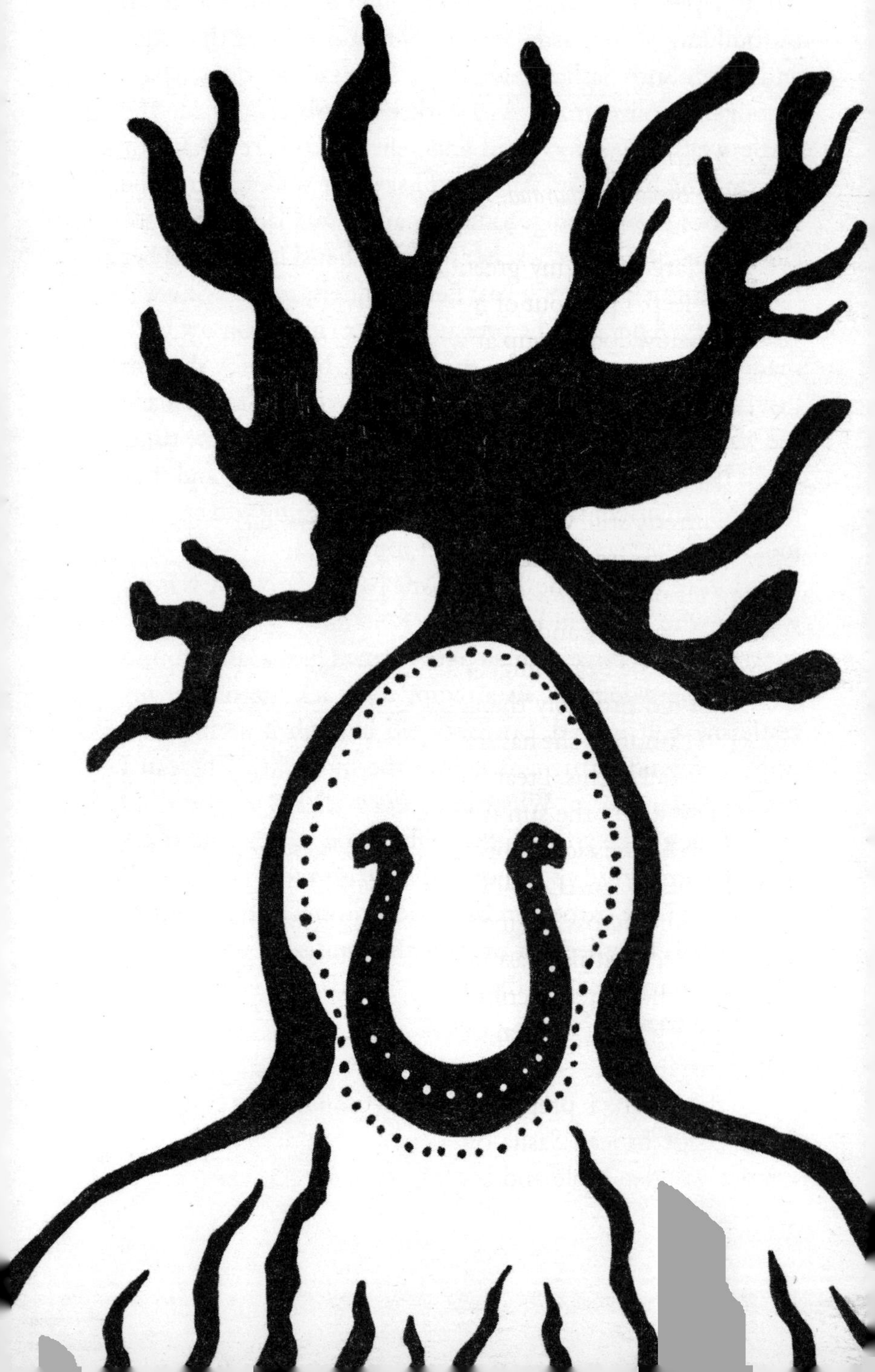

24–30 March
Lucignano, Siena – Ceparana, Liguria

It is still dark inside my green-walled bedroom. The castle remains asleep. I peer out of my window and see Sasha in the paddock below, looking up at me in confusion. The number 831 is just visible on his left flank, where the saddle sits. It was branded into his flesh when he was a foal, in accordance with the Polish tradition. He bows his head and crops the grass. The cypress trees appear blue and the olive trees grey. The sky utterly still. Coming over the hills on the far side of the valley there are streaks of yellow-and-clay-coloured light, burning off the night.

I shower quickly and leave a note for Savia on my bedside table: 'Is this the beginning?' Not entirely sure what I mean by it. I should probably thank her for all that she has done and for the kindness she has shown me and Sasha, but there is no space for all of this. I tear out a pastel drawing that I made of a sunrise where the sun is blue and the sky is red. I wish her luck on her mission to become the first female to win the Palio. 'IN BOCCA AL LUPO.' She is one of the best riders I have ever come across. I remember us riding through the oak woods on her lightning-fast horses, curving and gliding. On the back of the pastel, I scribble that I wished that she could have come with me, '… even if it were just for one day.'

Downstairs the kitchen is empty. Sunlight faintly floods the room. I prepare and cook some breakfast and head outside to lead Sasha over to the stables, *la scuderia*. I find a wooden table and bring it into the early morning sun so that we can eat together. Amando, Savia's favourite thoroughbred, stirs inside his box and wonders what it is we are doing. He is dark, fine and fiercely fast.

On one end of the breakfast table I place a bowl of chopped up apples and carrots and on the other I lay down a tray of scrambled eggs, bacon, sausages, toast, jam, milk, a pot of tea, orange juice and a bottle of prosecco. Together, Sasha and I eat as the morning rises.

By eight o'clock we are ready to go. The calfskin leather of Ciro's saddlebags is warming up as the sun swells. I roll up my World War II German poncho and tie it to the top of the cylindrical cantle bag behind the saddle. Hopefully, I won't be needing it for a while. I am wearing old navy-blue denim trousers, Blundstone boots and a olive-green cotton shirt with buttons down to my sternum. On my head there is a brushed cotton stevedore cap made for me by a friend of my sister's. I love it, I hide underneath it. I am a stable boy and a Cossack general. It makes me focused. I've decided to bring a small rucksack, something I got from an army surplus shop in London, just in case.

Wrapped up in the cantle bag is a *ferran* that I bought in Kashmir, made from goat's wool. It is shaped like a dress, reaching down to my mid-shins. It stopped me from freezing in Mongolia and I think it to be lucky somehow. I have no tent and I haven't brought a sleeping bag, but I have a thick woollen rug and an Argentine saddle cloth that I can lie down on. I'll need to find shelter. On the left side of the saddle hangs my black *bota* – a tear-shaped leather wine sack from Andalusia. I have made sure to fill it half full.

Savia is in Paris. I say goodbye to Amando, awkwardly mount Sasha after putting on his bridle and bit, and then ride off into the bright light of the morning. The bottle of prosecco is empty.

We pass the lake beyond the woods and before long find ourselves in untrodden territory. I have decided to use an app on my phone as the route system. I don't have the space for paper maps and, worst comes to worst, I can always ask for help. I look back and see rooks circling the turrets of the castle in the distance, now almost a mile behind. Ahead, a railway track cuts up the dry flat land that has replaced the groves and woods of the castle grounds. Sasha's first test: a train shoots past and the earth shakes underneath.

Then it all changes. The dry pit of the valley is replaced with the Asciano hills and we pick up a canter over the lip of a ridge. Either side of us hillocks rise up and roll out like a carpet with green and lemon folds, unspoiled and unbroken but for the pale silver lines that guide our eyes, our route, far into the distance. A lone cypress tree leans into the wind. The land glistens.

At lunchtime we come across a cinnamon-coloured hilltop town called Mucigliani and meet a man who is gardening to the sounds of Pink Floyd. I find a small, sunken vineyard, where Sasha can roam freely, and I remove his bridle and bit to ensure that he can consume as much grass as possible. One day I will get rid of the bit so that he can travel just with reins and a head collar, but we are not there yet. I have never ridden with him on a road or through a town or city. We have only known each other for five full days now. We need to take it slow. I lie down and listen to the comforting sounds of my horse cropping the grass with 'Shine On You Crazy Diamond' drifting as naturally as the breeze.

Is this the beginning? The words I wrote to Savia play over in my head. Perhaps I should have tried to kiss her. I don't think I love her. I do want to travel with her though, somewhere far. Perhaps I should have waited for her return.

But I was getting restless. Using some local contacts she gave me, I managed to secure the first couple of nights of paddocks and stables for me and Sasha.

The first night comes and we are greeted by Julio, a friend of Savia's, who breeds thoroughbred horses for the Palio. Together, we make up a stable full of straw and hay for Sasha and light a fire that burns all through the night in view of the horses. Sasha's neighbours are a Hispano-Arab stallion and an elderly Arab. The three of them watch us with curiosity behind their stable doors, lacustrine eyes glinting in the flamelight when it gets dark. Sasha's ears are pricked forward all the while, following me as I move around the yard. Working out who I am.

Julio's friends arrive and we have local red wine, spring truffles and steaks on the open fire. At two o'clock in the morning Julio teaches me how to shoe a horse using an old cob of his called Alfredo as the patient. It is a great success. We then don beekeeping outfits and go in search of honey. It feels as if we are off to climb the moon. I wake up in the cold morning in a nest of straw, my lips sweet from the nectar and my tongue as dry as cloth from the wine. Sasha's head is propped on his stable door, staring at me inquisitively. The stallion next to him stirs and begins to push his chest against the wood. A new day has sprung.

The yellow light of the sun stretches over me like a warm blanket. Around my neck hangs a necklace that I have never seen before. At the end of the chain there is a hoof nail.

'I made it for you,' says Julio, as he tacks up his horse. 'It is the first nail you used on Alfredo's shoe, remember?'

We travel underneath the speckled light of a 200-year-old oak tree tunnel. The antique branches call out to each other above our heads and dye the shade of the track dark blue, their fallen leaves are silver in the dust. A breeze causes the shadows to tremble.

Before lunch we find flowing water. A river. Horses and humans take a long drink and I submerge my face. A black icy whirl circles my existence and I then emerge, feeling the river water drip down my temples, my chest and spine. I mount Sasha and attempt to ride across the current. He is unsure of what to do, doubtful as to whether this moving liquid mass is to be trusted, doubtful whether to trust his rider. Perhaps there are no rivers in Piacenza, where he came from. I disembark and lead him slowly to the other side on foot, the river crawling up to my waist.

'By the end of this ride he will be swimming,' I shout to Julio.

'I think Alfredo has more chance of winning the Palio,' he replies.

We ascend the far bank to find a dried-up labyrinth of vineyards far and wide. Amongst the views of harrowed earth and dust I spot a green oasis in the distance, a cluster of tall, dark poplar trees clutching at the sides of a hidden villa, watered each morning with sprinklers. Meanwhile our path crumbles under the horses' hooves. Fossils lie flat like baked fish at the edges of the brown track. The owner of the vineyard is a friend of Julio's; I remember him from the night before – he provided the wine and the truffles. His thick black hair is unkempt. There is despair in his voice as he wonders how this ageless land of grapes and produce has come to look like a desert.

'It will never be the same,' he mutters to himself, kicking a fossil by his foot. 'Look. Now only rocks grow.'

'Would you like some water?' asks Julio.

'Yes. My head is killing me. What the hell are you two doing riding horses?'

'Here, have some of mine.' I offer our friend my *bota* of wine and await his reaction. He grins and drinks on.

It is five miles later when Julio points me in the direction of the fortress of Monteriggioni. I say goodbye and thank him and brave Alfredo. They have been kind to me.

The trail rises up upon the side of a valley. Down below I notice a Palio track lain out like a copper ring upon a green pasture. More than fifty horses are grazing on the grass. I look up and in the distance I make out the real Torre del Mangia, the fourteenth-century tower that overlooks Piazza del Campo. If all goes to plan, our route will take us west towards Siena and then north, just in time to avoid the madness of the medieval city.

By the time evening comes the light on the land is butter and the medieval town of Monteriggioni glows upon its ancient hill like an orb. I sleep soundly in the house of my host, a young Tuscan who, along with the help of her mother, is desperate to keep her late father's almond farm alive. A dog like a black bear snores at my feet.

Sasha and I head on towards the town of San Gimignano. We come across a deep pool filled with thrashing water that pours down the rocky face of a hill, collecting at the bottom and sparkling in the sunlight. We try not to disturb a silent crowd of people lying on their backs, meditating in the open air upon a grassy bank. There are over thirty of them. I drink from the water and wash my body and face, and then make sure to cool Sasha's legs for as long as I can. Eventually he drinks too. We both need to remember that water can be scarce and every opportunity we get to drink should be taken.

In the afternoon, I make my first big mistake of the ride. Too distracted by the people and the streets of San

Gimignano, I forget to keep an eye on our route. It isn't until five o'clock that it dawns on me we have been travelling four miles in the wrong direction. I turn back, Sasha as angry as I am, and the sun starts to go down.

Eventually the track hauls us up through teal and ashen groves and the moonlight begins to reflect upon the dust underneath our trudging boots and hooves. I dismount and walk on foot in self-punishment. Three times I see a wooden sign with the sacred word 'TRATTORIA' painted across it, but each time there are no lights on inside. Finally, we come across a farmhouse and I knock at the door for some water. An old lady and her granddaughter come to our rescue. We both drink as much water as we can.

On we travel into the night. The silhouettes of cypress trees accompany the moonlit path and the only other animals I see are sleeping sheep and an enormous beaver with eyes like the ends of burning cigars. We drift upon a rim of land that is taking us down into circles of an underworld. How dark it can get in the seclusion of the hills. We reach the humming town of Gambassi Terme and the eerie night becomes an electrified jungle; men and women pouring out of bars with stretched out hands clasping drinks in their fingers, cigarettes to their lips. Sasha stays close to me – we stay close to each other. Take me back to the darkness of the endless hills, the depth of the silence.

We leave the neon lights of the town and the night encompasses us once more. The beat of Sasha's hooves does the talking. Five miles later we reach our stables. My mind wakes up. It is midnight. The kind owner and her daughter show me to Sasha's box. I brush him down, feed him and then make my way over to a portacabin-cum-clubhouse, lit up from the inside by an old steel stove, with a hole for the wonky chimney cut out in the tin roof.

Around the fire is a man with smooth grey hair to his shoulders and a crafty smile. He is smoking a joint, and has bony knuckles and long fingers that clasp together and open up like claws. An older man leans back in a wooden rocking chair with a pipe, and then there is the owner and her daughter, who have spread out a blanket for me in front of the stove. I am fed *spaghetti alla puttanesca* and given a bottle of red wine to drink, and I drink and eat until I am too tired to keep my eyes open. We speak about the places I am to go. And of the beauty of the horse. After a while the smokers and the talkers take themselves away into the nearby villages, leaving me curled up next to the soft glowing stove. Two old black dogs are here too. Whether these dogs were left behind to accompany or guard me I cannot be sure, but their presence warms the room.

In the night I get up to go outside. I pull back the glass door of the makeshift clubhouse and, to my horror, the entire frame dismantles. The door smashes down upon me and the dogs snap up in fright. They bark and snarl as I remove the glass from my hair and off my body. I think I see Sasha looking at me from across the dark, his marble eyes glinting from a single electric light.

I wake up long before sunrise wishing it all to be a cruel dream and then, disappointed, hastily begin to brush up the broken glass and prepare an apology. The beginning of the working day arrives. The first car rolls down the dusty track. Holding back her disbelief, the owner tells me through gritted teeth that it has happened before. She is lying, of course. I insist on paying and offer to find a replacement door. Not knowing how else to deal with my mess and frantic efforts, she eventually erupts in laughter. She tacks up a horse with her daughter and I prepare Sasha. I hug her before I go, repeating my apologies. I hug the man with the long grey hair too. Naturally, he is completely oblivious to the missing door. The daughter accompanies me all the way to a place called Castelforentino. She is sixteen years old and helps her mother every day with the horses, before and after school. She wants to ride through Italy. Why stop at Italy? After she leaves me, it isn't long before I get lost again. The technology on my phone isn't quite as reliable as I had hoped.

The hours and days begin to shed. Tuscany strikes me as a space of unnatural order. The woods are sculpted, and the tree heads severed. The texture of the land is fabricated through rigid lines of vineyards, drainage ditches, and in the uniformed fleets of groves built into the earth. The hills have become upturned porcelain bowls with ribbon wrapped tightly around them to form paths. In contrast I feel more unruled each day. While nature grows domesticated, Sasha and I sink further and further into an earthier sense of living, dirty outsiders to the control. Now stepping into the unfamiliar, we are weightless. I lean down to pat Sasha's neck three times with my right hand and then keep it there, thinking of nothing, listening only to the sound of his hooves. Already my hair has begun to twist and curl. My skin wears two layers of clothing – one is fabric and the other sweat.

We come across a deserted house with a beaded portiere entrance. It sits lonely on the summit of a domed hill. The building is two storeys high, completely square, and has windows either side of the entrance. While Sasha grazes freely, I pull aside the beads to see what lies inside. I am careful to walk slowly upon the dust of the wooden floor. An old box television sits in the middle of the room on the left. I can see all the way through its broken-glass face.

A camp bed lies next to it with a children's book and a flaxen woollen quilt strewn over the imprinted mattress. Photographs and dirt mix themselves on the floorboards and in the next room there is an old cooker that has become overgrown with creepers. A dishevelled wicker chair stands upon the threshold of the door, looking out to an imagined kitchen garden.

A day later we rest at an abandoned chapel called Colle di Val d'Elsa. The solitary building has the face of a warrior, black-and-white striped, as if thousands of giant leopard moths have been stuck to it as a warning. Inside, only the stone altar still looks holy. The carmine-coloured sanctuary lamp, which once held a candle to symbolise the holy spirit, is shattered, and the wooden congregation chairs upended. Time and its violent breeze have dragged the people away and left their lives behind. Or perhaps it is the human trace that refuses to go, rinding to the air, pressing onto walls. The crafted hills around us are the things that now seem dead.

On the evening of the fourth day the omniscient presence of these deserted places is left behind. We travel towards the peopled town of Montopoli. Here a man named Valerio is waiting for us. I found him online, on an old site dedicated to equestrian folk in Tuscany. An apricot light shines down upon the approaching track as couples walk hand in hand, young and old, and I ride past them like a ghost. It's as if they do not even hear the sound of Sasha's hooves. They are well dressed and have kempt haircuts and clean shoes. The dusty track evolves into cobbles and then the groves disappear to leave a patchwork; terracotta, mustard and crimson houses loom above us like painted giants. We travel through these streets and then take a left, walking down a narrow alley that leads us to the bottom of a basin-shaped valley, cut out, it seems, from the land. At the valley floor there is an expanse of dry, wisping paddocks, fenced in by sawn-up bamboo. I stand with Sasha, strangers to this oasis for horses. A breeze shudders the grass. I look up to the town. White and yellow box-like apartments have been wedged upon the steep sheets of rock. The view must be good from there. From down here the sight of those apartments appears forced and fragmented. A pained and ugly face upon the smooth, dark shoulders of the headwall.

I find Valerio on a tractor with a little girl hanging off his shoulders like a blonde monkey. He is a strong man with a black twisting beard and skin the colour of the earth. Together we find Sasha a very green and curious-shaped paddock, one that zigzags up the talus slope and peers down at the grassland below. I put down my blanket and Ciro's saddle bags upon a huge bale of hay. With Sasha settled, Valerio drives me up to the town in his tractor.

'I once rode with my wife through these streets when I was first married,' he exclaims, a wry smile spreading across his face. 'It was the day of the wedding. We left the people behind at the church in Val d'Elsa, and we began to canter. I think we must have ridden the same way as you did today. The trouble was, the closer we got to my paddocks, the faster my horses ran. They became like bullets. We galloped down the hill. It was the greatest ride of my life. The foals of those horses are alive today. The marriage didn't last more than a year.'

The night unfolds and we place a table and some chairs in the centre of the town square and drink and eat as locals come and go, and the little girl with long blonde hair, his niece, plays with her cousins. We drink negronis. Valerio captivates everyone with his tales of history, Akhal-Teke horses and his proclamations on change. His booming voice rings around the square. He is a character that belongs in a book, and this makes me feel at ease.

When the wholeness of night takes over from the evening, I collapse into my nest of hay and wrap it over me for warmth. Sasha's Argentine saddle cloth acts as my pillow and I stare up at the sky that has a swarm of stars. I scan the maze to find the Orion constellation, and then I see great Sirius, the strongest star of them all. All through the night I fall in and out of a heavy sleep. I dream that I am aboard a small boat and that I am rocking upon the waves of an open sea. In the distance I notice a dark body of land approaching and the jagged shape of its silhouette fills me with dread. I know that my boat will crash into this land. In my fear I look up at the sky and Sirius is the only star that shines.

I awake to see a horse standing over me. It is Mithra, Valerio's Akhal-Teke horse. I was told to expect this. The Akhal-Teke is one of the oldest breeds in the world, with ancestry that can be traced back more than 3,000 years. Made famous by the tribes of Turkmenistan, they are notorious for their almond-shaped eyes, serene temperament and extreme physical endurance. In the past they have been called 'The Golden Horse', probably in reference to their dun coats, which shine like lacquered metal.

Mithra wanders through the basin each night, a ghostly ship, never thinking to escape due to the love she has for her home. The sentinel of the valley floor. She brushes her nose against my feet, sniffing me to understand what I am, and then lies down just beyond me, keeping her head up to look out through the night.

When the early morning cockerel crows, Mithra rises. Sasha calls to me high up in his steep paddock. I wash my face in a bucket of cold water, tack up and say goodbye to Valerio. He hugs me like a bear and tells me to always listen to my horse. 'Listening will take you as far as you need to go.'

I have been invigorated by Valerio's kindness and his sense of living. He is an advocate of the Journey – the ride to nowhere. He thinks the nature of a horse is often an indication of the character of the owner; they mirror your emotions. I ride away from Valerio's arcadia basin and feel limitless. I know with every inch of me that I am lucky to be living and to be making a journey with a companion as gentle as Sasha.

Before Valerio no one in Tuscany seemed to quite understand what I meant when I said I was riding to the Atlantic Ocean. So far, only a handful of strangers have taken the time to listen; an old man in a chequered shirt toiling in his perennial dry vineyard; an old woman seeing to the death of her husband in a hillside cemetery; a young barista trying to leave the countryside, desperate for life beyond the one he has been told to know. For most of these Italians, bewilderment at the distance I have to travel strikes first and then, as if in need of a plausible explanation, they usually ask where I am from. '*Scozia*.' Wherever I go – and wherever I have gone – this answer always seems to justify the adventure.

From Montopoli the sun beats down hard upon dried-up canals and stumped, naked grapevines strung up with wire. I feel as dry and hungover as the earth we ride on. The route takes us along flat, irrigated plains before slowly ascending into the cooler foothills of the Apuan Alps. After passing through the town of Altopascio, the vegetation around us enlivens and the oak and beech trees grow wider and older until, after meandering up and beyond the flats below, we come across a fountain in a square green cemetery. Cemeteries almost always have a source of water. I wash my face and pour water on Sasha's back and legs, now purple with sweat. I breathe deeply and look east as he poaches the dense grass on the sides of the gravestones, gardening for the dead. We are high up on the brow of a hill. The land beneath us appears like the Sargasso Sea; an immense mass of hazel, alder and chestnut trees unfurling themselves as far as the eye can see, with algae-coloured crowns reaching bold for the spring sunlight. If we stepped upon this mottled sea it would take us all the way to Florence. It was near these hills, upon Monte Altissimo, that Michaelangelo found the marble of his dreams, in 1517.

That evening I find a stable just beyond the cemetery that I discovered online. An attentive lady has inherited her wooden-beamed house and yard from her late father, in which she has created a riding club for the young of the city of Lucca. We are greeted by a colossal Hanoverian horse called Aldo who charges like a black bison in a round pen that extrudes over the never-ending forest below. I wonder to myself how many times this scene has been witnessed before in the archaic life of this country; this majestic horse, careering in the sands of a late-afternoon sky with his black nostrils flaring and with the unchanged tree crests dispersing the horizon. Sasha stays clear of Aldo, unsure of what to make of him, and I find him a paddock further down. The owner insists that her ancient stable had once been lived in by Michaelangelo himself.

After a very starry night where Sirius is drowned out by the others, Sasha and I descend west towards the coast. Before long, it becomes clear that everything around us is changing. The sculpted hills are being replaced by darker, rougher shapes and the very bark of the trees begins to spell a sense of the Alpine. Armies of pine forests spread left and right from the single tarmac road, and the sporadic cottages and farmhouses are stiffened by wooden beams and narrow smoking chimneys.

By late afternoon we find our way to a riding club in the town of Pietrasanta, one of many places once made rich by the discovery of Michelangelo's crystalline rock. There are almost fifty horses here. Children run around covered in hay and chase each other in the sands of the arenas. A man with a belly that almost fits perfectly into his wheelbarrow directs me towards a box for Sasha, out of the sunlight and next to eight other horses. They all eat and sleep calmly.

I am told of a woman in town who has an affordable bed and breakfast and, for the first time since this journey began, one hundred miles ago, I leave Sasha and walk alone. Beyond the rising rooftops of Pietrasanta I see the soaring pinnacles of the Apuan hills rising in the east. It is getting late. The sky is turning from orange to a lilac black. Those porcelain shapes of Tuscany have been shut up and put away for good. I bow my head and take a long shower, my first since leaving the castle, and then fall into a dreamless sleep upon a hard, clean bed.

Up to this point I have been walking on foot for about a third of the journey and together we have been averaging a distance of twenty-two miles each day. If I want to make it to Spain with one horse, then the walking will have to continue. If I were to ride Sasha the whole way, we would need to lower our mileage and take many days of rest. This slower way would lead us well into the white heat of the summer. Once upon a time a traveller would swap horses every hundred miles. This time it is just me and him.

*

It is a dark, wet morning and I walk quickly through the electrically lit streets of Pietrasanta. Adrenaline bubbles through me. Sasha's eyes are gleaming anthracites in the shadows of his box. I give him a light breakfast. He can sense the eagerness in my blood. After he has time to digest, we leave the riding club in darkness and take the road heading west, towards the coast of La Spezia. The mission is to ride up the beach for eight miles or so before heading inland. With our backs to the sea, we will then need to pick our way along the south bank of the Fiume Magra before attempting a crossing. I have calculated that the day will be thirty miles long. This is why we set off at 5 a.m. The rain continues to pour.

Since listening to the advice from the priest-trekker I have set about contacting anyone and everyone I can in the Ligurian mountains. Two days ago, a woman named Serena Berton reached out to me on social media. Serena is an experienced horse trekker who has lived in the foothills of the Ligurian Alps her entire life. Ten years ago, she journeyed into France in the bright, hot months of summer with her two quarter horses. As we head towards the grey beach, she sends me a text.

> The rain falls down heavily. If you cannot make it to Ceparana, below is the address of a town closer to you. It is called Avenza. You can sleep there tonight. Come and find us tomorrow if you cannot make it across the river Magra.

I unwrap my German poncho. It covers me, the saddle, Ciro's saddle bags and almost all of Sasha's back. We put our heads down and keep going. I am eager to push on in one day, knowing that we are both fit enough to go beyond Avenza, the halfway point between Pietrasanta and Ceparana. I know too that there is a rest day waiting for us upon arrival. Our first rest day. As if in response to my silence, Serena sends me the exact location of the only crossable section of the river by horse.

The grey sheen damply lights the shoreline as we canter on firm sand. Sasha's first time on a beach! The waves crash down on our left and he accelerates in fear at the sight of the water being dragged back into the sea. Perhaps this is what he thinks will happen to him if he gets too close. We ride fast along the Spiaggia Libera, the Free Beach, and pass the early morning tractors harrowing the sand. The bars are all closed up and the restaurants deserted. It is only us, the tractors, the rain and the sea. The mauve Apuan Alps striate the eastern distance.

We turn east and find the Fiume Magra, our thread to Ceparana. Serena instructed us to keep close to the riverbank, following the water for twelve miles until we reach a place called Santo Stefano di Magra. It is here, where Tuscany meets Liguria, that we will need to cross.

I make sure to cover ground as fast as possible on the Free Beach because I know that the river crossing is going to be difficult. I am concerned about the rain that continues to fall, Sasha's apparent fear of crossing water, and, as always, I want to allow time for my poor sense of direction.

With La Spezia now to our west and the Ligurian Sea directly behind us, I discover signs to a section of the long-trusted Via Francigena that keeps close to the Magra. We canter upon built-up canal banks with cars racing to our right and the swelling river raging behind bare trees to our left. We then descend an alluvial track, fertile and soft from previous floods, that guides us through darkened tunnels weaved together from dripping bamboo, and we ride in and out of thickets and bogland, everything heaving with the rain.

By two o'clock in the afternoon we have reached the point of the crossing. Slowly we push our way through the tangled-up riverbank, dense with cobwebs, plastic and the debris of burnt-out cars and parties. I scrape our way into the open air of the river and the big stones that layer the southern side. The water hauls before us, full flow. I find the point that Serena must be referring to. Here the Magra runs a fraction lower on each side of the bank, the colour of the water lighter. Like a blind man, I try and lead Sasha into the current.

The river has already soaked my knees and I am only a quarter the way in. Sasha is stuck still, refusing to move, several metres behind. I wade back to him, tie up his reins to the saddle so that he won't trip, and then continue alone, leaving him to watch me cross.

In the middle of the river, the water reaches my waist. It is flowing hard. I stand rigid for a moment, digging my feet into the stones. I wonder if this is the right thing to do. And then I hear a scuttle. I look back to see Sasha taking a step towards me. I wade on. Sasha keeps coming, his speed quickens as he feels the force of the current against his right flank. He stumbles and then stands dead still, finding his hooves in the rocks. He is scared but his eyes are fixed on me. I reach the other side and call to him. Once more he moves. The Arabian water horse!

Dripping and exhausted, we drag ourselves on through the late afternoon like two outlaws washed up ashore, the adrenaline now gone and the light beginning to fail. The rain continues to fall. Even on foot, the cold wraps me up. Sasha is tired. His eyes droop and his mood is low. After thirty-one miles and ten-and-a-half hours, we meet the glaring lights of Serena's pick-up truck and follow her up through the concrete town of Ceparana. Together, we have made it to the foothills of the Ligurian Alps.

165 miles, 7 days

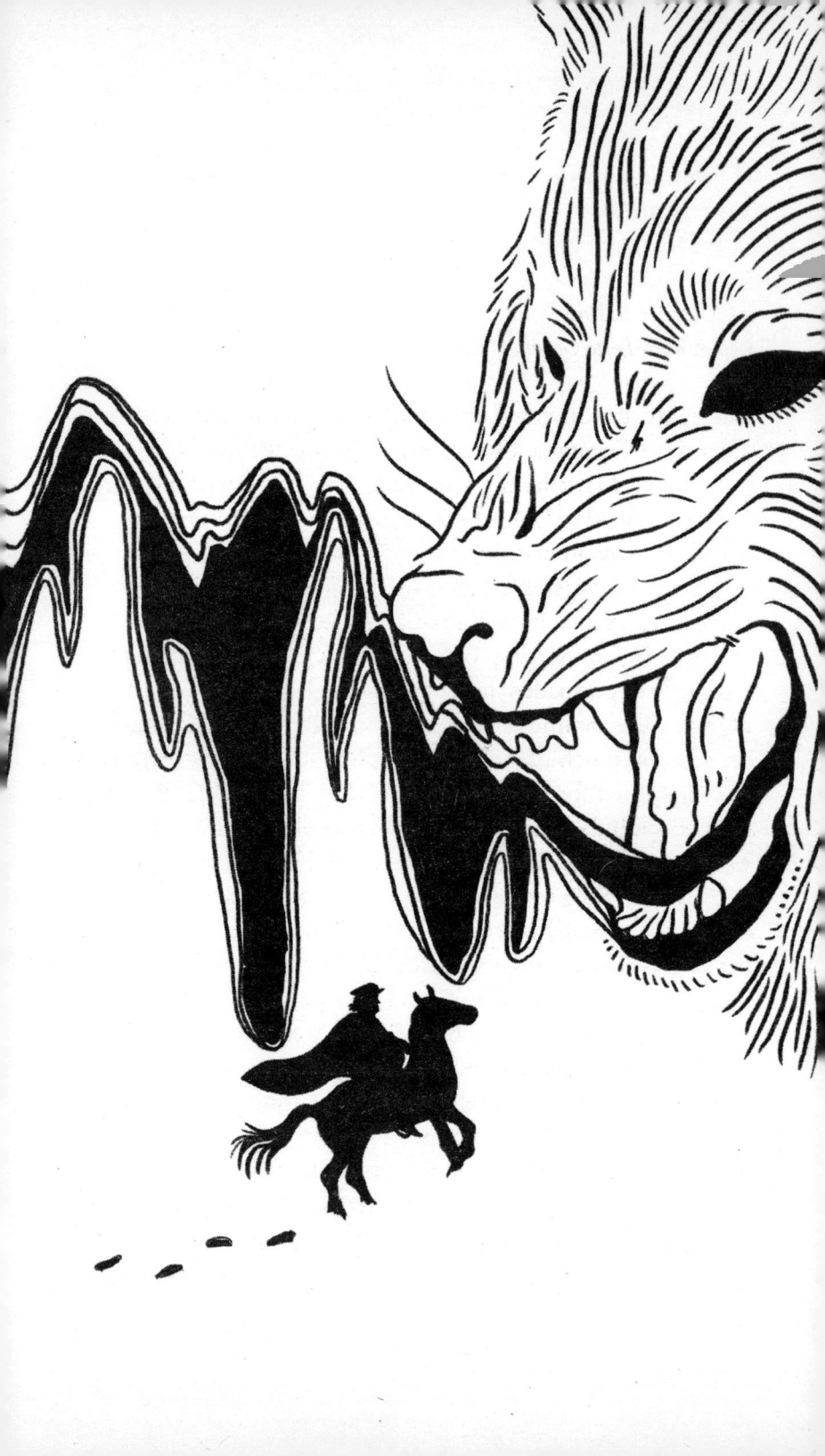

31 March – 9 April
Ceparana – Forte Geremia, Liguria

The lights of a car crawl up the steep slope that leads down, down into Ceparana, out of sight. I look out through wide glass doors. Mariella, my younger sister, has driven all the way from Scotland in a blue four-by-four Freelander. She managed to avoid crashing until the very last corner, where an oncoming vegetable truck removed the left-hand wing mirror and scraped its way along the side.

    Days before setting off from Castello del Calcione I somehow persuaded her to come out and meet me in Liguria. The ominous hinterland of the mountains had become too much of a dead zone in my mind. Most of all I was concerned for Sasha, my sole responsibility. The priest-trekker reminded me of the likelihood of snowfall, which would mean no grazing.

    If we are going to make it into France at the rate I intend to travel then Sasha will need extra feed. If we were ambling, pausing for many nights, adrift and with no set course, then finding feed as we go would be a feasible option. But I can't risk that. I don't want to reach Spain in the searing heat and I don't want to linger in the mountains for longer than is necessary. It is odd though, writing this. I have always thought I would like nothing more than to sink into the waves of a moving landscape with no set destination, walking and sleeping wherever we can. Just like the kind of journeys Valerio reeled off that night in the square of Montopoli. But it seems I am incapable of doing this. I depend upon a set horizon to keep me sane. Without it I have to face all the things that are around me, with no excuse of moving on.

I made sure that Mariella understood I didn't know anything about the mountains or Liguria and had no idea how I was going to cross them. Yet still she decided to come. For this I love her more than ever. I don't think she quite knows how much faith I have in her, in all things. She is one of the strongest human beings I know. She may be my little sister, but I find so much power and home in her. She is an old soul. In her eyes, I am no doubt an archetypal fool.

The car pulls up. Her blue eyes pierce the grey day, her long auburn hair shines on her shoulders, her denim jeans, cowboy boots and wool jumper are unmuddied, and her pale, freckled face breaks into a nervous smile.

'I didn't know it would be so bloody far.'

En-route she managed to pick up almost twenty bags of specialised feed. Each bag weighs twenty-five kilos and contains green dust-free briquettes, dense in fibre and easily digestible. 'DESIGNED FOR ACTIVE HORSES', the briquettes are made up of alfalfa-grass forage, toasted soya-beans, beet pulp, sugar cane molasses and flakes of maize, barley and oats. When we locate some checkpoints, and if I manage to reach them, this feed should see Sasha well into France.

◆

For three days the rain falls. The world is blurred. Mud collects from the hills and streams down upon the solitary tarmac road. Occasionally, when the sky clears, I can make out villages nestled into the hillsides opposite. They become glowing bowls of fruit in the brief gaze of the sun. Underneath us, the mechanical lights of Ceparana are muddled up with lorries, and the tapping sound of rain mixes with the sporadic choke of a freight truck. We are a long way from the olive groves.

Fortunately, there is a plan. For years Serena has been desperate to create a conclusive horse trail over the Ligurian massif, an '*ipo via*' as she calls it. A route for any rider. Little did I know that by contacting her I had inadvertently volunteered myself (and Sasha) as the guinea pigs for the undertaking. Serena has a friend, Leila Dorello, who is equally keen to make the *ipo via* a reality. I don't care how I cross these mountains, I just need to do it as safely as I can. If I need to shapeshift into a horse-riding rodent, then so be it. Importantly, Serena and Leila are both experienced riders – they too may be able to see the routes through the eyes of the horse.

Hour upon hour we plot through the heavy light of the day and through the night with wine, boar meat, venison and grappa to sustain our attentions. Looking over the meandering red trails and the tightly knit contour lines of the maps, I begin to appreciate the size of the task. The main route that Sasha and I are going to use, the Alta Via dei Monti Liguri, is 280 miles long. Some days we will climb higher than 2,000 metres. Mariella surveys the maps to work out where her road and my trail might collide. This isn't going to be easy.

'You will need to buy a handsaw from the town,' states Serena. 'The trails have not been cared for in almost two years now. Ever since everything went into the "lockdown".'

'A handsaw? For what?'

'There will be many trees that have fallen. There will be mudslides too. And wolves of course, many more wolves than before.'

Although the Alta Via gives a sense of the scale of the crossing, it is by no means a comprehensive guide. Almost a third of it is unpassable for horses. With all detours and dangers taken into account, we reckon it will take fifteen days to reach France. 'Unless it snows,' remarks Leila. 'If there is snow, then these plans mean nothing.'

'Like all plans,' adds Serena.

Along both the local routes and the Alta Via, I will be tracing the unforgotten trails of the World War II partisans.

'These mountains were once a home for *la resistenza*,' says Serena one evening. 'Many of the trails you see here are resistance trails, used to carry arms and food from one mountain to the next. The partisans would stay high up in these hills in the summer, ones that you will pass over, and then come down in the winter, to avoid being spotted by the Nazis and the fascists in the white snow and the bare woods. The villagers – the women, the old men and the children – risked their lives to help the ones who were able to fight. Especially *i staffettas*.'

'*Staffettas*?'

The messengers – women and children. They were the most important link in the chain. Once upon a time, communication meant something – it took courage.'

In the candlelit warmth of Serena's house, and with the rain and the wind shaking the world outside, there are moments when it feels like the only reason we are all here is because of the partisans. This uncharted trail that we are planning together, a route to satisfy both my Finisterre ambitions and the childhood dreams of these two women, is perhaps being carved for no good reason other than an expression of this freedom. I hope the partisans would agree with what we are doing. According to a book Serena lent me, partisans of *la resitenza* were motivated by 'a mixture of patriotic, ideological, idealistic reasons and self-interest'. They sound very human to me.

The enthusiasm of Serena and Leila burns through the dark afternoons and the evenings. I realise how lucky I am to have found them. A soft tranquillity exudes from their Ligurian voices and their delphinium-coloured eyes. With Mariella by my side, this Ceparana nest is the calm before the storm. But then sometimes, when the sound of the rain becomes louder than thoughts, I am silently afraid. When I am at my worst, I walk down and speak to Sasha. He eats and sleeps below the house in the warmth of a stable.

I arrived on Wednesday night and by Saturday afternoon I am equipped with a handsaw, a new set of shoes for Sasha and a delineated five-day route. Serena and Leila will configure the remaining tracks in the days to come. They will then send them to me by phone. Mariella has the coordinates for the designated stops and aims to deposit feed to those reachable by car.

As far as I can tell, all things within our control are prepared. Satisfied, Serena and her boyfriend then announce that we have been invited to a country-and-western dance. We jump in the car and they drive us to Adelano, a village set high up in the clouds. A hoedown is in full swing. It's Saturday night, after all.

The dance in Adelano is madness. A Ligurian hillbilly romance. I wake on Sunday morning to see the shape of my breath in the air. My eyes close, as if to hide from the day, and I briefly escape to the rubicund faces and handshakes of the night before, reliving the sensation of my body being dragged through a room by women and men wearing suede Stetsons and denim jeans. An American flag is stapled to the wooden panelled wall; the varnished heels of leather boots clap the floorboards in the square dance; a thin sheen of smoke shrouds the air from all the cigarettes and from a long meat grill that sizzles the room alight; jugs of beer flow. I envy the country-and-western-styled moustaches adopted so accurately by these Americanised Ligurians.

Meanwhile, a foot of snow has fallen overnight.

I get out of bed and go down to see Sasha. I rub my hands down his back to get the blood flowing and to somehow reassure myself that everything is going to be OK. Outside is white and freezing cold. To my horror, Sasha winces when I touch his withers. I soften my hand and feel heat coming from a particular spot on his back, just at the point where the spine begins its upper curvature. There is swelling. For the first time this year the snow has settled below the summits, and Sasha is in pain. I am due to leave in an hour.

With the front saddle bag now removed to ensure that nothing is in contact with Sasha's withers, we ride away from the eyrie seclusion of Serena's home. I have removed the metal bit in Sasha's mouth, attached to his bridle. I am determined to continue only with a head collar and reins.

Already Mariella is well on her way up the steep tarmac tracks that clutch to the sides of the opal forms. She is anxious and I try to show her that I am assured and calm, and of course she can see that this is not true, but the strength of our hug means that we both know it is going to be OK. Somewhere in the mountains we have each other. After dropping off feed where she can, her plan is to meet me in a few days' time.

The snow stops falling and the sun creeps out. Serena and Leila are riding with me on their sturdy quarter horses. Sensible animals for these conditions, unlike Sasha. Although the stamina and intelligence of an Arab is arguably superior to most other breeds, their fine coats and sensitive natures are not synonymous with the cold and the mountains. They belong in the heat and on the flat. Spirit though, this is something all horses share; the further they wander, the greater it grows.

After two hours of ascending the foothills by road, we hitch up onto a metal railing that overlooks the villages laid out upon the muddied table. Far below, the valleys are wrapped up in strokes of cirrus and the Fiume Magra crazes under a renewed blue sky. My eyes then follow the curving shape of La Spezia coastline. I find the island of Elba floating upon the cerulean sea.

The two women lead me across the road and down the steps into a hidden bar.

'Only locals know about this place,' says Serena. 'This bar was once the secret bar. Partisans plotted here.'

The walls are painted scarlet and a silver disco ball hangs from the low ceiling. Pictures of wine-ridden tables, pine forests and wars are stuck to the walls and in the loo there is a letter from a nun violently declaring her love to an unnamed partisan. The woman behind the bar is fascinated by Scotland and curious as to how I have ended up in a place as 'forgotten' as Liguria.

We leave the asphalt behind and ride onto the Alta Via dei Monti Liguri proper; etched into the sides of pine trees and mounted upon dark wooden posts, the letters 'AV' begin to appear, painted in thick red and white. These letters will become our mountain waymarkers.

By midday we have ascended 1,100 metres and are riding with clouds below us. I can now only see the heads of mountains and the land that lies at our feet. Nothing in between. The air has thinned. Around us snow glistens on the tracks, reluctant to soften. To the south-east there are the tall, crooked shapes of the Apennines. Ahead stands an ominous-looking mountain that goes by the name of Monte Gottero.

Flaked snow then comes and goes and the hills around us are a rolling mantle, the white crust disturbed only by rocks and trees. There is silence but for hooves and the breeze and Leila tells me courageous and desperate tales witnessed by this land in World War II: the mass executions of the innocent villagers below, guilty of housing partisans in the summer; the betrayals of Italians upon Italians, fascists upon civilians; the constant threat of the marauding Nazis, desperate to grapple and control this elusive mountain network. I become conscious of how much blood must lie beneath.

We pass a stone altar that has been built into the earth. A maple tree shields it from the light of day.

'On here men and women were murdered,' remarks Serena solemnly. We stop. The horses, following our eyes, look towards the altar too. It is no bigger than a kitchen table.

'And now the young walk up here to make love on it.'

This 'forgotten' landscape is alive with secrets and death. It was from passes like these that *la resistenza* was born. The trees are hard and bare. The roots are incorrigible.

At the summit of our pass there appears a restaurant, and we tie the horses to a wooden fence. They stand together underneath the shelter of a pine tree and ahead of them, metres from their hooves, the terrain plunges into a valley that reaches far into the distance. Blue-and-leaden-coloured folds rise up either side.

A fire roars and the noise of the patrons crackles and hums. All around the room there are woollen jackets on the backs of chairs, furs draped on the sides, moleskin and wool trousers, heavy boots, and faces that are as weathered and rich as the wooden beams that hold this place together. The waitress with bare biceps and ruddy cheeks comes over to our table and in no uncertain terms tells us what we are going to eat and what we ought to drink. She leaves and returns with three bowls of piping hot wild boar *ragu*, a plate of chips and a carafe of dark red wine. She then asks if we have seen any wolves and leaves before we have time to answer. Leila and Serena giggle to each other, commenting on the forthright nature of these mountain people. I look at these two women as they speak to me. They are beautiful. Their cheeks have turned pink with the change of temperature and their blue eyes are even bigger than before. They both have sharp and heavy eyebrows and skin made ageless by the air. They have known each other their entire lives.

The conversation turns to how it is that we are all here. The horse, naturally, is the answer. But then there are life's reasons. I tell them about a fifty-seven-day ride I did down the UK, two years previously. Along with a need to escape the confines of the pandemic, I set out from the top of Scotland in memory of a friend, Leo, who died of cystic fibrosis.

'Everywhere we went people would stop, exactly where they were. Everything else would slip away. Traffic and police stopped too. And then they would reach out to touch Irelanda, the pony I was riding, and ask me where we were going, or how far we had come; what's the reason? The answer was always Leo. Leo and Land's End.'

'But what do you have to ride for here?' asks Serena.

I go to speak but then I stop. I can feel them watching me, waiting for something lucid and composed.

'This is a good question,' I answer, thinking fast. 'I want more of what I had – that feeling, the way I felt at Land's End. I don't want it to go.'

They both nod.

'*Don Quixote!*' I exclaim. 'Have either of you read *Don Quixote*?'

'When I was a child—'

'This gives me reason,' I continue, faster, 'so much reason. And then, I suppose, what happened down in Naples... I wouldn't be able to live with myself if the start of this ride had been destroyed by an Italian – no offence.'

They both laugh. I take a sip of my wine.

'Guilt,' I say.

'Guilt? Guilt of what?'

'Guilt for what I have... and death. Or, rather, gratitude and death. They are reasons too. I never want to take what I have for granted. To not use it, or, at least, to not make something of it... this would be criminal. I know that someone like Leo would have lived for every moment.'

The two women smile. There is silence between us and I drink some more wine. Leila drinks too and then her expression changes. I feel her eyes go through me.

'What we are doing here now,' she states, 'as a three, it needs to be done... I am serious when I say this.'

The previous year, she and Serena embarked upon a five-day ride to a place called Rifugio La Terza, the highest refuge for horse and rider in the Ligurian Alps. On the final day, as they approached the plateau, Leila fell ill. Serena insisted that she be taken down to the nearest hospital. After some persuasion, Leila was lifted into a four-by-four and began the 1,780-metre descent. The pain worsened and the roadless car journey became excruciating. She lost consciousness. Leila emerged one month later from hospital with a rare disease of the intestine. Her illness and the scar that now runs across her belly as a consequence of them opening her up have created a fierce and permanent reminder.

'This is why I am here. This is why I met you. This route. This first horse route across the Ligurian Alps. Our *ipo via*. It is important that you make the way across the mountains because I thought I was going to die. Do you understand? I have wanted to do this since I was a child. What we are now doing, together, here... it needs to be done.'

Outside a storm has begun to brood. The shape of Monte Gottero looms vast ahead of us.

'The mountain of hell,' remarks Serena. 'Tomorrow, this is where you go.'

Late into the afternoon our trail becomes exposed. Winds rip their way up the frozen ravines and snow blows sideways, hissing against the side of Sasha's body and drumming upon my poncho. I have to shield my eyes and walk on foot, almost blindly. The silhouettes of the peaks are silver-plated in the unclear light. The clouds are dark.

Eventually we reach a village called Chiusola. And then it all happens so quickly. A mess of storm and horses. Before I know it, Serena and Leila have gone. Their faces and words vanish into their friend's horse truck and Sasha and I are passed on to strangers that take us to their stables and, once more, into new lives.

In the morning the beaten earth is silent. The sun shines and the hills are enclosed with snow and scarred with scoria shapes of rock. I jump into Lodovigo's car. My host skids down the body of the mountain until we reach the stables that he and his wife, Roberta, have built up during the fifty-five years they have been married. There is an inky-black river running by.

Steam rises from a majestic Murgese horse that bows its black head from a wooden stable door. From Arab and Barb blood, these dark horses originate in the south, in the woodlands of Puglia. Historically they were used for farm work and, like many strong horses, by the military. Within the shadows behind I see its foal, eyes like glass. The hair of the proud mare is knotted and draped like a wild gypsy and the other black Murgese horses are mellow in their stalls. Sasha looks rested and warm. Little does he know that he is sharing a stable with his ancient cousins. Roberta has found him a rug, lots of hay, and fresh straw for his bedding.

For their entire lives Roberta and Lodovigo have lived in the ridge-top village of Chiusola, home to twenty yellow-and-saffron little houses that cling to each other so as not to float away. The setting is mesmeric. A bottomless valley engulfs the north. I am unable to see the land at the bottom because we are so high up. To the south, the view is cut in two by the serrated line of a rugged sierra, leaving sunlit basins either side, forbidden from ever meeting. Chiusola is the floating portal between the two chasms.

Thanks to the fire in Lodovigo and Roberta's home, most of my clothes are now dry. They are gentle and kind people but wary of my route and how far I intend to travel; the volatile conditions on Monte Gottero... the snow might shift underneath me... and then there are the newly fallen trees, mudslides, and, of course, the danger of being unreachable. All that way to France and then to Spain... it isn't possible. It shouldn't be done.

As I tack up Sasha, the worry in their voices makes me rethink the situation. Roberta touches Sasha's withers and shakes her head. She cuts the beginning of his mane to inspect the swelling more clearly, and then places my saddle on his back.

'It does not work,' she states.

Roberta explains to me how this saddle is not capable of dealing with the terrain and pressure of a mountain crossing. The weight is not evenly spread. I cannot climb Monte Gottero with this.

'But I will walk with him—'

'It is not right.'

I sense a stubborn fear in her. To avoid dispute, I agree to alter the route. But this is not what I want. I am sure that Sasha and I are capable of climbing this mountain together, side by side, and the assumption that these people have about what horses should or should not do is difficult to hear. But they are my hosts and I am in their land and country. I understand too that their caution is not only driven by their fear of the unknown – the most habitual form of fear – but also, I'm sure, from experience. In these conditions, this overrides all. 'The mountain of hell' will have to wait another day.

Together we map out a longer, simpler trail that descends from Chiusola and runs adjacent to a road. Eventually it will ascend once more onto the Alta Via trail. Lodovigo rides with me for two hours and, as I say goodbye, he points up to the far side of the steep, wintered valley, shaking his head at the foreboding sight of Monte Gottero that now roams above. I see a lonely black track stencilled across the silver side of the mountain's face, the traversing track we could have taken. As we watch, it is then swallowed up by a mass of cloud. The lore surrounding this foreboding body of earth is hard to silence. I would have loved to have been in the palm of that cloud.

'*In bocca al lupo,*' shouts Lodovigo, turning his olive-shaped Murgese horse back to Chiusola.

The only other marks on the new snow apart from ours resemble the paw prints of dogs. At some points the powder reaches the tops of my knees but, just as it seems too deep, my boots hit on firmer ground, uncovering the submerged pre-pandemic tracks. The sky darkens and we come across a large, square chrome-yellow building standing alone and surreal in the middle of a pine and larch wood clearing. Rifugio Passo del Bocco.

Funded largely by the European Union, *rifugios* serve as a place of mountain accommodation for hikers and skiers all through the Alps, with most of them accessible only on foot. Many of these *rifugios* have been abandoned since the pandemic. Fortunately, I have the help of Mariella. To ensure that Rifugio Passo del Bocco was still standing, she called ahead a couple days ago to inform them that her brother and his horse are on their way. For the first time in two years, the *rifugio* agreed to open.

We give each other a mountain hug. She looks well. Her own story is full of obstacles and solutions, understanding the Ligurians and their 'style' being the centrepiece. Unsurprisingly, she has survived the foreign maps, the storms, the snow-ridden roads and the heavy car to deliver Sasha's feed for the next couple of days. In doing so, she has also been making sure the locations Leila and Serena have pinpointed for me and Sasha to stay at are real and peopled.

Together we brush Sasha and cover him in a warm waterproof coat for the night ahead. There is no indoor shelter for him, only the tussled limbs of pine trees above us that interrupt the snow fall. After feeding him, we go inside the *rifugio* to eat like kings and queens, the only guests on a mountain in nowhere. We are served by a woman with fuchsia nail varnish, lipstick and enormous red hair to match. As it gets dark, the lonely building changes. A stranger trudges through the wooden door.

'*Mio fratello*,' the woman explains.

The tall man wears a patched-up grey woollen overcoat and a macabre expression that is heavy like the rock-faced mountains he comes from.

'*Il freddo è ovunque*, the cold is everywhere,' he utters without elaboration, stamping his boots on the brush-mat in the doorway. '*E così sono i lupi*, and so are the wolves.'

He makes his way to the bar and orders a large Asinello and whisky. I get up from our table and ask him if what he says is true. The man looks at me and then glances to the window by the door, which now shows nothing but his slumped reflection and the blank night.

'It may not be true for you, but it will be true for that horse,' he concludes.

I pitch a tent from Mariella's car in a position that allows me to see the full silhouette of Sasha through the canvas. Initially I fall into a deep sleep, but then I wake to the disturbing sound of barks. Wild boar roam, running through the forest that encloses us. The barks cease, and then there is an uneasy silence. My eyes open and close with my woollen blanket wrapped around me.

Suddenly my senses are wired. At first it sounds just like a patter, like the paws of a whippet on snow or the soft fluttering of wings, but then it becomes too near and too heavy to ignore. My eyes are fixed on Sasha's silhouette, waiting for him to see what I can't. His head whips up in fright. I scramble out of the tent and shine my headtorch. There is nothing. Only the naked tree trunks and the veils of snow. I calm him. He settles and I return to the saddle-cloth mattress of my tent. Three times he jolts and three times I hear the animals come close and then disappear. We are at the centre of a nocturnal game.

In the morning the snow around us is covered in the pugmarks of wolves. They circled us in the night. I am glad I slept next to Sasha. This year has seen the most deaths in decades with regards to sheep, chickens, calves and foals. With the growing absence of the human in these remote parts of Italy, the wolves have grown in number and desire, reclaiming their woods.

The trees ebb away, and the land is stark once more. With fresh snowfall in the night, the wintry landscape rolls formlessly. The howling sounds of the Maremmano-Abruzzese sheepdogs echo through the cold air and wolf tracks pepper the sides of the track we walk upon. Indigenous to central Italy, the lion-like Maremmano dogs have been guarding livestock for centuries and need to be given the space and respect they deserve. As tempting as it is to befriend them, I think against it.

Before leaving I decided to leave Sasha's saddle in the car. I need to give his back a break while I can. If I ever want to ride him again, the swelling will have to go for good. I recall Roberta's voice in my head. Her intentions were only for Sasha's well-being. The saddle doesn't fit. Despite Ciro's changes, it seems the saddle wasn't designed for journeys beyond three or five days. It was bought when all things were being prepared for a horse that wasn't ready and for a journey that was not meant to happen. When anxiety and pressure were food and water. This saddle has harmed Sasha and I will not ride again until I find something that fits. It's the least that he requires. Besides, I like travelling with Sasha beside me, I can see where his eyes look, and I can hear his breath.

Mariella drives on. I don't know when we will see each other next, but I hope soon. Already she is growing in confidence in her wayfinding, her smile is warm and her hug is tight. She is unpacking the mountains, one by one. I put the most essential of mine and Sasha's belongings into my rucksack and set off on foot. *In bocca al lupo.*

The last time we communicated, back in Ceparana, Kiki said she would join me with her horse in France. Then she called back to say it would be sooner. I have no idea how long it will be until this person arrives. I'll believe it when I see it.

To be honest, I don't let myself think about it for too long. I need to keep the focus on Sasha and on getting through these days. The idea of someone walking next to me, sitting near me in the evenings, sharing this little world that is being forged, step by step, doesn't fill me with joy. Kiki will not know what it is we have gone through. Only Sasha and I understand what it is we have done to get to where we are.

After following the red-and-white-painted Alta Via signs, Leila and Serena's route takes us into the shadows of an old quarry where ten or so wild horses roam like bandits. The sounds of barks and howls now drift away. We are alone but for these glaring horses, standing indifferent and separate from each other upon a plateau of scree. I wonder how on earth they survive in this desiccated landscape. Sasha sticks close to me. Silently we pass through. Our route steepens and then narrows before we reach a point where we can go no further.

Ahead of us a waterfall thrashes down through a deep gorge in the mountainside. Smooth rocks shimmer in the reflection of the light upon the flowing water. The remnants of a wooden bridge lie scattered either side. There is no way we can jump this. We turn back upon the narrow path and zigzag our way down the snow-covered slope. The gorge begins to shallow.

As we reach a possible place to cross, I notice that the far bank is blocked off by a ramshackle barricade. A single line of rope is tied between two trees, while a collection of loose coils of fencing wire and cut up branches are purposely laid on top of each other. I choose to ignore this warning sign and begin to cut. We need to cross – there is no other way.

Up to this point Sasha has been remarkable. He has followed me into this wintry tundra of snow and mountain and has stayed by me, trusted me and has never stopped moving and taking in all things new. But now his nerves have caught up with him and he refuses to cross the flowing water. He stands with his nostrils flared and his legs rigid.

I saw up the branches, roll away two big grey boulders that block an easy passing, cut the rope and clear the shrub and the wire. Tentatively, after watching me wade through the water and jump up onto the cleared far bank of the gorge, he places one hoof in front of the other. As if electrified by the water, he then loses control and races towards me, cutting his legs on the rocks. I calm him as he stretches up onto the other side and set about to disinfect and dress the worst of the wounds that drip scarlet on his front-left leg.

We rediscover the red-and-white star signs and the path rashly begins to climb. Railings guide and fasten us to the mountainside and the waterfall rushes underneath. The drop is horrifying. We slip together and clamber on. Like nuggets of hope, every twenty metres or so, we find a small pile of horse manure. If bandit horses can roam here, then so can Sasha.

At 1,100 metres we plateau upon Monte Gosciona and look back to see the crystalline vista below. Only clots of trees and veined bodies of water disrupt the lifeless mould. From a recurring dream, the landscape is sliding into a nightmare. Beyond the plateau we reach a pinewood forest where the sun hasn't yet shone and human life hasn't touched for months, years, it seems. We examine the ground for any reassuring signs of horse manure but see nothing. Only wolf tracks have disturbed the deep snow. The forest rises sharply above us.

I take time to breathe. All around us cast-iron faces of mountains conceal the horizon. We are alone.

To climb safely up through the forest we have to take it slow. But it is important that we keep moving. I kick my toe into the ground for purchase, and begin wading my way up through the snow that tackles me at the knees. I fall and start again.

At the base of the first tree, I latch my arm around its trunk and wait for Sasha to follow, catching my breath. Loosely, I hold his lead rope in my free hand. Sasha's black coal eyes glare at me in discontentment. At least he is not afraid. In normal circumstances, there is no way that I would have endeavoured to climb this wood, let alone with a horse. The gradient must be forty-five degrees at least. If he could speak, Sasha would be questioning my sanity. I watch him as his chest pounds and his body ripples, and he digs his hooves into the snow to force his way up to me. The process goes on. The dig-in, the climb and the anchoring to the trees. Soon it becomes too steep to go back down.

After an hour and ten minutes we reach a lumberjack track that shelfs out from the steep wood. According to the map it is the old road to the village of Cabanne. The descending road to civilisation.

A low tolling bell pulses languidly through the afternoon air, a haunting salute. Like many of these Ligurian villages, Cabanne is deserted. I ride Sasha bareback past the empty church and down the main street. We are in search of a hostel or a *rifugio*. A person. The sound of Sasha's hooves shudders off the walls.

A face appears from a first-storey balcony. I glance up and the stranger hurriedly withdraws. Moments later a street door swings open and an old lady emerges into the cold. Her smile wraps itself around me. Softly, her hand touches Sasha's neck.

'You have a wonderful sister,' she says in perfect English. 'She told us that you were coming. Follow me.'

The old lady leads us into a stable full of hay and straw. An ancient Arabian mare wallows in the shadows, at peace, it seems, in her isolated world. She and Sasha share the shelter and munch on hay all through the night. The woman gives me a bottle of white wine, some bread and some cheese, and I sleep in the cobwebs and cover myself in hay.

In the morning I am awoken by a man tapping at my shins with a stick. He then gestures me to follow him, leading me outside. The sun has not yet risen and I can't feel my toes. We reach a tap, and, with the energy of a magician, he turns the handle and stands back in delight as the water that flows steams in the frozen morning air. I place my feet in a bucket below and stand tall, feeling my toes thaw. I do the same with my rigid boots.

This day holds the first view that completely takes my breath away. I say goodbye to Cabanne and the kind couple, and we travel back into the hills. Along the ridge of Monte Larnaia there is a steep rock face that projects out into the open air like a pier to the sky. It is too dangerous for Sasha to climb, so I leave him grazing and then clamber up to see what I can find at the top. The expanse below is an illusion of waves; white-peaked breakers blurring the lines between sky and earth. Monte Caucaso stands tall ahead of me, a portal into the Rapallo and Genoa shores that shudder somewhere beyond, the far-off ocean now a shadow to these mountainous rollers. Sasha scales up to meet me, curious to see where I have gone.

I cry. This is something I haven't done for a very long time.

We stand together and breathe in the interchanging shapes of the terrain. For a moment, this makes me feel as at home as I imagine the wolves to be; just as the trees and the rocks. I feel close to Sasha, my fellow traveller, trying to decipher the house where we are.

I acknowledge how violently this unending landscape can oscillate between wintry dream and iron-faced nightmare. But the hellish moments have their own beauty too. They become coordinates in memory, proving that we are moving forward. The crumbling walls of the palace are now a long way behind us. This makes me proud.

For that night we head to the town of Torriglia, in the upper Trebbia valley. I am worried about Sasha's withers. I think of little else. The swelling remains. In the night I see an image of his back being torn apart while he stands on the crest of a ridge. Limbs of trees erupt from his spine, reaching for air. I must keep walking on foot, allowing his back to rest and for the blood to flow as he moves.

But for how long can this go on? My legs ache and I have started to get a pain that shoots down from my right hip at random intervals. A knuckling pressure squeezes at my temples. I only have myself to blame.

◆

Configuring where I am or what I am doing has been replaced with the mantra of step by step. Scree now resembles shattered bones, just as the fossils in Tuscany had replaced the roots of vines. The trails worsen. The handsaw in my rucksack is used daily. Mudslides have charred the routes and even the astral red-and-white Alta Via signs have morphed into signifiers of suspicion. The shoulders and jaws of mountains are walls. The ceilinged sky remains low and metallic. I am in the season of dead spring, a season that bears dead skin on the bottom of my feet. Amongst it all, however, my exhaustion has produced something of an indelible determination. A steely myopia in the hoary light. I believe this applies to Sasha too. We have entered an unshakeable state. All we have to do is to keep climbing, keep going. Dream or nightmare, we *have* to get out of these mountains. Wherever that might be. The horizons are a sackcloth wall. Exit-less. It's strange how we can be so confined in so much space. This is a new form of vertigo. The only thing that breaks the monochrome is the silverware of bells and the glugging of cold black rivers that Sasha drinks from. There are no birds in the sky. There are no stars in Liguria. The cuts on Sasha's leg have begun to mend.

I am steadily losing weight but am growing fast in muscle and strength. Whenever I see my reflection, my eyes appear like someone else's. I have succumbed to coffee. The tea here doesn't work. I begin to associate coffee with river water, like a fish might do. The villages I pass are solemn and mostly empty, fading away, but the people – when we are lucky to find them – have warm hearts and are full of a charged life. At times it feels it is only their work and their nature that keep the mountains standing and the rivers flowing.

I finally meet Mariella again in the hamlet of Crosi, a very difficult place to find. Leila is there too. All morning I have kept loyal to the invisible path that traverses the untamed slope of Monte Badriga, cutting my way through and digging my heels into the ground to avoid slipping down the fresh mudslides. Finally, the trees part and Sasha and I emerge into the full bright daylight with my handsaw in front of me like a torch in the darkness. To our right, four mouse-coloured donkeys approach us from behind a wooden fence line, presenting me and Sasha with their soft noses. To our left, Monte Badriga continues skyward.

Crosi is a collection of six stone buildings situated high up on the south side of the Molino Vecchio valley. The buildings have been resurrected by a man called Emmanuele. All over eastern Liguria his name is known, almost to the point where it seems that he must be a myth, or a wandering spirit. As Sasha and I sweat in the sunlight, covered in cuts and mud, it feels like we have sidestepped into someone else's dream. A warm and earthen one with, hopefully, some hay and water at the end of it. I am exhausted, Sasha is unimpressed. We have just endured one of the steepest climbs of the journey so far. An 800-metre ascent at a near 50-degree angle.

'*Il mulo e il cavallo!*'

Emmanuele puts out his hand and shakes his head in disbelief at the size of my rucksack and at the unsaddled back of Sasha. His eyes greet me like mad swaying trees.

'You will be stronger than him by the end. No one walks next to a horse like this.'

He is young with rosy cheeks and has auburn curly hair that escapes from the sides of his green felt hat. When he was a boy he lived in a nearby town. After school he would roam this valley, replacing his loneliness with the limitless possibilities that the shadowed side of Monte Badriga had to offer. One day he came across some forgotten farm buildings, wrapped up in ivy and brambles, and here his internal world became something tangible; he finished school and university, got a job in Genoa, and it came to pass that the land of his secrets was being offered up by the local government, to recover and to be cultivated as a project for whoever had the energy and mind to want it. Emmanuele set about to claim back the hamlet from the mountain.

Sasha wanders in the midday sun and Emmanuele finds some hay for him from the donkeys' barn. The buildings are interlinked with creepers, wooden beams and stairwells; most of the roofs are still crumbling and the insides are full of hay, cows, donkeys, sheep, chickens, tractors and tools. Hidden in the centre of it all is his home. We climb the wooden steps that hug the side of his eyrie house, the heart of his promethean kingdom, and we duck our heads as the door creaks open.

Inside the low ceiling glimmers with iron pans and hand-painted plates. The floor is covered in loose tiles. I turn a corner and weary leather yokes and brass cow bells protrude from the stone walls. Mariella and Leila are sitting with beaming smiles at the kitchen table. A large clay bowl of swollen snap beans stares at us from the middle of the red-chequered tablecloth, while plates of hard cheese and focaccia wait left and right. An unlabelled magnum bottle of dark wine stands like a well-trained dog at the head.

Emmanuelle sits down and pours the wine into four small glasses. We eat and speak in broken Italian, and I soak up the enigma of this room and this man like he is a rare thing on the point of extinction. Stirrup leathers, copper ears of corn, string onions and another green felt hat hang above us. The belly of the ceiling slumps between the beams as black-and-white photographs flag like leaves along the termite-ravaged bodies, the figures in the images dimmed with time.

'When you ride here, nothing is ever certain. The mountains don't owe you a thing. This is why you have everything.' Another snap bean bursts in Emmanuele's hands. I have come to get used to this succinct, prophetic style by which the locals communicate. It seems to somehow be appropriate to the environment that surrounds them.

'The Ligurian people are not rich. We live off very little. We work for our food and fight hard to stay warm in this valley that is fighting too; fighting for life.' Leila translates his local dialect as we talk of the people and the crossing. He then enquires about what Sasha and I have seen. I make sure not to leave anything out. By the intensity of his voice, I can tell that he cares a great deal for these mountains and their paths.

'*Ma perché sei qui?* But why are you here?'

'To reach Finisterre,' were the words about to tumble from my mouth, but I stop myself and think.

'To find... to find places like this, people like you... to learn something.'

Emmanuele drinks another glass of wine before getting up from the table. He takes us outside.

After waving goodbye to Leila and Mariella in the Freelander, Emmanuele takes me down an old mule track, Sasha in tow. He points to a clearing below, where felled beech trees have been hauled aside and velvet, rich soil upturned and sowed two years previously. The launches of a meadow have slowly begun to take shape, sunlight drenching the new space. We pause to take stock of his work. He turns to Sasha, placing his hand upon his neck.

I want to say more throughout our time together but all I can think of is, 'What you have created is important, Emmanuele. I believe it is important.' I am absorbing more than I can give. This man has made noise and brought life out of rock and silence.

We walk on to a bone-white fountain that he made from clay when he was a boy. It collects water that flows down from the ridge. I submerge my head in its basin. A faint blue image of Mary Magdalene is painted upon the clay bottom.

'I will see you one day,' I say to him, drying the water from my face. He shakes my hand and looks once more at Sasha and then back at me. His swaying eyes now still and distant.

'I want that I can come with you,' he says, his expression now serious.

'If only we could be in two places at once.'

'*Sì*... *In un altro momento.* Yes... at another time. *Cammineremo insieme in un altro momento.* We will walk together at another time... good luck on your search.'

With the fatigue of the afternoon and with the wine making my head slow and unclear, the lunch at Crosi begins to feel all too much like a staged diorama of Ligurian life. A very different reality presents itself later in the day as we trudge into the town of Casella. From across a busy road people laugh at us, drivers beep in anger, and a dog jumps out from the boot of a car and clings to the back of Sasha's leg, biting him and making him bleed. I kick the animal as hard as I possibly can. With a yelp the dog collapses onto the pavement. At first, I think I have killed it. The animal then rises to its feet and slopes away.

That night I burst four blisters with the sharp end of a hoof nail. The swelling on Sasha's withers looks bad. I think it has worsened. I can't be sure. His thin Arabian hair is beginning to fall away and open skin is starting to show. I can feel my ribs clearly now.

A fog sets in and smothers the next two days. It soaks us and makes the mountain passes dangerous. But I don't mind it, it reminds me of Scotland. Occasionally the weather lifts, pushed off by the southerly wind, and an entire new landscape uncovers itself, just for a moment, before once again disappearing into the damp blanket. At the top of Monte Taccone an enormous mass of water reveals itself just below us, the dam of the Rio Lischeo, and beyond; blue hills tumble over each other as if they are fighting to be seen, to be close to us. And then to the south, for a second, I see the far-reaching form of the Ligurian Sea. I can trace over it with my finger. Sharp rocks leer above our heads, trees leaning away from the rancour of the wind that is always present, always loud. It is only in those brief moments of clarity that I notice how steep our trail has become. And then the danger is covered up and once more there is nothing but my steps and Sasha's hooves.

It is getting late. I am hoping that we are expected at an old fort, the only point of refuge according to the maps. But the phone reception has been so bad that I can't be sure where Mariella is or if the fort is still standing. Either way, we have to try and get there before dark. Sasha needs rest. I could sleep for days. I have reached a new layer of exhaustion. My rucksack and my clothes are drenched.

Forte Geremia is situated on the large eastern peak of a mountain called Bric Geremia, from which it gets its name, and overlooks the Turchino valley. It was constructed in the late nineteenth century to better control the Apennine Pass before being abandoned after World War I. At one point it could house up to a hundred troops. According to the map it isn't far, but nothing seems reachable within the mist.

I ride Sasha bareback through an avenue of trees. Branches grope at each other with wooden fingers. We are apparitions cantering along the ascending trail. Everything is mute but for our breaths steaming in the air and for the clang of Sasha's shoes. The canter swifts to a gallop and the cadaverous avenue curves to the south, clutching the body of Bric Geremia, and then, in an instant, our tunnel of trees disappears and the mist is white and smothering once more, the shape of the land impossible to read.

Before long, a black form begins to dominate the near distance. The looming mass seems elevated, the size of a ship. We climb a path that crawls up to it, still only able to be sure of four metres ahead of us, and the thing grows bigger and darker. Graver. We have reached Forte Geremia. It exists.

Sasha roams the eerie plateau and I knock three times on the metal door of the fort, the taps echoing like hammer blows. I stand back and wait. The wind squalls across us. Finally, a shuffling sound of movement escapes from inside and I hear the shaking of keys and the sliding of bolts. A tall, gaunt man appears in the doorway and, without uttering a word, opens the door wide enough for me to come inside. I promise Sasha that I will be quick.

   A fire roars. Stone steps climb high up to a wooden gallery on the first floor. I immediately remove my rucksack and poncho and hang them from the stair bannisters and turn to follow my host. The silent man leads me through a narrow door frame on the right side of the hall. Beyond, there is a bar that glows with a low-hanging light and candles that twist their necks out of empty wine bottles, pools of wax stuck to the wood. Muskets, swords, shovels and a Phrygian hat are hung confusedly on the stone walls and old photographs of soldiers and mountain excavations are framed above the bar.

   '*Sono sorpreso*. I am surprised,' says the man in a quiet, lisping voice. He is young, perhaps thirty, with thinning hair, sharp shoulders and a narrow, beaked nose. He speaks and moves like he has lived in this fort for sixty years, the dissatisfied palimpsest of a night watchman. I sit down on an old church bench that is propped up against a trellised window facing the bar. My body is cold from the mist soaked into my clothes. '*Mi aspettavo un gigante*. I was expecting a giant.'

'*Gigante?*' I reply, trying to understand what he is saying.

'*Tua sorella è molto alta.*' I nod in agreement, warmed by the mention of Mariella. She has been here.

'Where are you from?'

'*Scozia.* When was my sister here?'

'Before the fog. And the other girl. They were here before the fog. *Questa mattina.* They have gone to the place where your horse must go, La Nuvola sul la Mare. You will then return here to sleep. There will be dinner.'

'Is it far, where we have to go?'

His pale fingers clutch and pull down on the tap of the solitary beer dispenser. The word 'Peroni' is crudely engraved onto a wooden placard that hangs from the neck.

'It is difficult for you and the horse to travel tonight. But then... you travel here, to the fort, and not even the farmers travel today.'

A sickness fills my stomach. I need to find Mariella and the place this man is speaking about. I am starving. In my mind I imagine us blindly wandering all night through the mist, just moving to keep warm.

I drink the pint of lager and retrieve my poncho and rucksack, half dried from the hall fire. The man explains to me where I have to go and then shuts the metal door behind me. The echo remains.

The wind roars across the plateau. Sasha is huddled next to the wall of the fort, unamused. His ears prick up and once more we move. It isn't long before we are descending the far side of Bric Geremia, the fort behind us, disappearing into the mist like flotsam. The track traverses and then switches right, through woods with trees that shake manically and with branches that creak. The way clears and we find ourselves on an asphalt road. It is dusk. I now can't see beyond two metres.

Cat's eyes overlap the white painted line in the centre of the road. To our right there is an amorphous cascade of rock. I can't make out where it begins and ends. To our left, on the far side of the road, there is a metal barricade. From what I can see, only an abyss lies beyond. On we walk.

The headlights of a car circle towards us on the far side of the road. Shark-like, they wallow past. I keep looking back, twisting my neck while moving as fast as I can, preparing for the inevitable to creep up behind us. It soon comes. The round eyes arrive, glaring through the dense fog. I shine my head torch from the back of my head and then flick it on and off in a desperate bid for the car to slow. But the machine is blind to us. The headlights come closer. Quickly, I jump off the road with Sasha, pushing him against the rock face. The car drives through. Our bodies remain out of sight, hunched up until the danger passes.

◆

After wading on through the fog, I spot an opening in the rocky cascade. We follow it and reach a track that takes us three miles towards a field. There, in the far corner, I find a shelter with hay and water. A storm has set in. I feel weak. At one point delirious. I need sugar. Once the shelter door is shut and Sasha is out of the rain, I turn to walk back across the field, before collapsing in the mud. A shepherd sees me from the track and drives me to the fort.

The noise of shrieking girls and music leads me into a room with a cobbled floor and old skis criss-crossed on the walls. A fire roars. The ceiling is low, wine barrels serve as lamp stands and a table is laid with tall candles. A sewing machine draped in brocade cloth sits in the corner. Red-and-olive hardback books about partisan weapons lean in shelves and, cross-legged on an old church bench with cigarettes in their mouths, cowboy boots on and woollen tunics turned up to the chin, sit Mariella and her friend from art college, Raffi.

By now Mariella is confident with the process. She has managed to locate the stables and paddocks suggested by Leila and Serena and convince the Ligurian locals that the horse and the boy are real and that what they have heard is true, he is indeed riding to the Atlantic Ocean. She hasn't crashed the car again, she has safely dropped the feed and, for the majority of the time, has kept to the right-hand side of the road. She tells me that her height is proving an advantage for getting what she wants. To the typical Ligurian she must appear as a Viking.

As a three we sit down at the table. Giuliano, the peculiar guardian of the fort, drifts in and out of the room clutching bowls of *ragu*, tall carafes of dark wine, shots of grappa and plates of sugared *torta Sacripantina*. The room rolls with music and glows in firelight. The wind and the rain rattle at the turret windows.

I become mesmerised by Raffi's smile; it is the biggest one I have ever seen. She has captivating, maroon-brown eyes and hair that is thick and dark. I feel so calm with these two friends, so relieved to be out of the weather and to know that Sasha is safe in the warmth of a stable.

283 miles, 17 days

LIBERTÀ 1944

10–12 April
Forte Geremia – Giovo Ligure, Liguria

The quiet village of Giovo Ligure is home to a haunted stable built by Napoleon that goes by the name of Terra di Mezzo. Over 200 years ago the stable housed French troops, mules and horses as they sought to divide and overcome the Piedmontese and Austrian armies. They used the hostile Ligurian Alps as their earthen accomplice. After over a century of neglect, the buildings were later recycled by Germans to torture and kill Italian partisans during World War II. Forte Tagliata del Giovo, a nearby fort constructed by Napoleon for garrison reserves, is said to be the home of a phantasm soldier who ambles down from the hill and into the stables of Terra di Mezzo by night. As well as a hotel for ghosts, the fort has become a hotspot for teenage sex and Sunday afternoon picnics. The stables are still in use today.

Sixteen miles beyond Forte Geremia, Sasha and I turn off the track leading to Pontinvrea village and walk into the yard of Terra di Mezzo. Once more, I can only hope that Mariella has warned these people of our coming. The weather has made a turn, and I see creeks of blue in the sky.

Two young boys chase each other around a tree stump on push scooters. Tawny dogs hurtle through the dirt in pursuit of a frontrunner and, on my right, girls are riding gypsy ponies in a sandy arena with no bits on the bridles. They wave and whistle at me, and then carry on.

I am greeted by Mattias, a stocky twenty-something-year-old man with a black t-shirt that has 'ANARCHY' printed on the front of it in white letters. He takes me through the arched doorway of the stables, with peeling malachite-coloured paint, and as I cross the threshold I am forced to stop. I have been here before. I know I have. The smell is the first thing. A smell I once knew well. An inborn scent, before everything, untraceable to a specific place. For a moment, time withers. The malachite-green paint seems the most natural colour in the world.

The stable building is long. There are twelve looseboxes running down the right-hand side, which leaves a pass on the left. At the far end there is an enormous bale of hay, keeping company an old chestnut horse that roams free. Mattias leads me down the pass and one by one we are greeted by the inhabitants; the heads of eleven curious horses lean out of their boxes to inspect who these itinerants might be. No horse is the same: Cob, Friesian, paint horse, quarter horse, Pinto, Andalusian. Girls, boys and women chatter and roam among them, birdlike, passing by the stranger and Sasha. They stroke his neck and flank like one of their own and nod at me before moving on. I feel strangely calm. That force of pressure: the worry and the self-destructive expectation that squeezes upon my temples, cold sweats that stick to my spine – for the first time since Ceparana, it lifts.

After finding Sasha his box, Mattias introduces me to a woman named Luna, the owner of Terra di Mezzo. Luna is young. She has a kind, tired face with pink cheeks. As she shakes my hand, she exudes an instant warmth, a blurred glimmering, softening the sound and the edges. Her pale blue eyes are round and mellow, her lips are finely shaped, and she has long blonde hair.

'*Tu sei il mulo.* You are the mule,' she laughs gently, feeling the weight of my rucksack. I smile and thank her for her kindness in letting Sasha stay.

'*Dov'è il cavallo coraggioso?*'

I take Luna to Sasha's box. She is visibly impressed.

'*Brilla,*' she exclaims, '*brilla e i suoi muscoli sono forti*. He glows and his muscles are strong.'

I explain to her why it is that I am not riding, and she asks me how difficult the journey has been. She is fascinated to know the route I have taken and questions me on certain points that she thought were unpassable except on asphalt: from Adelano to the 5,000-feet ridges of Passo Bocco; the sheer climb above Cabanne and across the oak and chestnut woods to Torriglia; she has heard that the mudslides and the trees have destroyed the trail through Crosi. Is Emmanuele well? And the wolves? How have you not got frostbite yet?

She tells me of a man who attempted to cross the Ligurian mountains last year, but from west to east.

'When he reached Terra di Mezzo,' translates Mattias, 'he stayed here for a week... which then turned into three months. He then hired a horse trailer and drove all the way to Ceparana, before riding down the length of Italy.'

'*Afferma di aver cavalcato dalla Francia alla Sicilia.* He claims that he has ridden from France to Sicily,' interjects Luna, '*ma se non puio passare per Giovo, non puio passare per l'italia.* But if you can't pass through Giovo, you can't pass through Italy.'

At this point in time a three-month holiday and a trailer ride seems like an attractive offer. Luna is surprised that I have managed to make it so far on foot and, of course, baffled as to why I have decided to make the journey across the mountains in April. I just shake my head in a shared disbelief, relieved at accepting the fact that I am lucky to be here and foolish to have left so early in the year. It is my fault that we left on 24 March... and it is my fault too that we left at all. But it is by the work of both me and Sasha that we have reached Terra di Mezzo.

Luna rubs her hand down Sasha's strong chest and checks his feet. She remarks on how handsome his head is and how friendly his eyes. She wonders where he is from as he appears stocky for an Arab. I tell her that he was born in Poland and that I bought him from a stud called Bosana, near Piacenza. She strokes his mane, his neck, his withers and then, with her fingers, feels her way around the swelling. The hairless skin shines greyly in the falling light of the stable. Luna goes very quiet. My worries return.

Outside the stables, horses roam the brown, grassless paddocks like self-proclaimed rulers of the land. They charge and circle me with matted manes and hairy legs. Mud is strewn across their flanks and faces, and they have moustaches and plaited tails in the style of pixie monarchs. When their dance is over, I approach them. The herd is wily-serene. Rugged and warm.

A woman with three teeth offers me a joint. Two teenage girls run towards me with a tub of Nutella spread and force the wooden spoon into my mouth. It tastes delicious. A Romani woman with matted black hair smacks me on the back as if I were her long-lost son. A girl riding in the arena wolf-whistles at me while cantering in a long, slow circle, and a voice calls out in anger from inside the stables, reluctantly preparing horse feed for the next day. Mattias grabs me by the arm and leads me down the road to the house of his parents.

'It seems they have been waiting for you to come here for a long time,' he says, shaking his head. 'I have been here for six years and they don't even look at me. You arrive for six minutes and they fight like cats.'

'Who?' I ask.

'*Le ragazze!*'

'A boy and a horse bring people together,' I respond, licking the Nutella from my lips.

We are interrupted by the crackling sound of a motorbike that rumbles past. The Romani woman raises her hand in a wave and motors on with her hair trailing in the air behind her like blackened reeds. Her eight-year-old son pursues her in the same lane on his plastic push scooter.

Mattias introduces me to his mother and his stepfather: Gabriela and Roberto. They live in a two-storey yellow house with chickens and an old grey Arab horse in the back field beyond a veranda. Chicks are due to hatch in the shed.

Roberto is like a Genovese gaucho; he is small, tough, moustached and has the unruliest wit that I have come across in a very long time. Gabriela is Chilean. Her round face beams with kindness. And with stories. She is a mother to everything. She hugs me and shows me to my room on the bottom floor. Soon, Mariella and Raffi arrive, and we all eat upstairs in the kitchen. Roberto pours wine and we dive into a huge bowl of spaghetti bolognese. There is nowhere else in the world I would rather be. Something has been released in me. By arriving here, something has passed and gone, and space has been created. The sense of swaying in and out of what was real and what was not, feeling and unfeeling, has come to an abrupt halt. We are now in the real hands of human love. Strangers' love. But this will have its price. I can sense it coming. The suppressed dust of these past days will settle and I will have to endure whatever it is that I have been ignoring within me. Somehow, it feels like I am no longer passing through.

Roberto and Gabriela speak of the first time they met. They recall weekends spent in the mountains north of Genoa, Gabriela's arms clutching Roberto as he drove his little blue motorcycle out of the city. Freezing hands and the smell of leather and oil. Gabriela recounts all the lovers she once had and the heat of life in Santiago and Chile. She describes it like a trembling repository of music, katydids, streetcars and moonlight.

'Men and sex were things to play with, not to live by,' she recalls. 'That was until Roberto.'

They tease each other all night. She reprimands him for bad English and rolls her almond eyes at us as he sets off upon another anecdote. His knowledge is relentless and bizarre; the complete London Tube system, the life of Boudica, Mel Gibson's parenting, the mining of silver. With everything, he finds a way to make us laugh. Gabriella and Roberto are glowing in the autumn of each other. Their love holds up the roof.

'You cannot ride him, she says. You must not ride him for two weeks.'

'Two weeks, but—'

'You must rest here. That's what she says.'

'But can we walk – is Sasha OK to walk?'

'Walking for him is the best thing that he can do. But *you*... you need to rest.'

We stand together in Sasha's box near the far end of the stables. Luna's expression is severe. A pang of nausea gushes through me. I feel a clamping pressure on my temples. The sound of horses munching their breakfast quickly morphs mechanical in the air. The manic cogs of a factory. With every day gone by, and in almost each hour within, I have been telling myself that we are walking towards recovery, that the swelling will go and that soon I will ride. Somewhere, somehow. I am so tired. From Ceparana to Giovo we have walked an average of nineteen miles and ascended 1,062 metres a day. We have travelled 134 miles in the last week. There are still some 125 miles remaining of these Ligurian Alps, and then there is a whole new country. And another country after that. I glance at Sasha's swelling and the hairless skin that has now fallen away to form a wound. I close my eyes in anger.

'Yesterday I rode him bareback with a sheepskin rug I found. My hip was in pain.'

Luna nods tolerantly. We both know that it was this that opened up his sensitive skin.

She takes me to the pharmacy to buy a tube of Hypermix and a tub of zinc oxide cream for Sasha's wound. I am to apply the zinc every morning and night, and after ten days or so I should begin to apply the Hypermix. She calls a vet who comes to inject him with an anti-inflammatory.

I pack my rucksack, pay the vet and say goodbye to Gabriella and Roberto. I hug them hard. I explain to Mariella and Raffi that I need to go, I need to leave and take the problem – the problem caused by me – elsewhere, away from these good people. My horse will recover if he walks, so I will walk him on. A shooting pain darts down my leg as soon as I leave the stables. The other horses stare at us from the top of their badland mound.

Trees watch us sweat and trip on the auburn leaves they have shed. The track is steep. A cult of vast metallic wind turbines soar above. For a moment the sheer size of the propellers fascinates and the oceanic currents they generate wash over us, blowing away the pressure, wheezing down my spine. And then later, when we sweat silently once more into the humus of the wood, something in my mind starts to pull me, almost physically, it seems, back to Terra di Mezzo. I pause for breath and hold Sasha's face in my arms. I look down at my boots and then up to the revolving metal arms for an answer. In my head I feel the safety of Napoleon's stables; the eyes and the spirits of the women and the children, the scent of belonging that washed over me beyond the malachite-painted door. I picture Mattias and Luna and the bosom smiles of Gabriella and Roberto.

But then it all loses colour and something pulls shut. I turn and march on. We can't find what we are looking for if we don't go forward.

The woodland pass opens up to a rich green bank that sees a vista of mauve wavelet hills below. The sky is delicate in the afternoon light. Together we stop. My hip is in agony. Sasha crops at the grass and I lie down and close my eyes.

It is 9.30 in the evening when I arrive back at Terra di Mezzo. I thought I would never see this chimerical place ever again. But I couldn't go on. It would have been risking too much. We both need rest. I sleep the soundest sleep in the yellow house of Gabriela and Roberto, deep in the knowledge that Sasha is sleeping too, somewhere in a haunted stable.

In the days that follow I learn many things from Luna and Mattias. We compare ideas, practices, saddles and stories, and converse in depth about the terrain and the challenges to come. They want the best for Sasha and for me. They don't care where we finish, they do not mention Finisterre once. The only thing that is true to them is our well-being.

As the hours seep into me, my body rests. My eyes see things as if for the first time and my mind allows itself to dwell in the falling dust. By watching and listening I notice how integral Terra di Mezzo is to this remote Giovo community. Horses have come to save this place. The horse has brought together many lonely people into a family. Luna as the mother.

In a bar with music playing and with three men hobbling around drunk in the corner, I order three Aperol spritz.

'She won't drink it,' mutters Mattias, 'she can't drink.'

I buy a bottle of Coke instead and sit down opposite Luna. She is weary. She has such a tender-looking face and it makes me sad when she appears so tired. I feel helpless. But we are all tired this evening.

'She does not drink because of a sickness she has.'

'A sickness?'

'A disease. Although it is not a recognised disease by the Italian government. It is too rare.'

With the help of Mattias, Luna tells me of an incurable autoimmune disease that she suffers from. The illness was triggered by the trauma of a sexual assault inflicted upon her by a local *carabinieri* officer. After moving to a new house, she then spent three years trying to convict him before he was finally sent to prison. Eleven months later he returned to Giovo, and Luna. Her body reacted. She is now perpetually tired. Her body is almost unrecognisable as to what it was three years previously. She is in constant agony. As a form of protection for her and her ten-year-old son, Mattias offered to move in with her. They have remained close friends ever since. Luna's boyfriend, Marcello, is a strong, kind, coolheaded man who sells timber and mules in a valley to the west. We make plans to meet each other later on the ride, should I pass near his town of Costa.

'Our stables is not a business, it's a family,' Mattias tells me another time, a hand running through the golden-brown mane of Ulric, his favourite gypsy horse. 'It's a reflection of Luna – the things that come from her.'

He is right. The wild girls, the children, the parents, the local vets, the mongrel dogs, the cats and the wanderers that come and go seem ignorant to superficial notions and needs. They have each other. They have Luna and Terra di Mezzo.

Day by day Sasha's inflammation decreases and his skin slowly heals. For two hours each afternoon we walk up the hill that leads to the wind turbines. I ride with the girls and help them in the yard. Two of them – twin sisters distinguishable by one having a black eye – wear, at times, almost nothing. I am told this has only started happening recently. As I find a routine, Luna and Mattias suggest that after this journey is done I should come back and live in the old house of the generals that stands deserted in the shade behind the stables. It is mine, apparently, as long as I am able to rebuild the stairs and cohabit with ghosts.

◆

On the fifth day I feed Sasha in the morning. He is looking rested. His eyes bright and curious. I then walk down the pass to the old chestnut horse standing loose in the last stall. I brush my hand along his neck and open the back doors. Before me I see the house of the generals, dove-grey, sun-deprived, square. It appears it was constructed entirely for the purpose of keeping an eye on the horses below it. I approach the wooden arched doors, which are loosely clasped by a padlocked chain. The word '*LIBERTÀ*' is inscribed into the wood. The engraver has left a date underneath it: 1944. I slip through the gap in the doorway and make my way into the dust and the mess.

Resting on the floor at the top of the broken wooden stairs, I find piles of letters and photographs, black-and-white images of undecipherable faces, and creased sheets of paper, smudged with ink. In a small bedroom there are crumpled covers on a single bed, the cloth reaching for an ageless body. Brown leather boots stand like statues on the floorboards with woollen socks forced inside them, and a pair of dark brown trousers are hunched on the back of a chair. The room appears like it has been caught in time and fossilised in wax. The walls are an unsettling green.

In the dining room a table is half set. A silver spur, an Italian almanac from 1929 and newspaper cuttings that are now the colour of sand make up the rest of the empty places. A black gilt cabinet sits underneath a silver mirror which murkily reflects a taffeta armchair standing in the corner, apparently being lived on by the weight of the air. The golden scene on the cabinet depicts a wild storm disturbing the manes of horses and the branches of trees. The old house of the generals is inhabited by everything else other than life and somehow this makes it feel more alive than me; it still survives, breathes, moves in its undisturbed story. Being in this room suddenly fills me with a heavy, longing feeling. A sadness. The lonely lived-in shapes of these objects are everything I am not – still. For months I have been driven by so much want and ambition that I have compromised almost everything. The pressure I have put upon myself has blinded me to the pure, changeless thing that remains as clear as moonlight – Sasha. My faults have hurt Sasha. His condition is the embodiment of my choices.

A shrieking cry pierces through the silence. I jump down the broken staircase and run into the stables. A plastic bucket of water is placed on the pass outside one of the horse's stalls and there are scattered tissues drenched scarlet. I approach the scene and meet eyes with the black-eyed twin. Tears are streaming down her face. Her sister is weeping too, and two other women watch on, funereal like gulls. Inside the stall there is the straw and on top of the straw stands a man wearing a pair of tracksuit bottoms and a fishnet string vest and trainers that are no longer white. His biceps are bursting and a distending vein pulses from his temple like a black worm. The horse's head seems almost separate from its body, clamped between the man's arms. Mattias, meanwhile, has his left hand gripped tightly on the animal's short mane and his right shoulder is dipped into its ribs, pressing the horse against the side of the box so as not to allow it to wince or move. Slowly the vet forces a long plastic tube up the horse's nose, but it splutters blood back like an old man trying to speak, unable to make sense. The vet turns to me as she hears the women mention my name and her darkly twisted hair reveals blood smeared across her headband, nose and chin, and a cigarette hanging from her mouth. She juts her jaw up as if in pride, gesturing to the scene.

'*Ragazzo. Benvenuti in Liguria.* Boy, welcome to Liguria.'

When it is clear that there is nothing lodged inside the horse's trachea and that perhaps mother nature is trying to tell us something, or that the horse has a urine infection, throat infection, ear infection or a thousand other unknown ailments, I offer to walk it out onto the grass. Perhaps it will try and eat; perhaps it might make the problem more obvious to us as its old body gets moving again. Never before have I seen so much blood pour from a horse's mouth and nose, from its entire grey face it seems. The twin with the black eye enquires as to whether I have a girlfriend or not and tells me that I should not continue on my journey but instead consider staying here in Giovo for the foreseeable future. Her tears have disappeared. I assure her that I will not make any rash decisions but, for now, we must keep walking in circles because her horse is drowning in its own blood. She winks at me and then tries to hold my hand that clutches the drenched lead rope.

The horse is dead by lunchtime. For her own sake, I am glad Kiki was not here to see this.

283 miles, 20 days

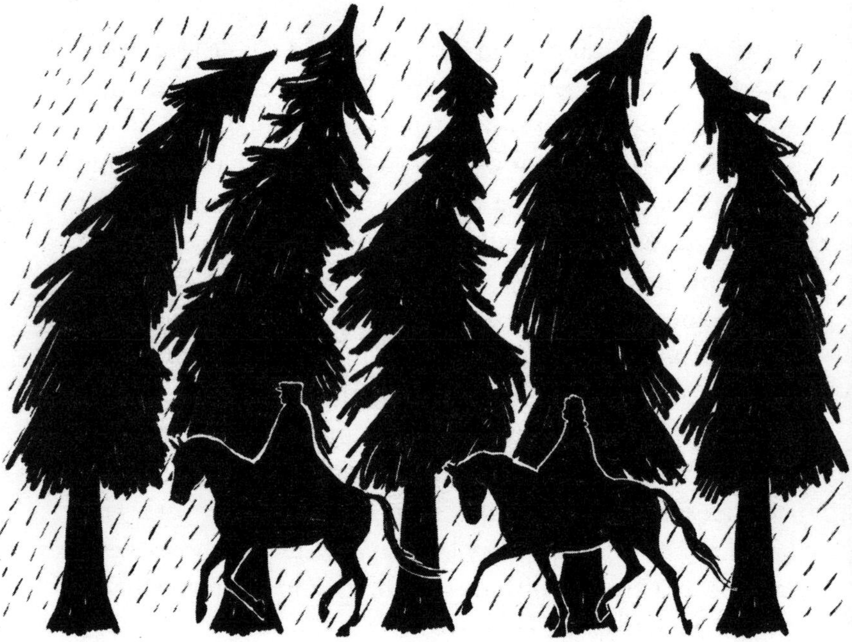

13–23 April
Giovo Ligure, Liguria – La Brigue, Provence-Alpes-Côte d'Azur, France

Sasha and I are standing in the bright light of the afternoon when her entourage pulls into the yard. They drive in loud and fast. Doors are flung open and slammed, and voices follow limbs. I did not expect them to come now. In my head it was always going to happen in the evening, in the dark. I see Kiki. She walks towards us across the sand of the arena, her own horse in hand. She is slim, small and has olive-coloured skin. She wears pristine navy-blue jodhpurs, grey-and-red striped socks pulled up to her knees, white trainers and a tweed cap slanted upon her head. She is noticeably clean. Istia, her bay Arabian horse, glows like the colour of an autumn afternoon. Her coat is satin and full, and her belly healthy. There are no cuts on her legs. Her back has no swellings. They both appear like they have been transported from a different country and time entirely – one where horses are kept with grooms.

    We embrace and say hello. I am embarrassed and anxious and this makes me quiet. Kiki and Istia look inappropriately full of life. She needs to know that none of this is easy and that Sasha and I look as dejected as we do because of all the days and nights we have gone through and all the things that she hasn't. Mercifully, the horses do the talking. Their nostrils touch and flare and they nestle their necks, remembering one another from the Apennine lands of Piacenza. A different life.

In a very short space of time, hands are flying in Italian gesticulation and proclamations are being thrown across the sand. For twenty minutes I nod, close my eyes tight or put my head to Sasha's neck. Kiki's entourage: people all connected to her and unknown to me; her mother with sharp, arched eyebrows and deep-looking eyes that survey every inch of us; her indifferent aunt, grinning at what I have become and then staring expressionless at Sasha; and an old-school horseman from Bosana who has a loud voice, strong opinions and a well-versed ability to hear only his own thoughts.

Sasha stands coolly with his body being talked about. I feel all of their eyes move over him and over me.

For a moment I look at Luna, seeking out some form of comfort. She moves over to stand with me. Next to her, Mattias has adopted a cutting, monotone voice in response to the intruders. His expression is unwavering.

Eventually the old man runs out of things to say and the car and the trailer disappear. Kiki's mother and aunt remain. As the sun begins to go down, everything seems to breathe.

That night the fire is lit and I buy meat from a butchers so that we can all share something together. There is a full moon that shines like a silver mine. The stars are made crisp and strong in the cold air. I see Sirius and think of Mithra, the night-time sentinel, and of Valerio.

Kiki has brought me a bottle of whisky and I ramble on about all the things that I shouldn't. I tell her about my time in Mongolia that follows me and has led me here. And, in my drunkenness, I let go and tell her about Ido and Frank. How Frank is the greatest friend I have, while Ido made me want to die.

Just as I start trying to leap through the fire, Kiki clambers on my back and I carry her back to Gabriella and Roberto's yellow house. At least that is what I am told in the morning.

It is agreed that we are going to leave on Monday, the day after Easter Sunday. I will walk on foot and Kiki is going to ride. I make it clear to her that her horse doesn't look ready. I make it clear to her that she needs to ride and leave me to walk. It's a good thing for her to begin to make her own way. I would do the same.

All my words are coming from fear, from so much uncertainty. I am afraid that the world that Sasha and I have been inhabiting will be somehow taken from us. Stolen. Just as Ido stole what I loved most. And what I loved most stole Ido. Stealing something not only removes what we have, but it redefines its very existence. Treading on someone else's dreams means all things after will never be the same. Kiki's dark eyes look scared. I want to touch her shoulders and to look at her, face on, but the reality of this seems impossible.

With her openness, she is stronger than I am, and with my worries I must appear arrogant at best, heartless at worst. It was *she* who embraced me when she arrived. Her strength earnestly covers a shaken place. Soft feathers over broken bones. I cover nothing but a puerile fear. How can I be so selfish as to not think of her? All I think of is myself.

I stand in the shower of Gabriela and Roberto's home and acknowledge each toe below me upon the tiled floor, the feel of the water on my body. I clear my head of everything and try hard to envision Kiki's circumstances, her life. She will surely feel lonely. Lost. The death of her only sibling, just six months ago. I can't imagine it. I can't even pretend. The relentless, the suffocating parasitic grief. And then what... your entire living existence is altered forever: drowning confusion, incandescent anger? Kiki is confronting the greatest pain of her life; who am I to know what to do?

I am very concerned about how I am going to adapt to her presence. I don't want to fracture her healing with my insignificant issues. I would rather a hundred nights of wolves. Solitude is easy; I was the interlocutor of the mountains. The sole ambassador of the human race. Along with our hoof-and-boot-drawn tracks, conversations between me and my horse were the only things that I shared. But now I must face the change. Be more like Sasha. Embrace the struggles of this stranger, if I can. This small, dark-haired, dark-eyed, fine-lipped stranger.

Perhaps it's the fact that she is beautiful that makes me wary.

The rejuvenating lights of Easter couldn't have come sooner. The day is soft and the sky is pale blue and lemon-yellow. The girls wear dresses and I don a cream linen suit that crumples up to the size of a small hand towel in my rucksack. I took this suit with me when I rode down the UK too. We pattern a white tablecloth with daisies, yellow daffodils and a potted gardenia underneath the veranda behind Gabriella and Roberto's house. Mariella and Raffi take us by car to the church of Parroquia Santa María, Sassello. I pray for Kiki's sister, for Ido, Frank, Mariella and for Victoria, my young cousin who has just been diagnosed with cancer.

After the service, Kiki lights a candle and we return and have lunch, like a family, and the afternoon sways gently into twilight. Chilean and Cuban music rumbles through the air. We drink and dance, but Roberto can't dance for long on account of his gut being 'twisted like a mullet's'. The early signs of gout, I fear. The daffodils are raised to our noses and to each other and then torn apart. Petals drift through the air and rest upon the floor so that it appears as if we have only been eating flowers. The hens peck upon the dead grass and Roberto shows us, with a father's pride, the nine chicks that have successfully hatched.

*

We spend the next morning tacking up and preparing to go. I add to my rucksack new supplies of zinc oxide and Hypermix cream for Sasha's hair and skin recovery, devil's claw for muscles, Reparil for the swelling, and Mobic pills to reduce any pain or stiffness. He appears rested. Luna is happy. The swelling is now only visible on the left side of his withers, with the right side having gone down almost completely. Quietly I pray that he hasn't broken a vertebra.

A famous French saddler and a friend of Luna's comes to Terra di Mezzo to offer some advice on what saddle – when the time comes – I might look to buy. He concludes that I will need a lighter, 'treeless' saddle. He says it will cost me at least 3,000 euros and that my estimations are all wrong: I should expect to reach Cape Finisterre in six months' time.

'But I can walk,' I reply, shocked. He laughs.

'Walk? Why would you want to walk when you have the horse?'

It is very hard to leave. I give Luna and Mattias the biggest hug that my body can muster. I promise that I will return. Luna hands me an old, thinning red halter that she was given by her father when she was a little girl. It is her lucky halter. She tells me that she wants to come with me and that she wishes things had been different. I see tears collecting in her eyes, which today are as dark and deep as sapphires, and I quickly look away as tears begin to gather in mine. I clip the lucky halter to the back of my rucksack – if only I could put it on a saddle – and then say goodbye to the wonderful inhabitants and spirits of Terra di Mezzo. It isn't until I reach the road that Kiki points out that I've left Sasha behind, tied up in the arena. What a competent first impression I must make.

Alone, I weep after saying goodbye to Gabriella and Roberto and their little yellow house. I have been cared for, so deeply, by their generosity and their warmth. I don't want to look back as I travel away, but I feel the air becoming stifled again with that smell that washed over me so naturally the first time I went beyond the arched doors of the stables. No matter where these characters or horses come from, how we got here, who is young or who is old, how much paint is on the malachite-green door or how many ghosts, murderers or victims are viewing us from the shadows, Terra di Mezzo is the stable house of love. I will always be lucky just to have known it.

The roaming horses flock to Sasha upon hearing hooves disappear up the road. Solemnly they follow us until a barbed wire fence makes it impossible for them to continue. Kiki travels on ahead, her backside trotting up and down into the distance like a dressage rider. I remain shoulder to shoulder with Sasha all day, all the way to the town of Ferrania. We retrace the steps we made exactly a week ago when we tried to leave for the first time. I gaze with anger upon Istia's hoofprints.

The metallic windmills return, peculiar and monstrous, but definitely dead and not like giants, as Don Quixote claimed. The weather then turns wet. I put my head down, my eyes on my boots.

'*Luis! Luis!*' Sasha bends down to take water from a low flowing stream. A man with a silver pointed beard rides towards us along the road. He is wearing a brown suede jacket with a gardenia in his breast pocket. A slanted suede hat is placed upon his silver hair and his donkey is clad with magenta-and-blue-patterned saddle cloths. As if it is rehearsed, Kiki then emerges delicately behind him, from a break in the wood. She must have got lost. I watch her approach. Her position upon Istia, as I couldn't help but notice when I first saw her ride in Giovo, is impeccable. Her tack, too, is top of the range.

I put out my hand to greet this wintry-looking man upon his donkey. He informs me that he found Kiki and her horse in the woods and asked her if she knew of a boy called Luis.

Proudly he leads us to his house, which has been painted pink and cream by his wife, who is an artist. It reminds me of the witch's house in Hansel and Gretel. Inside, modern cornices layer the corners of the rooms and scenes from *The Odyssey* line the walls and ceilings. Cakes, pies, wine, chocolate, ice cream and chicken are laid out on a floral table. It is a fairy tale. Our bellies are filled, and we sleep like drugged children, ready to be thrown into a cauldron. Even the flames in the wood-burning stove are the colour of roses.

The boy in me clenches his fists in resentment. We follow the mocking shapes of Istia's prints. Sasha is frustrated by her lingering scent. There goes the benthic duo. We are lost and washed up at the bottom of the Ligurian massif. I am not able to ride Sasha because I made a mistake and it is no one's fault but mine. We travel behind a matched pair, rider and horse, journeying west. It would be better if we were always alone.

The sound of Sasha's breathing and the feel of his muzzle upon my right shoulder calm me. Did I ever envision finishing this journey alone? I don't know. How far could I have actually gone before I would need to feel someone, tell someone, need someone? Only a ghost can ride solitary forever. To share in the river-like spirit of the horse – is this not what I have always wanted?

I cross the border of the Apennine-Alpine pass on a donkey called Tina lent kindly to me by the man with the gardenia. Sasha walks behind us, put out by my new companion, unimpressed with the rain. Our week of convalescence in Giovo had appropriately been adorned with healing sun, but now everything is turning the colour of ash and mud. Each day I tell Kiki to ride ahead and each evening we reconvene. Istia and Sasha find it heart-wrenching to let each other go in the mornings and for an hour or so Sasha pursues her scent like a hound on heat. With the routing of Sasha's amorous nose and with the stench of Istia's sweat and droppings thronging the misted air, we could probably shape our way to night blindfolded.

The red-and-white Alta Via signposts have now all but disappeared in this uncharted stretch of Serena and Leila's route. No land stars now. The night skies remain barren.

'NO BORDER. NO NATION' is graffitied onto the side of a deserted power station high up upon the mountain of Monte Burot. Sasha and I have now travelled over 500 miles together.

Two nights beyond the arms of Giovo we arrive at our stop soaked to the bone in a remote *rifugio* in the Muschieto valley of Bardineto. As promised, Marcello, Luna's boyfriend, finds us in his old Defender and takes me to see the biggest mule I have ever seen. While Kiki showers and sleeps in the *rifugio*, Marcello and I roll across and up the other side of the valley, the mountains now black and silver under the light of the moon, and we arrive at his hillside farm in Costa. The mule wades towards us through the darkened olive groves. At 166 centimetres tall and 600 kilograms heavy, he is much bigger than Sasha. My imagination begins to wander, and I think of all the mountains of the Alps I could ride over with him, all the pain that I could avoid. He is a unique creature.

A combination of jackass and mare, the mule is the oldest hybrid in existence, yet is forever unable to reproduce itself (they are 99.9 per cent sterile). The intelligence and endurance of these animals has been harnessed by humans since 3000 BCE. From the pharaohs to the Romans, from Marco Polo to modern America, from the construction of the Panama Canal; through wars, empires and revolutions, and to the pre-industrial development of almost every country on earth, these indomitable animals have enjoyed a vital part in our history. Known to cover fifty miles a day while needing only five hours of sleep, mules are stronger, hardier and more resilient than donkeys and horses; their skin is more resistant, their hooves are rock hard, and they can survive the harshest of environments on very little feed. Marcello prizes his animal like a world-class boxer. I have now become possessed with the idea that I need to buy a mule. Somewhere, somehow.

Once more, Kiki rides ahead of me. The rain persists and each path looks the same, drowned out by dead leaves. For the first time, my emotions begin to really darken. My main concerns have so far always consisted around the physical, but now I feel moments of hollowness. I am sad too that Sasha and I are alone. Many times, Kiki has offered to stay with me, to walk with me, but my pride responds with distance.

Sasha and I cascade a dry riverbed entombed with boulders. So far, the province of Savona is proving to be muddied and obstinate. Each day we traverse paths of engulfing woods neglected for years, fallen oak trees the size of train carriages; slumped beech sepulchred to the bleak earth, backs holding up a wheezing mudslide. The handsaw is helpless. We climb and descend like goats, our legs falling deep into ponds of leaves and mud. At the bottom of the riverbed, with fresh cuts on Sasha's legs and with my hip providing a renewed shooting pain, we arrive onto an expanse of lime green. The light in the sky brightens. We walk through the cobbled commune of Bardineto and follow the sun to the side of a soft sloping hill. In the distance I see crumbling stables, horses and the shape of Kiki. There is someone else there too.

As the two horses graze in the spring paddocks of a dilapidated fifteenth-century stable, Kiki, R and I light the fire in a small house in Bardineto. *Prosciutto*, bread, cheese, olives and wine sit in bottles and plates upon a rust-coloured table. R is Kiki's boyfriend – the link between me, her and this ride. We know each other from school, although we haven't seen each other in person for years. He has hardly changed. He has olive skin, a curved, handsome nose and wavy dark hair that comes down to his shoulders. His face belongs in Florence, during the Renaissance. We eat and drink, and after Kiki says goodnight R and I stay at the table.

'Kiki told me that yesterday you gave her your food when she forgot hers.'

'Yes, I think I did. I'm sure you would have done the same,' I reply.

'Yes, I would. But that's not the point.'

'Well, it wouldn't have looked great if I hadn't.'

'Either way, thank you... She says it's important that she does this alone. Without me.'

We pause and take sips of the wine.

'It's funny that we are here now,' he remarks, leaning back and looking slowly round the room and at the shadows of the flames that flicker on the walls. 'After all these years, we meet each other here.'

'Yes, strange, isn't it?'

'You know, people said I was mad to let my girlfriend come on a ride with you.'

I laugh and take another sip of wine.

'It seems she has let herself,' I reply.

'Yes. Of course she has. It's just all quite difficult. You know?'

I nod.

'And I was there when it all happened, with her sister... I have been there ever since. I only want to give her what she wants. I'm an altruist by nature.'

We hug goodnight before he goes up to Kiki, their double bed on a mezzanine landing above. I lie down on a sofa in front of the fire. I watch the flames and try and work out what it is I am feeling, what I can conclude. I like R a lot. Him being here makes me feel light. His character is soft, inquisitive. His clothes clean and ironed. He is attractive, in all senses of the word, and he is kind. But perhaps too kind.

There is love and care between R and Kiki. But surely there is now space and doubt too. She is riding away from something, towards an unknown. She is tearing herself up each day and discovering new things that keep her moving. With each step Kiki takes she breaks and reshapes. All the while he waits for her return.

I have had to look up what an altruist means.

In the morning something has changed in me. 'We need to walk together.'

'Today?'

'Today. We need to walk together today and the next because it's now too dangerous for you to go alone.'

Kiki and I set off and say goodbye to R. He drives on to find somewhere for us all to sleep that night. Mariella and

Raffi have driven further into the mountains since leaving Terra di Mezzo. According to Leila and Serena's plans, we are three days away from France. Ahead of us lies a twenty-two-mile day and a seventeen-hundred-metre climb. Sixty-five mile per hour winds are expected, and snow too.

We begin with optimism upon Monte Lingo and we pass a deserted *rifugio* with shattered windows, terracotta-coloured walls and a dark, elegant bar still intact inside. A giant wind turbine revolves above us. We continue to climb.

The fog clears just for a moment and we let the horses graze and absorb the view. Like the turning of a new page, a tract of woodland smothering round-topped mountains idly reveals itself in front of us.

On we crawl along the rim of the mountain bowl and, as if the shutters to a storm have been unhinged, we find ourselves exposed upon the hunched ridges of Monte Galero (1,708 metres), Monte Fontanette, Monte Dubasso, Monte Pesauto and Rocca l'Arma. The barrage of promised winds disembark with violence. Kiki and I are forced to crouch and wade our way through the air. I am blown off my feet. Sasha has to trust me – he too is blown sideways but his four legs keep him standing. The dishevelled clouds scatter to reveal colossal lakes hovering at our fingertips, still and grey metal discs, and the amorphous shape of tumbling land folds that I have come to know so well.

With our bodies pressed against the mountain, I feel alive again. Kiki's smile reaches me from in between her beanie and zipped-up jacket. We are here. The danger has been restored – the adventure has awoken. All day we travel together on foot and all day we think and question and speak. As manes and tails flay wildly behind, she tells me that, last night, she dreamt of her sister. She said that her sister was trying to tell her something, to show her a thought, but no matter how hard she tried, Kiki couldn't understand, she couldn't hear her.

We talk about insanity, those in society who condemn others in their misunderstanding, and about art and Vincent van Gogh. Kiki tells me that the last book Siu ever read was *The Letters of Vincent van Gogh*. I describe my favourite painting of all, *Bedroom in Arles*. I was given a print of it when I was five years old. I was once told that the green shutters on the windows are closed, or closing, but I have always liked the idea that they are about to burst open. The scarlet, the wood, the walls of the bedroom are restless, waiting for the fostering air. I hope that we will pass through Arles, the city Van Gogh sought for its light.

The winds reach eighty-five miles per hour. The snow stays away. Is this storm the final tearing up of winter?

Stout black Mérens horses dot the bottom of the Nava valley. The winds soften. In the distance, directly west, the sky is foreboding. The dim mountain peaks rise like jagged rocks in a sea. Somewhere beyond those peaks is Leila's Rifugio La Terza, 1,780 metres high. And then there is a new country.

A fizzing sense of accomplishment flows between us. Just us. Davide, the owner of the trekking stables at the bottom of the valley, leads us into his office.

'The snow is coming. There will be ice on the tops. Where you wish to go, it is not possible,' he says gravely.

'Not possible?' I ask.

Davide looks at me and then takes a breath. He points to a detailed map of the area, pinned to the wall.

'If you are to consider it, then there are three ways. The first is to ride to Rifugio La Terza. Here you will freeze.

The second is to use Colle Melosa. Here you cannot pass. Mudslides have fallen this morning that now block the trail and disturb the mountain.'

'The third?' Kiki asks, tentatively. Davide steps back from the map and points to the black sky through his dirty office window. We follow the line of his finger.

'The partisan way.'

'The partisan way?'

'Yes. From here you take the Colle di Nava. After some time, you will reach Monte Collardente and then Monte Saccarello, the highest mountain in Liguria, 2,200 metres up. Look, those mountains you see out there.' He waves to the skyline.

'You must go around the summit of Saccarello, and then you will reach France. You will not know that you have crossed the border—'

'France? We can reach France tomorrow?'

'But the route is long.'

'How long?'

'At least fifty kilometres from here. I have not used the pass in over a year. As far as I know, I'm the only one who rides it.'

'Do you think it's possible?' asks Kiki. Davide squints his eyes towards the muddled form of mountain bodies through the window.

'What are your reasons?'

'I have no reasons not to,' she replies sharply, perhaps without even thinking. I notice then that she has the same, arched eyebrows as her mother.

Davide looks at her seriously, and then to me. I stay silent.

'If you leave early,' he continues, slowly, 'and if there is no snow, you can make it in time for the light to be with you. With a lot of luck, you will reach France tomorrow night.

But the risk is high… if you are caught in a snowstorm no one will find you. You are out of reach.'

'*In bocca al lupo,*' mutters Kiki.

That evening, a friend of Davide's comes to see the horses. From the back of his old Defender he lugs out a saddle made by an Italian company called Prestige. I recognise the name from Luna. 'There isn't a better company for trekking,' I recall her saying. With caution, he places the saddle on Sasha's back. One by one I call Luna, Leila and Serena and send them pictures of how it sits. I cannot make the same mistake twice. I ask Kiki for her advice too.

We are all satisfied that the weight of the saddle is distributed evenly. It has a high pommel for Sasha's withers and the whole thing weighs just 6.8 kilograms. The man states that I am most probably never going to get a chance like this again: a world-class saddle being offered at a discount price the day before I cross into France, with Sasha almost ready to ride. It is hard not to agree. The original price for this saddle is 3,000 euros. Davide's friend is willing to sell it to me for 1,400. Up to now, my money saved from the stables in London is holding well, but this saddle was not part of the budget. We shake hands and agree a long-term payment plan that will take me to November.

R finds us and we sleep in the forgotten mountainside town of Mendatica. Our little house winds up a stone staircase. A wood-burning stove sits in the middle of the kitchen, our chimney the only one with smoke rising into the sky. Five chairs are clustered around a square wooden table, and a wide-reaching window gives light. Beyond the rooftops of the terraced houses we can see only the Arrosica valley, dim in its wintry greens and browns. The grey and white Alps continue somewhere else, above and beyond our temporary home. One black cat passes over the cobbles of the street.

I tell R and Kiki that they are lucky. That this is romance.

'Romance?' replies Kiki.

'Yes. I'll remember this little place. One day I'll take someone here.'

Our fire rumbles and the town holds us close together in a pocket of a time gone by. Mendatica is ours for the night. R and Kiki sleep soundly upon a bed in the far corner of the room. I envy it, from my single mattress on the floor.

By 7.30 a.m. we are on our way to France. With Sasha's back still not entirely healed, I leave the new saddle in R's car. The pass we set upon, the Colle di Nava, drags us up four hilltop peaks – Poggio Possanghi, Poggio delle Forche, Poggio San Martino, Poggio Forcarau – before reaching the 1,300-metre-high village of San Bernardo.

The bruising skies from the night before have ruptured. So far, it is just rain. I wear my German poncho and Kiki pulls over her red one; both of us are soaked to the skin. The horses appear as if they are draped in purple velvet. We find a bus-stop shelter for the horses and trudge into the only café in the village in a bid to get out of the weather. Monte Sacarello remains somewhere far away in the clouds above us. Kiki informs me that coffee and grappa make a *caffè corretto* and so we have two of these each. The woman who serves us asks where we are going. Kiki says we are travelling to France and then to Spain. The woman is puzzled.

'*Perché vuoi arrivare così lontano?* Why do you want to go so far?'

'A good question!' replies Kiki, warming herself in front of the electric heater.

'A mixture of patriotic, ideological, idealistic reasons and self-interest,' I answer, remembering the line from

Serena's book on partisans. The woman smiles, unsure what to make of us, and hands us two *caffè corretti*. The rain worsens.

With grappa in our blood, the trail rises steeply above San Bernardo village and then drops down. I see a sign to the *frazione* of Piaggia, a hamlet. I have heard of this place – in the autumn of 1944 it was used to help the resistance retreat into the French town of Fontan, the same direction we are headed. The fascists had surprised the partisans in Mendatica, and units in the area were forced to scatter. But the partisans regathered, a rising that culminated in Italy's liberation.

Kiki is knocked to the ground by Istia, who jumps on her when clambering down a rock. They are both OK. Fog saunters with the rain and cold trickles of water begin to seep down our backs and into our socks. The horses are drenched. We have to keep moving. It is below freezing. Our feet begin to shuffle almost mechanically. Avoiding the sheer summit of Monte Saccarello, we straddle the French border and head south towards the eastern side of Monte Collardente. Here, when the rain finally turns to snow, we come across a sign to Refugio La Terza, '4hrs and 25mins'. I think of Leila.

The cold and the snow take grip and at 1,800 metres we can see nothing in front of us. I pause for a moment. Sasha presses his soaked muzzle into my back and pushes me on.

The pass hardens into a flat track that intersects the side of Monte Collardente, and before long we find ourselves inside a freezing-cold tunnel that runs 800 metres long. Now out of the sky's reach, Kiki wants to stop and rest, but I take her hand and pull her up from the stone and grit floor. Her skin is cold on mine. We have to keep moving – for the cold and for the horses.

After emerging from the dark of the tunnel we trudge forward, our footsteps making the noise of shovels. The inside of the horses' hooves now collect with snow and earth. Everything is suffused in a damp whiteness. Our way is shaped only by the bend of a track jutting out from a snow scarp above, a hidden drop below. The day is becoming clotted. Too hard to see. Too wet to stop.

Davide was right. There are no signs, no lights, no people to tell us that what we are doing is right or wrong. At 2.54 p.m. on 23 April we breach an intersection of paths and leave Italy behind us. The only ones to notice are a wood of heaving pine trees camped on the French side of this invisible border. Horses and humans travel together like soaked leaves. The moment we pass into this new country, I shout back to Kiki to tell her what we have done. Like it was when our bodies were hiding from the torrents of wind, I can see her eyes smiling, this time from within the thin gap of her red poncho. Together, we run down into France.

Into French woods we go and the horses go too. Our day began at the bottom of the Nava valley at 7.35 a.m. and it concludes in the cobbled village of La Brigue on the western side of Mont Saccarel. Only in 1947 did this old Italian commune become French. Yet suddenly, in the knowledge that we have crossed a border, intangible though it may be, all things appear remote and new. The buildings are shaped differently. They are taller for one, and their bodies encroach on each other. The colours are a pink and a cream that I am not used to and the tone of the six o'clock bells that chime through the alleys are higher in pitch. There are more people here. Their voices are lively and their accents a world apart. Now off the mountains, the snow has turned to rain and it jumps up with force from the ground, filling our boots. Glass jars upon the windowsills are vases for water and drowning flowers.

We trudge through La Brigue and R finds us in his car. I don't know what it is, but something small breaks in me when I see him. Kiki grows silent. He tells us of a mute man named Favi who has a small shelter for the horses, three miles north. He drives on ahead.

I think of Mariella and Raffi. I miss them. The last time I spoke to them they told me the front right tyre on the beloved Freelander had blown up on a motorway. They don't like it when R is around as he has taken their role.

To the east and west the curtaining shapes of the mountains materialise high up into the drab clouds. We have descended a long way from the shoulders of Mont Saccarel and now the fierce peaks all around us are indecipherable. The adrenaline in me begins to subside and a heavy fatigue drips in. Can Liguria really be gone? Everything has come full circle; the whorl is pulling in the tide. Now beyond the maze of the mountains, I feel lost.

Today, as we made our way from Italy into France, Kiki and I escaped somewhere. We may have been alone on that crossing, but we were alone together.

Favi's shelter is made up of wooden planked walls and a tin roof and inside it steams with the heat of a colossal donkey whose coat is the colour of melanin. Upon hearing the approaching beat of hooves, the donkey's enormous velvet face leans out into the rain. It is shaped like a dark crescent moon. I hold Sasha tight as he eats his hay and as steam smokes from his neck and back. I never thought my greatest companion in the world would be an Arabian horse.

I rest my soaked head on his back and close my eyes. I try and think about nothing and to clear my thoughts so that only the sound of the rain, and the horses and the donkey eating the hay, fills my mind. I open my eyes and I think Kiki is watching me through the darkness, but I cannot be sure.

400 miles, 31 days

Kiki's diary
17 April, Giovo
   Sunday morning, perhaps before 08:00. Easter. In a house with people that I don't know in a place I have never seen, getting ready for something I have never done before. Before we even set off – tomorrow – it seems like I have lost quite some weight already. Job quit, money raised, travelled, trained, bought a horse, and now here. At the place of departure. With a young man whom I cannot see through or sometimes don't even understand. I only half trust him.
   My mother seemed stressed on the phone. She asked me earlier to promise her not to take my own life. To stay on this damned earth. I refuse to promise anything.
   That same young man enters the kitchen and starts making that typical tea for himself with all that milk and stuff that British people put in it. They call that normal tea. Centre of the world. Navel of the planet. They say they believe in God, but one can't really tell from the outside. Feel very lonely. Don't want to cry because I don't know them.

II

Death of the Dorado

'This is how he grows: by being defeated,
decisively, by constantly greater things.'
Rainer Maria Rilke

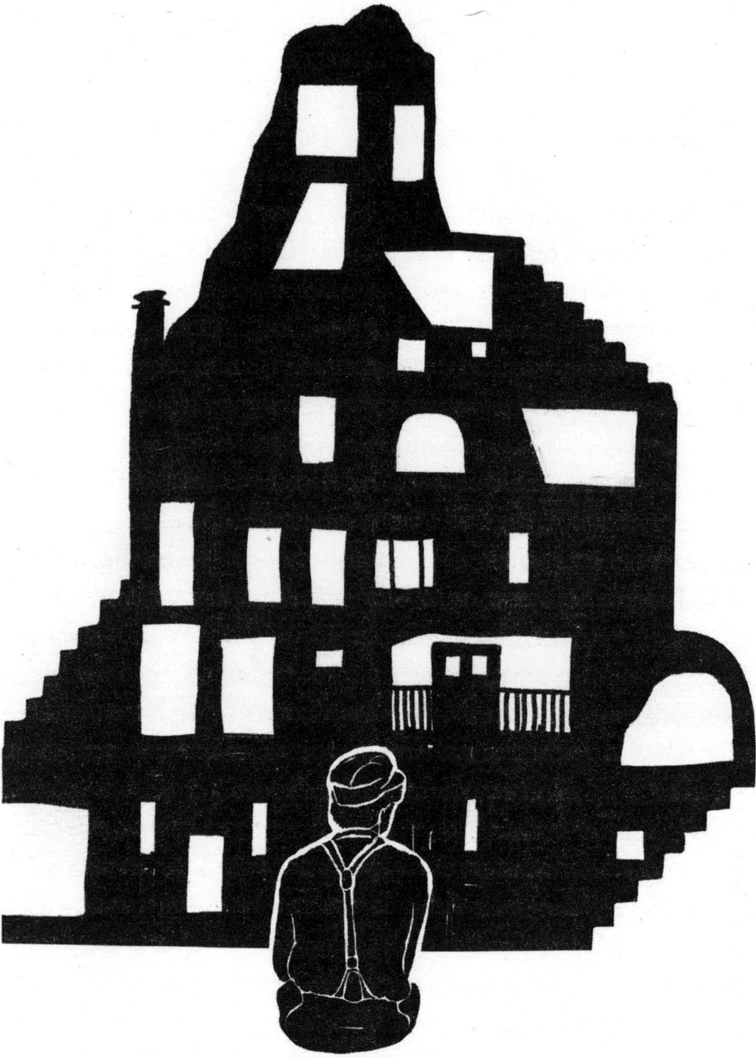

24 April – 1 May
La Brigue – Trigance, Provence-Alpes-Côte d'Azur

The beginning of France means the end of Leila and Serena's faraway help. The routes we formed back in the Ceparana nest, twenty-two days ago, have reached the end of their road. I have managed to locate stables for our first couple of nights after La Brigue, remote and high up in the Maritime Alps, but after this I have no idea where we are going to be.

The Roya river is the colour of absinthe and it tears through the valley and all the way down into the Ligurian Sea, thirty miles south. Soon after the first sight of light in the morning, Kiki and I travel beyond the rich café scents of La Brigue, the market stalls assembling. We follow the river for two hours before stopping to rest upon its eastern bank. The crests and broils of the water teem below us. I look ahead and upon the other side there is the site of a broken village, Fontan, once the harbourer of convalescent partisans. The buildings have been recently hit by a devastating flood. Many of the locals did not have time to escape and the banks have become depositories of furniture, silt, bricks and dead things. A complete cross-section of six houses stand opposite us, their fronts stripped away for the world to peer into. In one house the bed is still made up on the top floor. The duvet is taut. There are towels hanging in the bathroom. Tables wait and mirrors watch.

'Do you think rivers have souls?' asks Kiki. I consider this for a moment and then reply that if they do, they have souls that are nothing like ours. Rivers are indifferent, destructive, fertile; rivers are just born to flow and never remain the same. They have no choice.

'If we had no choice would we be better?' she asks.

'I think we would. I think choice can take away everything—'

'Like last night.'

'Last night?'

'Yes. We had no choice but to leave the horses with Favi and the velvet-looking donkey – and it was the most perfect place in the world. There was nowhere else we should have been.'

'That's right. But then it changed again, didn't it?'

'Changed?'

'Well... when we then found R... and the place we had dinner. There was choice there. The moment vanished. Don't you think?'

Kiki looks away, silent.

We sit and watch the water for a while as the horses find some grass to graze. The air is filled only with the river sounds. I survey the destruction of this village and think about cycles, death, loss, and of Kiki's sister.

Kiki's smile was so delicate when we crossed the French border into the tunnel of pine trees. She holds so much sadness and life behind such a fragile surface. Sometimes, when she is not watching me, I look at her face and see a secret that no one else will ever comprehend. Before me there are vast dolls' houses emptied through death, and beside me is the living embodiment of grief. I roam in the middle, a useless dog, peering into deserted rooms and amongst the river's glacial light, desperate to find a place to sit, to give everything a meaning. The horses don't do this. They have no choice. They move, they react. They flow.

*

Along the concave side of a mountain we come across the fourteenth-century village of Saorge. How different this new country already seems. We pause for a beer at Le Heinze Café and the horses drink from a fountain that overlooks our new home, Les Alpes-Maritimes. Strangers approach, drawn to us through their seclusion and need to speak. Their faces are wrinkled like the veins of leaves. Once useful in the salt trade, this isolated village has now become a medieval mountain homage to all things narcotic. The scent of marijuana wavers in the air. One man, with a striking aquiline nose, recalls a melancholy memory of burying his horses at the end of his garden.

'A lot of life is about learning how not to cry,' he stutters.

The houses and chapels of Saorge are extensions of the cliffside itself, crawling over and mimicking each other. The blue-mauve tiles of the rooftops take the role of fallen scree, wittingly placed. The stained windows of belltowers gaze their cycloptic eye across the air to the western side of La Roya valley. They watch the black choughs in the distance, clutching the cornices of Cime de Pesourbe. Chapelle Notres Dames des Fontaines looms astral above.

We descend to the valley floor, met by the inevitable entrapment of the tarmac road. We are like aliens as we trudge through a motorway tunnel, head torches on the backs and fronts of our heads, and we inhale the fumes of the cars.

'At times I feel like there's someone watching me, like a reflection or a shadow, sitting on my shoulder in the scene of the moment.'

'The scene? Do you only see everything as a scene?' asks Kiki.

'No... just sometimes. Only in as much as the shadow or the presence makes the moment seem fake. It's proof that nothing really matters.'

'What do you mean nothing matters?' repeats Kiki.

'Like it doesn't count. Real pain and laughter. It doesn't have to get to you if it doesn't really count. The sitting shadow finds it amusing when I'm sad and hysterical when everything appears normal.'

'And so it protects you—'

'It comforted me when I thought of taking my life down by the docks of Bristol, after what happened with Ido—'

I stop myself from continuing. I close my eyes. I remember how that shadow hugged me like a fire blanket when I finished whisky bottles alone. It was with me when I woke each morning to a pillow of dead ladybirds in my room at university. For some reason, the ladybirds would crawl up the outside wall of my residence block, pass through my open window, and then fall down from the plaster ceiling above me.

For the first time since we have walked together, Kiki speaks about her parents and her sister. There is anger in her voice. There is frustration and there is loneliness. Perhaps it would be simpler if there was someone or something to blame. I try my best to listen carefully, always to listen and to hear her speak, and then, if I can, offer another point of view. One looking forward. Despite my efforts, I feel wholly inadequate. Mentioning that bullshit about my shadow and my betrayal-induced thoughts now seems puerile. Pathetic and inconsiderate. I'm frustrated on another level too: I want desperately to make her smile more.

We must start working together – burrowing and retrieving as much as we physically can from the precious hours of each day, each single moment.

*

A man named Alessandro hammers on the last nail of Sasha's new shoes and shows us the cheese he has made from his seven goats. We converse in French, Italian, Spanish, gibberish and English all at the same time, the language of the Latin borders. Ten horses stand proudly in their boxes, as proud as Alessandro, and a stallion becomes untamed by Istia's presence. R arrives in his car, and then later Mariella and Raffi. Together we try and understand the eerie landscape around us. It is tantalising.

As we watch, the hues of the Roya valley constantly renovate. The late-hour sun is disturbing the stolid rain and fog that has accompanied us to Alessandro's stables and the evening now rises in the air like a silk fan, unfolding itself from the bed of the mountains. The tall flanks of spruce and pine trees are drenched an olive-ink colour, feathering mist spreading from their bodies, and the sky above is now streaked in scarlet and blue, dyeing the daytime with the night.

The stable, Les Ecuries de la Roya, juts out upon a clay-coloured tableland, a stepping stone into the sky, a stone that has taken Alessandro many years to shape. But he is still young. Like Serena and Leila, he has delphinium eyes filled up with the vast living environment that encircles him. He wears a felt beret and breeches and has thickly arched eyebrows and tanned cheeks. With our bellies full of wine and raclette, Mariella, Raffi, Kiki, R and I sleep as warm as all of the animals on the other side of the wall. Our bunk beds surround a fire in the middle of a square, wooden room.

Today Kiki wants to ride alone. I think she wants to be alone with her sister. We say goodbye in the morning with an embrace that seems to communicate all the things that we have not been able to voice. But perhaps this applies only to me. Her legs lift up off the ground and I can feel her fingers dig into my shoulder blades. For a fleeting moment, everything is in one place: the tapping of rain upon plastic, our breath heating up the humus air in the black tunnel of Monte Collardente, the scent of wet horses and soaked hay and all the things, now known only to us, since leaving the obscure, loving arms of Terra di Mezzo. We hold each other, the Alpine kaleidoscope rotates. For that single moment we are the sole two things that can ever be still.

Together Sasha and I travel side by side along soft, silver tracks into the Parc National du Mercantour. It is warm, at last. The sight of Istia's hoofprints makes me curious; the self-loathing has gone, somehow, and as I travel I wonder where Kiki is, what things she might be seeing. I haven't ridden in so long that the thought of it seems absurd. But I think the time is getting close.

Sasha's muscles have grown and his coat shines. He is in exceptional condition thanks to his Ligurian training. Since leaving Ceparana, we have ascended 16,572 metres on our hike. Not bad, considering the peak of Mount Everest sits just below 9,000. Thanks to time and movement, the swelling on Sasha's withers has steadily reduced and the hair on his skin is growing back well. I feel good too – my back and shoulders have hardened with the weight of the rucksack and my hip no longer hurts. I am in a continuous process of being broken down and changed. My face is gaunt.

The sun bends down to meet our eyes and, to the south, the medieval village of Sainte-Agnès beams back at the cloudless sky, a doorway into the French Riviera. Upon a hilltop, the Church of Notre-Dame des Neiges has a glazed belltower that shines like fire embers. The tower is enamelled in gold, red, kyanite blue and a deep green plating. The Mediterranean Sea as the backdrop.

Sasha halts suddenly and peers across to the far side of a narrow valley. The trees are dense and there is the soft rustling of leaves, but nothing more. I follow his eyeline as accurately as I can manage and then, from amongst the shadows, there is a flash of white and a clattering of hooves. Two horses canter around the bend of the valley to meet us. Sasha and I run towards them. Lex has arrived.

Lex is a motorbike fanatic; founder of motorbike community Petro Camp. A very old friend and a wildly kind individual. Brown curly hair, big wide eyes, the drumming pat on the back and a huge toothy smile; from the outside, he is the same as I have always known him.

After contacting me a week or so ago, he booked a flight. He would never use this word himself, but his mother recently passed away and I think he wants a place to 'escape' to, even if just for a few days. I never for a second doubted that he would find us.

Tomorrow there is a long path ahead, twenty-six miles, and it is going to be made a lot harder by the ascension of Mont Férion, a steep-rising 1,400-metre mountain that stands as guard to the ancient village of Levens, our next refuge point. I option that we go around the mountain, Kiki is adamant we go over.

'You do as you wish,' she says decidedly. 'But tomorrow will be my sister's birthday. I will meet her at the top.'

The two of them march in tandem in front of me as they share their experiences of loss: a mother and a sister.

Silently I listen, travelling wedged between the bay flanks of Sasha and Istia. I am struck by how lucid and considered these two people are in their thoughts; they have fluency over a pain that I can't even imagine. This grief, this ultimate grief, seems a state that is so poignantly human and helpless. And yet, within this, in the face of the unescapable reality, there appears a man-made strength. The love and the faith – this is human too. There can be so much life created through death.

The shape of Mont Férion remains in the distance all day, blackly approaching. An oncoming storm made of stone. We come across a fountain in the village of Coaraze. Kiki goes into a little chapel to light a candle and Lex and I fight off two drunk locals attempting to lure the horses into the bar. We reconvene and march up the vast east side of the mountain. Kiki leads the way, climbing the wave. My body feels tired. Everything in the past 470 miles is finally taking its toll: the pressure on the balls of my feet, my calves, the weight on my back. Suddenly I am the most exhausted I have been, and then angry that I am exhausted on such an important afternoon for Kiki.

As if it were predestined, Sasha stands on my heel and I am forced to continue alone, on horseback. I couldn't limp on. Together, Kiki and Lex reach the jagged peak of Mont Férion, and I arrive later, cantering up the ridge on Istia, Sasha in tow.

I find Kiki lying on her back. Her legs are stretched long and her face is looking up towards the sky. The stratus sifts across the view like paint on water.

'A painting of a bird,' she smiles, her eyes opening and closing lithely. 'That was the last painting my sister ever did. A bird sitting upon the side of a mountain.'

I dismount and take in the view. The look on Lex's face is one of so much peace and satisfaction. Sitting on the rocks, he leans on his leg and takes in the rotating scene. The sun and the cloud play games with each other, folding the light so that the dark trees of the Alps appear and then disappear underneath us.

For the next two days my mind is unfocused, and my body remains tired. Sasha and I are not in tandem. I'm lost when I'm not in his rhythm. We are chased over a bridge by French police and I lead everyone along a shortcut that results in Sasha cutting his legs and Istia falling on her side. I am lucky it is not worse. Kiki and Lex walk on and I drop back. I feel like a stranger to where we are.

On Lex's final day we journey into a jungle of oak trees. Rocky paths guide us along. A river flows through it. Then the shape of the ravine shallows and the trees grow sparse and the river shrinks into a stream and then into a river of stone. The bush and the shrub become loose boulders, the grass is thin and brown. The light slants down upon the explorer's afternoon and we ride on into a rock-and-veld tundra. We are now on Mars. With a cowboy hat and a cigarette, Mariella finds us in the Freelander.

Lex says goodbye. We hug like brothers. I close my eyes as we embrace and I am sad that he has to go. So much seems always to be left unsaid on this journey. The hooves and the boots do too much talking. We look at each other and he smiles. Brown, open eyes. I want to hug him again, or to say something about what it means to me that he is here, apologise for not being present. I wish we had more time. He gives me his toothy grin, turns and jumps into the car. Off to the airport, back to his reality.

Kiki and I travel into the evening. Together, we see to the horses' cuts in a lilac-coloured valley. Chickens scatter the tracks, shuffling donkeys like old men. I carefully spread honey upon Sasha's legs with my index finger. We have been told by many that honey is the best thing. It keeps off the flies and protects the wounds. 'It always heals.'

A twenty-nine mile day.

◆

The bloodiest things seem to happen when the sun is at its highest.

The heat sticks to everything we touch. The path ahead is an old broken aqueduct made up of square concrete plates, each the thickness of a brick, terracing out from the earth. The drop below is steep, the village of Courmes now hidden behind a mess of spindly trees. I am in front with Sasha, Kiki and Istia are behind, single file. We take a breath, leaning into the mountainside that rises sharply above.

Firmly, with the heel of my boots, I test the first couple of concrete plates. They hold. Sasha then follows, his eyes wide and cautious. We continue like this for almost twenty metres, Kiki and Istia shadowing our movements, step by step.

And then I hear it. A foreboding crack snaps through the air. I turn round to see Sasha, falling. In an instant, his back left leg has dropped and disappeared from sight, breaking a concrete plate, down into the trench below.

His nostrils flare and he trembles. His remaining three legs clutch desperately at the ground above, keeping himself from falling further. I can't be sure how deep it is. I don't know how long he will be able to hold himself.

Slowly, with the help of Kiki, I somehow manage to encourage him out. With all his strength, he uses his legs to force his way free. I dread to see the damage done. He stands up on all fours, quivering all over, and, remarkably, there are no broken bones. Blood streams down his back two legs. Kiki and I set to work. We use all the disinfectant and bandages we have left.

On we traverse. Vigilant and fearful. There is nothing else we can do. Istia and Kiki follow behind, learning from our mistakes. As the concrete plates are then finally replaced by hard land, we cross over an ancient plain like Berbers. We leave the mountain behind us. Relief.

R meets us in the evening.

The next morning Sasha's back left leg looks awful. Our host for the night, an endurance rider with several horses of his own, insists that the swelling will be due to the shock of the event itself. I am convinced it's an infection. The sun brims above us and after an hour or so the man turns his sparkling grey Arabian champion back to his house in the village of Caussols. We thank him. Another friend now made.

Confident that Sasha's leg is not infected, Kiki suggests I jump on Istia and that she rides Sasha bareback. She is thinking mostly about my feet and hip, which ache with pain. Together we ride into the biggest expanse of flat land I have ever seen. Haute plaine de Caille. Over 700 acres of unblemished green carpets the valley floor before us. It reminds me of the valley plains in Mongolia. One single, pale track slices the stage perfectly in two. This track was once ridden on by Napoleon on his return from Elba and, before him, used as a communications road by the Romans.

The grassland is hyperreal and as smooth as water. The horses' ears point forwards, away from the Maritimes Alps.

All day Kiki teases and questions me, investigates me. She appears irreplaceable on the back of Sasha. Her riding technique comes into full show as he bows his neck and cups his chin into his strong chest like a dressage horse, stretching all of the muscles in his back. Whenever Kiki rides Sasha he looks like a completely different animal. It is a wonder to witness how a horse can speak through its body and then listen and grow with the rider. I try hard to copy what she does.

'Imagine your legs to be long,' she suggests, 'as long as they can be. But then think of forming a ball around his belly. Relax your body, your forearms and your wrists, and feel his mouth in your hands.'

Softly we travel as if on the crest of a wave through pine forests and tracts of algae-green and we make our way to a stable in Blacouas. Kiki and the man were right. The swelling on Sasha's leg has disappeared.

After the two of them kiss and say goodbye, R leaves for the very last time. We hug like bears. At first, I thought I would be secretly glad to see him go, allowing for the world that Kiki and I share in the day to be more complete. But I'm sad that he is leaving. I ask if he can stay longer but he has to return to Amsterdam.

As his car draws out of sight, an alarming realisation penetrates through me. It is not for wanting him here that I asked him to stay, but because the travelling world that Kiki and I share in the daytime is slowly starting to bleed into the evening and the night. The adrenaline of the ride no longer belongs only to when we are with the horses. For the last couple of days, everything and everyone else has begun to ebb away into the background. I want R to stay so that boundaries can remain.

This realisation scares me. It also excites me to my core; the fizz in the stomach before diving off a rock. The journey itself has a lifeforce of its own and I feel like I am losing a sense of control.

543 miles, 39 days

Kiki's diary
26 April, Levens
   Were you really there? I sat in the clouds. I saw the formation, a spectacle. You are everywhere. I ran back to the chapel to take back the feather but a part of you remains there. Our secret. My dearest big sister, together forever. I miss you on this physical damned earth. But I am learning from you. Tried to pay penance. Your suffering. Could be more. There is nothing more. Write tomorrow? There is so much I want to say. I am a skulker. Head head. Us together. No one else. Deep regret. Another day. Fuck. Hand hand. Do we stay together? Are we one? Cut all ties. Nothing left. Hold tight. The whole night. Eyes falling shut. Sleep close. I love you.

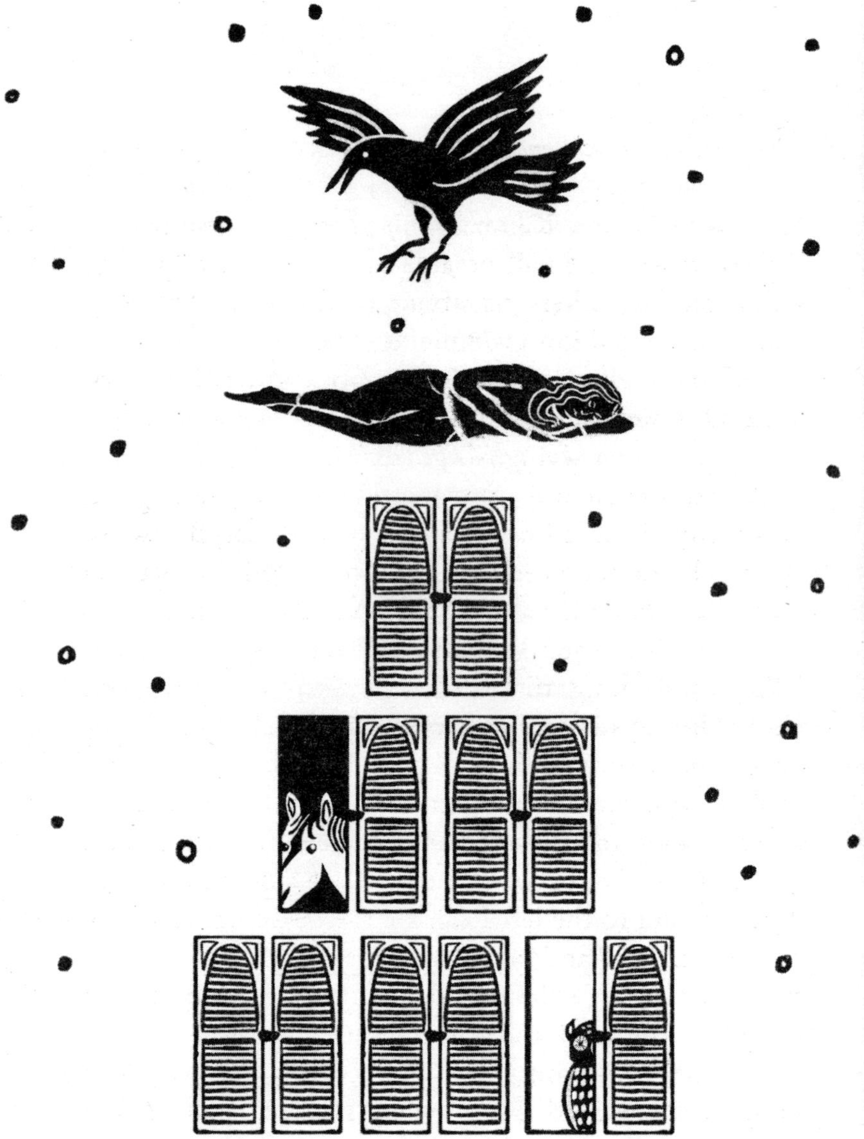

2–9 May
Trigance – Vestric-et-Candiac, Occitanie

Sasha is beside me. Kiki has gone ahead. It is surely only days now before I will be able to put his new Prestige saddle on, his withers just about good as gold. The hoof and boot companion-machine regrowing together.

I stop for a bowl of minestrone soup at Les Cavaliers, a dated restaurant that hovers in the air above the beautiful and terrifying Gorges du Verdon: 15 miles long, 700 metres deep and 1,500 metres wide. Sasha is given two carrots by a red-faced chef named Pascal. Below us, the coral limestone rock stabs like grey teeth in a gaping mouth of slate-blue water. All morning we have been stumbling over the rock and the desert shrub. I picture Kiki approaching the village of Aguines somewhere ahead. Perhaps she can already see the lake? Her head back, Aperol spritz in hand. I get up to go.

The tarmac road meanders away from the restaurant and the gorge and then there is a choice. Another choice. To our right the road continues straight all the way into Aguines, and to the left I can see the beginning of a GR trail (Grande Randonnée) snaking up the mountain. Both ways lead to the lake, Lac de Sainte-Croix. I look closely at the land above me: Le Grand Margès, 1,577 metres high. Kiki must have climbed this. She wouldn't have taken the road. From where I stand, the GR trail appears wooded, which is always easier to handle; the roots of trees make useful leverage for Sasha's hooves and my boots. The maps suggest it plateaus at the top. I imagine the view. I choose the mountain.

It doesn't take long for us to wind our way up to the plateau. We are met with harsh grassland and scree. The views are everywhere and the lake somewhere ahead. Sasha and I keep close. Every forty metres or so I find a flat-faced rock painted red and white with the letters GR scribbled in black. We are on track.

But then the ground underneath us begins to change. The tawny grass and rubble are replaced with larger rocks that we are forced to twist our way around. And then the rocks morph into sharp limestone boulders that begin to dominate the path. It doesn't seem right. These GR trails are designed to be simple. I lead Sasha to the side, away from the limestone pavement, and we cut our way through a warren of prickly shrub and agave plants. I need to find a safer route to cross this plateau.

Our path is cut short by a ten-foot-high barbed wire fence. 'TIRS PERMANENTS TIRS PERMANENTS TIRS PERMANENTS' is written on a bullet-shot sign. Beyond the wire there is a French military zone. Leaving Sasha in the shrub, I backtrack and run across to find the other side of the plateau, desperate to source a different way, an opening perhaps, an animal trail. I find only the precipice of the mountain. A 1,577-metre drop looms below.

Sasha is scared. We both are. He whinnies at me from within the shrub. I stand tall on a pointed boulder and look ahead. I can see that the plateau tapers. And then descends, surely to the lake. This gives me hope – this karst labyrinth cannot continue forever. I turn and look back at where we have come from. A mess of rock. Forward is the best way out. We keep moving, picking our way through the boulders.

With a little progress made, the land narrows into a twenty-metre-wide ridge. The gaps in between each boulder deepen. Our steps turn into strides, and then leaps.

Sasha trips and cuts himself on a rock. I tear off some skin that I see hanging from his back-right leg. There is a lot of blood. I dress it quickly. He becomes even more tentative. With each step I take I begin to worry that something real and awful is about to happen. He is going to break something. How have I not learnt from Liguria? We are completely isolated. No helicopter will be able to reach us. And then what? Only a bullet. The only animal I have ever owned is going to be shot on the top of a French mountain and it is going to be all my fault. Once more pride will defeat me. Surely Kiki has not come this way... she must have chosen the road.

I take another jump, my feet landing on a wide rock surface that projects out beyond the precipice of the ridge. I glance back, waiting for Sasha to follow as he has been doing so well. And then it happens. I hear the scrape of metal shoe on rock. His front left leg is trapped in one of the black holes between the boulders. He panics, he stumbles and I watch his entire body fall towards me.

The last thing I see are the whites of his eyes that beam down upon me in horror. My body tenses, and I prepare to be thrown from the mountain of Le Grand Margès by my own horse.

When I open my eyes, Sasha is standing above me. His neck pulses against me. I will never know how he managed to stop himself. I hold him to me as we breathe in relief, making sure not to move an inch. I turn my head to look out at the drop below. I can't see the bottom. The twists and scarps of Les Alpes-de-Haute-Provence stand vague and untouchable in the clagged light of the early afternoon. It's easy to mistake the mountains as things that have a heartbeat. If we had fallen off Le Grand Margès, this land would still remain, and life would go on. A gush of wind sweeps over us. There is a layer of sweat that coats my skin. We find our breath and keep moving.

Eventually the ridge mellows. The boulders give way to rocks and grassland and the trail descends. It becomes steep and we both fall down upon our sides, careless in our fatigue. We get up, a few scratches between us, and continue down the mountain. Pine trees replace stone and the ground softens, the air sweetens, and the path winds in orange earth down the lake side of Le Grand Margès. I kiss Sasha's neck and apply honey to his wounds. I release him from his head collar and he follows me, closer than ever. We travel together towards the magnetic shores of the lake.

As the white sun comes up Kiki and I swim in the cold water.

Our trail circles the rocky shoreline of the lake and ascends a sharp climbing hill on the far side. I look back at the charnel form of Le Grand Margès, glaring at us from across the blue. My heart quickens. In fear of somehow being picked up and deposited on the top of the ridge once more, I sit down on the ground and clasp Sasha's lead rope tight in my hands. I watch the mountain being swallowed up in its own black cloud.

'How was the view?' asks Kiki.

'Not worth the climb,' I answer.

'Do you think you would have still climbed it had you been alone?'

'I was thinking about that... I reckon if it was just me and Sasha I would have gone on the road. I've had enough of mountains. But it was the thought that *you* might have taken on the climb that made me want to do it too.'

'That's funny,' she says, looking away. 'I took the road because I thought that's what *you* would have done – the safe thing.'

Red-and-white GR signs lead us down into the town of Montagnac. It starts to rain and the water leaps up from the ground and slides down the narrow streets. The air smells of mud and lavender. We tie the horses to a railing underneath a giant plane tree in the square and run inside Café de la Colonne. The lone barman brings us two strong beers and a board of *saucisson* and Kiki takes out her knife to cut the meat and we eat and drink. For an unsettling moment she is the only person in the world that I have ever known; these afternoons and horses have been waiting an eternity for us to find them, tacked up and sleepy under a plane tree in the middle of a silent French village.

Finally, we reach a rest day. Raffi and Mariella have found a *gîte* for us near the village of Céreste-en-Luberon. We all kiss and hug each other like long-lost friends. I have missed them both in France, have wanted them to share in what Kiki and I go through. Being near to them is home.

After a long night of music, dancing and telling stories of our disasters and recoveries, we all stand over the maps and plan our route for the coming weeks. It's 6 May. We aim to cross into Spain on 3 June. Outside, the warm rain continues to trickle and fall and there is a leaning, breathing light in the sky.

Leaving the girls at the *gîte*, Kiki and I check on the horses before driving into the village to buy food. I love driving the Freelander on these rest days; the speed of this machine is absurd. I put my foot down and feel the engine roar. The effortless motion of the wheel between my hands.

We place our orders at a small pizzeria and stroll through the rain. Burly men shuffle inside underneath the scarlet veranda of a bar. Kiki pulls me to the side, and we sit down at a restaurant. The waitress looks at us in distrust, and the couples dotted around go silent at our ragged appearance, unnatural in this element. We drink two gin and tonics and get up to go, back into the rain.

I place my hat on top of her head and put my arm around her, keeping her warm. For a moment I feel her whole body relax into mine. And then, as if awaking, she pushes herself away and then leans up to bite my shoulder, hard. It hurts. I pull her into me and she giggles. I squeeze her waist in my hands. My heart beats fast.

Streams spill across the windows and the windscreen as we drive back to the *gîte*. The skies are heaving, mimicking the dense lavender that the rain falls upon.

'Suppose I'll need to leave then,' says Kiki after a long silence in the passenger seat.

'Leave?'

'Well, wasn't that what you said? "Once we reach Spain, we can part ways." Remember?'

For a moment I say nothing, keeping my eyes fixed on the road. To my right, I notice the crooked silhouette of a farmer, guiding his sheep through the torrents.

'I don't think we need to do that anymore,' I reply.

We are silent.

*

The day has finally come: I can ride with the saddle. Kiki and I cut up the pad that sits underneath so that no piece of cloth or rubber is in contact with his recovered withers, and I place the saddle gently upon his back. Abreast, we ride past a funeral march and a derailed train in the area of Apt. It feels unfamiliar being at this height. Sasha feels unsure underneath me, both of us awkward, getting reused to communicating in this way. During these past two days he and Istia have been close, almost solitary in their unity. We have been seeing different things.

We walk, trot and I try a short canter.

After an hour I make sure to jump off, giving his back time to adjust to the saddle. Manically I check and recheck his withers to ensure there is clear daylight between the healed wound and the leather. Nothing must undo his recovery, especially not me. Sasha and I have now been on the road for forty days.

An early summer breathes down on spring. The land is becoming flatter, warmer, the air thick and humid. We are leaving the Provence-Alpes behind us. For the time being, the mountains have gone. Arles is approaching, that city of light.

The rugged earth we have been moving over softens to rich clover green. A narrow stream runs by us and we follow it until we are greeted by a perfect house, just north of the village of Paradou. We dismount and go closer. The horses drink from the stream and then graze on the luminescent grass.

A dormant, brooding energy encircles the house, holding the walls and sifting along the unkempt lawn in front. The shutters are painted the colour of malachite, and the bricks are like the worn-out labels of wine bottles.

It is square, three rooms high, two rooms deep, and has a wooden front door. Unsure of whether it is lived in or not, we approach tentatively and touch the stone.

One day, we agree, we'll come back here. Together.

After passing into the old town of Arles we ride up the cobbled pavements of Rue Voltaire. Swarms of tourists panic and part, plastic camera sticks and flopping sunhats clutched in their palms. Unfazed, the horses take us through. We climb the stone steps of Emperor Tiberius' Arènes d'Arles. Built in 90 CE, the Roman amphitheatre was once an arena for hand-to-hand blood fights and chariot racing; it is now the Provence home of bloodless bullfights, plays, concerts and the annual Feria d'Arles.

We tie up the horses beyond the amphitheatre and survey the early morning from a café. The *jus de pommes* is fresh and the Rhône river flows. It swells. I feel the crude acidity of the apple on my teeth and bite down on my bottom lip. Strangers pat the horses. Strangers walking by. The river and pockets of conversation churn in my ears. I want to close my eyes and see and hear only horses. I think of Van Gogh's *Bedroom in Arles*. I open my eyes and survey the light around us. I wonder what Kiki's sister would have made of this. I wonder if she is somehow with us now.

'Do you ever think that when we're together, with the horses, it feels like some kind of story? And then when the day ends, the story finishes, and we have to go back to being normal?' I ask.

Kiki looks at me. For a moment she appears frightened by my question. Her lips part, her fine, arched eyebrows raise. And then she returns. I hear the metal of her teaspoon stir in her coffee. I feel her foot press down upon my boot.

Beyond the green light of the city we travel over a bridge with the blue-and-silver Rhône flowing underneath us. Two fishermen wave from their little white boat, shouting in triumph as a fish wriggles at the end of the rod. After the water there is nothing but poppies bending in the wind and lime-green leaves of juvenile vineyards reflecting the sunlight. Earth and stone tracks never seem to end. We gallop and gallop until the way lowers down into a fertile place made from long, untouched grass, stray lavender plants and an old oak tree that lives alone. We break for lunch in its shade.

With the saddles removed, the horses roll and roam freely in the grasslands. They look like buffalo on a prairie. We both lie down and look up at the sky and are pleased to be out of the heat. Wisping strands of rye and bromes stand between us and sway with a reluctant breeze, but our bodies are still visible to each other. I wonder what might happen should I put my hand through the grass. Kiki's arm is so close to mine. Her bare neck and her collar bone. I remember how she looked on the first day she arrived at Terra di Mezzo, how much she intimidated me, and now she is almost naked next to me, in the shade of the oak tree. I think of R and my fists and jaw clench in anger at myself. Lavender and sweat fill the air.

Impatient to go, I get to my feet and put out my hand to pull Kiki up. She takes it in hers and then jumps up. Her body latches on to mine and we hug each other. And then the hug doesn't stop.

Slowly, she leans back, away from my chest, and then

holds my shoulders, looking straight at me, into my eyes. My heart races. My jaw clenches. I twist away to find Sasha.

712 miles, 47 days

Kiki's diary
7 May, Vauvert
　An electric shock runs through my body when, after forty kilometres, we look at the map for the last stretch of the route for that day and he puts his arm around me. Electric perhaps from the beginning but I had good hopes that the initial tension would blow over. Now, in the last days, he spoke about a new secret and sometimes his wall is absent for a little longer than it was before. Back then his periods of silence and exclusion were much greater. A given, seeing his character.
　Yet, something different happened yesterday. I felt low and grumpy, as he once again shamelessly shut himself off and refused to pose any question in return. I wondered if I was truly frustrated but realised I wasn't. Surrounded by the green hills beyond Arles, he proposed to stop for lunch at some awkward turn of a dirt road. Unusually decisive, I said no and we cantered a little while further. A tree offered some shade beyond a dried-up stream. We jumped off the horses and sunk into the tall grass. The horses roamed free. The green was so high that we couldn't see each other. We lay down in that field. We spoke about life after death, of life

through death and life with death. About faith or destiny or coincidence that had brought us together. Every now and then we looked at each other but not for too long. When it was time to go, he offered me his hand to pull me up.

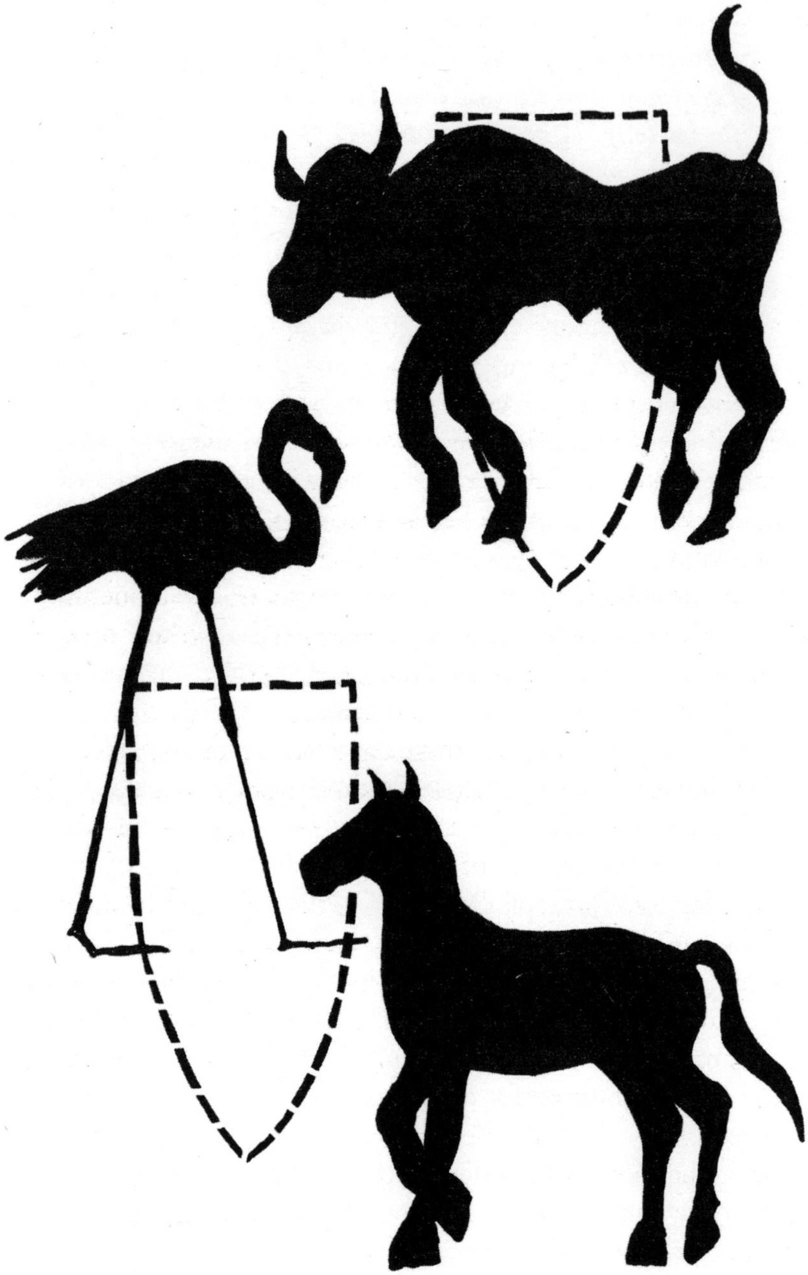

10–24 May
Vestric-et-Candiac – Lannemezan, Hautes-Pyrénées

No one really knows the origins of the Camargue horses. They are strong, serene and alabaster grey. They live in the wetlands of the Rhône delta and they share this vast ecosystem with curlews, clement Camargue bulls and pink flamingos. In the mornings there is often a mist that winnows the long grass, and within this breath I can just make out the swaying shapes of the wild horses, their heads floating, ears twitching like blackbirds.

In the village of Beauvoisin there are stencilled silhouettes of bullfights, bulls and long-legged birds painted onto whitewash walls. This *empègue* tradition began over a hundred years ago when boys were conscripted for national service. They would paint these signs on the walls outside of their homes as a mark of their duty and their departure.

There is a strong tradition of bullfighting in the Camargue, but instead of having the warrior name of the matador, *razeteur*, splashed on the yellow posters in thick red paint, there is only written the name of the bull and the farm from which it is born. No blood is shed in the Course Camarguaise. Instead tassels, cockades, ribbon and flowers are positioned in between the bull's horns and it is here that the *razeteur* must perform his magic, severing the ties of the objects from the bull's head with a four-bladed hook after tiring the animal into indifference. The bullfight is replaced with the dance. The greatest of these occurs each year in Emperor Tiberius's Arènes d'Arles.

We rest for two days beyond the stencilled Beauvoisin and the horses stay a stone's throw from our bungalow cottage in a gold-and-white-painted round pen once used for the bull calves. At night I lie awake listening to the cicadas beyond the doorway and I think about Spain. It feels close now. I can smell its heat. I remember how it once felt hopeless. An impossible, faraway place.

But there's a long way to go. I cannot become complacent. We still have to cross the Pyrenees. Now sweating in the encompassing heat of the Camargue, the cold and the snows of the Alps have faded away. The nest in Ceparana, Serena and Leila, Terra di Mezzo – the eyes of Savia wane from memory. Tuscany is dimly lit, represented only by the image of Mithra standing above me as I lay in a bed of hay.

The air temperature increases as we leave our bungalow with dust on our boots and dust upon the horses' bodies. Istia's back has become hard and she has developed saddle sores just below her withers. Kiki walks and I walk too.

The horses peer over the sides, down into the cerulean gorge of the Hérault river. We mount and ride over Pont du Diable, the Devil's Bridge. Shaped with two Romanesque arches, it seems as inherent to the landscape as the granite, schist, limestone and dolomite rock from which it unfurls. I am informed by a man with a moustache and a globular head that the bridge was built in the early eleventh century by Benedictine monks. Reverently, the man goes on to suggest that its construction served two purposes: to link the abbeys of Aniane and Gellone, and to exercise good against evil.

'The monks worked tirelessly, day in day out, yet the Devil came each night to tear down their labour,' the man begins, his hand stroking Sasha's muzzle. 'In their desperation, they then called upon a young novice named Guilhelm and sent him to reason with the Devil, hoping that he might persuade him to stop his sabotage.

'Young Guilhelm presented the Devil with an offer: if you help us finish this bridge – and if this bridge is indestructible to all – I will give you the body and soul of the first creature that crosses it. The Devil, hungry for death, agreed at once and the bridge was completed that night: an unbreakable crossing over the gorge, linking the two abbeys. Upholding his side of the deal, Guilhelm then found a stray dog and sent it over, tying a cooking pot to its tail in mockery. Expecting a human, the Devil couldn't believe the deceit. He flew into a manic rage and attempted to destroy the bridge that he had created. But, of course, it was impossible. The Devil clambered up the sides and hurled himself off, down into the water below.'

The man points gravely to the river. We fall silent. The horses are sleepy in the daytime heat.

Breaking from a spell, the man then looks up at me and squints his dotted eyes. He scratches his head and asks where it is we are going. He then asks why.

'Why not?' I answer. 'It would be a shame to stop now.'

'If you are travelling to Santiago de Compostela,' the man continues, 'you must throw a stone off the bridge. You must keep the Devil at bay. He, too, is indestructible.'

Kiki and I have no stones, but instead we walk down the path and jump into a pool of the river. The horses drink.

Beyond the bridge, the cobbled streets of St-Guilhelm-le-Désert entrap us all. Mariella reaches us and we find a little apartment with stone walls. Raffi has returned to England to surprise her father for his birthday.

In the night I get up for some water. I walk across the room and see the outline of Kiki's body in the bed opposite mine, her shape underneath a single sheet. Her eyes glimmer, still open. Mariella sleeps soundly in the next-door room.

I fill my glass and drink from it. I fill it once more and walk back to my bed. Kiki's arm awakens. It reaches out in the dark as I pass.

'I'm thirsty,' she whispers.

Her fingers find the glass, and she sits up to drink. Gently, I come down to her mattress.

She puts down the glass on the table between our beds and I touch her arm with my hand. She then touches mine, pulling me ever so slightly towards her. We hug and are still in a fraught silence. She then pulls me hard with her hand and I bring the rest of my body onto the bed. Softly, I kiss her neck and lower my chest against hers and then my waist and my legs, so that all of me is pressing against her. She holds the back of my neck with her cold right hand. I brush away dark hair that sits upon her forehead. I kiss her cheek, and then take myself away, back into my bed.

We both lie in silence. My heart pounds in my chest. All I want is to go back, to travel through the darkness and to feel the shape of her body underneath me once more. To hold her.

The figure of R flashes through my mind, through the room it feels. I have crossed a line.

The sky is cornflower blue in the morning, and we ride through the heat towards the old sister of St-Guilhelm-le-Désert, the ceramic village of Saint-Jean-de-Fos. The beauty of the south of France continues to enchant.

After sinking their muzzles into the fountain, we tie the horses to a bench on the side of rue Ancienne Ville and Kiki walks in under the veranda of a bar. I buy two yellow apples for the horses and a punnet of strawberries from a market stall. Swallows warble like children and sycamore trees stand around the square, having seen all this commotion many times before. I return from the stall to find Kiki speaking with a tall elderly woman.

'When I saw you with the horses,' says the lady, her voice soft and her accent delicate, 'it took me away to what it was like when I was three years old. There were no cars here, you see, and the square was made from... from earth. Only that. The men would play boules – here – and we would run around in the dirt. The bar and the fountain... *this* bar and *that* fountain: that is all that remains from back then.'

There is something disarming about this woman. The touch of her hand is ice cold, her eyes pierce. After speaking to Kiki, she insists that we stay with her, that we bring the horses and that they roam in her garden. Her house, she states, is just around the corner. We follow her. Her name is Marie.

There is a Bechstein piano in the hallway which she lets me play before dinner. Outside there is a pool, green with algae, and a shower that has been built into the dead body of an oak tree. At dusk we light candles and sit outside. Bach is Marie's musician of choice and Picpoul her wine. As it often is in places that have seen so much time come and go, each room in the house is traced with a different story.

That night I don't sleep well. There is a draft inside our bedroom, sweeping through the still night-time air and across the old walls. But when I turn to watch the contours of the tree that stands outside the balcony, the branches are motionless. I can't understand it. The wind shudders in the hallway, flying along the blue wooden floorboards, weaving amongst the strings of the piano, covering the house from the inside out. I hear Kiki sleeping in the far corner of the room. We have barely spoken a word to each other since last night.

*

The next day we get lost. Exhausted from the heat, we find a shaded forest in which to lie down. Every single evergreen tree is watching us now, collecting us with their roots. We are both drunk with fatigue. There could be a violent downpour of thunder and lightning, a white raging bull being chased by a band of flamingos tumbling round the corner, and still we would remain, sinking listlessly together into the forest floor. Dripping in and out of sleep.

I reach out to find her hand and she grabs mine, tight.

We rise up, lighter than before it seems, and push on to the village of Prémian. Mauve hills of Le Parc naturel régional du Haut-Languedoc peer down above us as we travel on a *voie verte*, green way, sheering right through the valley. The green ways are a network of cycling tracks that crisscross Europe. The going is flat and soft underfoot. The horses are guiding us, it seems. With summer now in full rage, our heads bow into the west-falling sun.

It's a Sunday and we only have twelve miles to travel. Montpellier is somewhere to the south-east and Toulouse is directly west. We are 619 miles from Italy, some 700 miles from Spain and over 1,000 miles from where this journey began.

We stop to eat under a tree on the verdant banks of Le Jaur river. We undo Sasha's girth; Istia's back remains too sore to ride. The horses start to graze, filling their bellies, and we dig a hand into a saddle bag, hoping to find something for lunch. Nuts, *saucisson*, carrots, apples, cheese, berries, half a croissant, whatever remains from the day or night before.

I lie back upon the ground. Kiki stays upright, dissecting the ryegrass between us and peering into the moving water.

'You don't ask many questions, do you?' she says, looking away from me as she throws a tuft into the ground.

'What makes you say that?' I reply.

'Well, do you? You imagine things just the way you want them to be.'

'Just because I don't ask questions doesn't mean I'm not listening.'

'That's not what I'm saying. You don't ask questions because you don't really care.'

'What are you talking about?'

'You keep things in your mind so that you can understand them your way. So it works for you. Are you not curious how *I* feel? What *I'm* thinking? Don't you want to know more about why I'm here?'

I sit up and look at her, her amber-brown eyes glowing in the shade of the tree.

'I'm sorry... I hadn't realised—'

'I don't care if you're sorry. Do you often try and kiss other people's girlfriends in the dark, pretending it doesn't matter—'

'Of course I want to know more of you!' I shout, interrupting her before she can go on. Rooks scatter from the branches of the tree.

'That's all I want,' I continue, quieter. 'Look, I'm only able to deal with these things practically. I just walk. I'm not equipped. I don't know *how* to ask you about why you are here. It seems like a different language to me. Something foreign. Do you know what I mean? I've tried to imagine what you're going through; what it is you feel. But I can't. I'm sorry. I want to know more, but—'

'I am not asking you to "feel" it,' she interrupts. 'No one on earth needs to feel what I feel. I'm just asking if you... care. About me.' She looks up at the clouded sky and I see water in her eyes.

'And about my sister,' she continues. 'About Siu.'

Kiki lowers her head and tears fall down her cheeks. I try

and take her hands and put them in mine but she throws down the grass and keeps them to herself. I tell her that I am sorry, and I reach out to touch her arm. She looks up and says that she is sorry too. What are you afraid of? she asks. If *she* is able to do it – to face each day, experiencing something that only she knows – then surely I am able to walk next to her, with her, opening my mind just a little more to what she is living.

We cross over an old stone bridge patrolled by tall scarlet lampposts with gold-tinted faces for their bulbs. On the far side we reach a campsite for French holidaymakers. An acre field has been organised into perfect squares, each section bound with three walls of high laurel hedging. Campervans drive in and out like trawling boats in a harbour. The campsite manager bursts out from the door of his Portakabin office. His rubicund face beams at the sight of the horses, his glasses almost falling off the end of his nose. Mariella stands next to him, a cup of tea in hand.

He leads us to our square patch of land, stating that he will charge us only for the tents, and that if everyone rode horses then the world would be a much better place. I like this man. Sasha and Istia sniff at the laurel leaves and rip at the short grass, bemused by their lodgings. To make the fourth wall we tie two lunge ropes to trees either side of the open entrance and crisscross our reins like a saltire. Secure enough, we leave the horses and all drive into the village for food.

During supper Kiki tells me about a documentary that she has made. It is the first time I have heard of it. I think of how little I really know about her, about what matters to her.

'It'll be premiering soon.'
'Soon? Where?'
'Amsterdam.'
'Will you have to leave?' I ask.
'Don't you want to know what it's about?'

'Of course. I just didn't know—'

'It's about the Dutch colonisation of Surinam,' she interrupts. 'It's about what happened after they left.'

I don't ask any more about it, embarrassed in my ignorance. My mind turns to the idea of Kiki leaving, even if it is just for a short time. It sits uneasy in me. Perhaps it is the realisation that she is going back to the home and place that only she knows and where I don't belong, where Sasha and I don't exist.

'Will you see R?'

Before she has time to respond Mariella's phone starts to ring. It's the campsite manager.

'*Les chevaux!* I hear hooves!' he shouts. 'I hear the sound of hooves on the road!'

The horses have escaped. We run from the table and jump into the Freelander. I drive as fast as I can.

Seven miles later we see traffic ahead. My heart sinks. Kiki holds her head in her hands in the passenger seat. A queue of twenty cars or so is being held up by two figures in the distance. The horses.

I feel sick at the thought of what might have happened. I slam my foot on the brakes and we jump out of the car and run down the line. Drivers emerge from their car doors, pointing ahead, muttering. It all seems too static.

We continue running round a slight bend, a blur of cars blotting the way, and then we see it. I stop to catch my breath. Kiki halts too, behind me. There, in the middle of the road, unmoving and damp with sweat, guilty beyond recognition, stand the panting escapees. Unscathed.

We approach slowly and take them to the side. Out of the corner of my eye I see a woman get out of her car with a baguette in her hand. I expect her to stop and speak to Kiki, but she continues, heading straight towards me. I turn away from her and brace myself, fully expecting to be hit across the head. I open my eyes to find the woman looking up at me, confused, offering the baguette to Sasha.

The village of Saint-Pons-de-Thomières is covered in dust and sewage and the chimneys are painted the colour of corn. Music runs around the empty corners. Since the conversation by the river there has been a distance between Kiki and me, how we speak. Or perhaps it is since that night in St-Guilhelm-le-Désert. Today we have decided to ride separately.

I haven't been alone with Sasha for so long. At first it is trying, like meeting an old friend you no longer understand, but after some miles I begin to feel a sense of the free, shared solitude that drove us through Liguria. I take him into a trot and then a canter. His ears prick forwards. My mind clears as we ride together on a flat, gritty track with long grass either side. I pat the side of his neck with my right hand and scratch my fingers into his black mane. There is nothing else. Just us. These past days my head has been a fog. I can't let my feelings for Kiki distract from the journey. It is pure ecstasy to experience living in an animal herd.

We veer away from the route and ride down to a stream. We follow the water's edge, shaping our way around shrub and tree, and then come to an abrupt halt. Standing alone in a sharp crevice of light, we see a horse. A stallion. His coat is stippled, like a tiger's.

Tentatively, the lone animal comes down towards us. His face meets Sasha's. They sniff and rub, configuring friend or foe. Assured, the stallion then circles us, one step at a time, before promptly returning to his island of light. Then he walks on through the woods.

His path at first is simple enough to follow and the wild grass does not prove too difficult, but then this changes. The stallion meanders left and his track climbs higher, and then, speeding up, he swerves right. Sasha and I cling together. Before we have time to catch up to him his dark tail disappears into the open air above. Carefully, I pull back the thorns of a rose bush and, after two clambering steps, we surface from the wood and find ourselves at the edge of a moss-coloured mesa.

We step upon this new place, both of us making sense of where we are. The tiger-coloured stallion stands in the middle, staring at us, dead still. He then turns and continues walking, leading us forward, it seems, his shoeless hooves noiseless on the grass. We follow.

Our guide takes us along a track beyond the open space. Prickly arms of rosebushes and swelling bodies of rhododendron thicken the way. The track then curves and rises and, before long, we reach the head of a domed hill. This, it seems, is where the stallion's journey ends.

Before us stands the giant wooden structure of Moulin de Pesquies of Saint-Sulpice-sur-Lèze. The windmill is stout and old, dark and wise. His back is broad, straight, his belly firm and rotund, and his russet wooden eyes wander far, far, into western provinces. This is the beast that tried to kill Don Quixote.

As the stallion watches on, I bring Sasha underneath one of the windmill's weary arms. We hover, perfectly still, admiring the aged contours of his limbs, before I cannot resist but to climb. Slowly, I raise myself up onto Sasha's back and stand on top of the saddle. With my right arm outstretched to the sky, I reach up to touch the windmill's hand. I hold it there. All those seasons it has seen. The colossal shape of the round sky must be his television, coming and going; the pigeons bomb at full speed, the blackbirds taunt his figure but, of course, he doesn't waver. He finds the red admiral butterflies a wonderful distraction from the rooks that misshape the light of the sun.

My reach up is interrupted by the sound of an enormous bee. A hornet perhaps. A trumpet. I look around. An electric drone hovers above the windmill's head. I tense. Sasha tenses too. The stallion becomes anxious. The drone then circles the windmill, investigating, before descending slowly but surely towards us. A middle-aged man appears from around the corner, remote control in hand, and Sasha leaps in fright. The stallion runs away. And I fall to the ground.

Mariella finds us and we all agree that Istia is ready for her saddle. Her back has softened; the stiffness has gone. Gently, we place it on, making sure there is no pain. Kiki mounts. Immediately, Istia's ears switch forward. The pair reunited. With both horses fully tacked for the first time together, Kiki and I set off. How long we have waited.

We pass through the idyllic village of Sorèze and then down a meandering track that leads into a jungle. We emerge the other side, wet and hot with our arms cut. We gallop along the canal into a field of grain that flows in the wind, silver-green shoals. R is a shapeless form in my head; with me, behind me, waiting in the distance and watching me from the end of each road.

That night we pitch our tents at the side of a lake and the horses drink from the water and eat long damp grass upon the banks. Raffi has returned. But only for a short time, she says. She has to go back in a week. Her warm smile beams, her brown eyes overflow. I have missed her. We all swim in the eerie light of a full moon.

We lie by the fire and I recite extracts from *Don Quixote*. Never before have we felt like more of a family.

Early the next morning a farrier comes to change the horses' shoes. The final set before Spain. Up to this point we have made sure to ask farriers to put protruding nails in them, preventing the horses from slipping on the concrete. This time, unthinking of tomorrow, I forget.

> 'Destiny guides our fortunes more favourably than we could have expected. Look there, Sancho Panza, my friend, and see those thirty or so wild giants, with whom I intend to do battle and kill each and all of them, so with their stolen booty we can begin to enrich ourselves. This is noble, righteous warfare, for it is wonderfully useful to God to have such an evil race wiped from the face of the earth.' 'What giants?' Asked Sancho Panza. 'The ones you can see over there,' answered his master, 'with the huge arms, some of which are very nearly two leagues long.' 'Now look, your grace,' said Sancho, 'what you see over there aren't giants, but windmills, and what seems to be arms are just their sails, that go around in the wind and turn the millstone.' 'Obviously,' replied Don Quixote, 'you don't know much about adventures.'

994 miles, 62 days

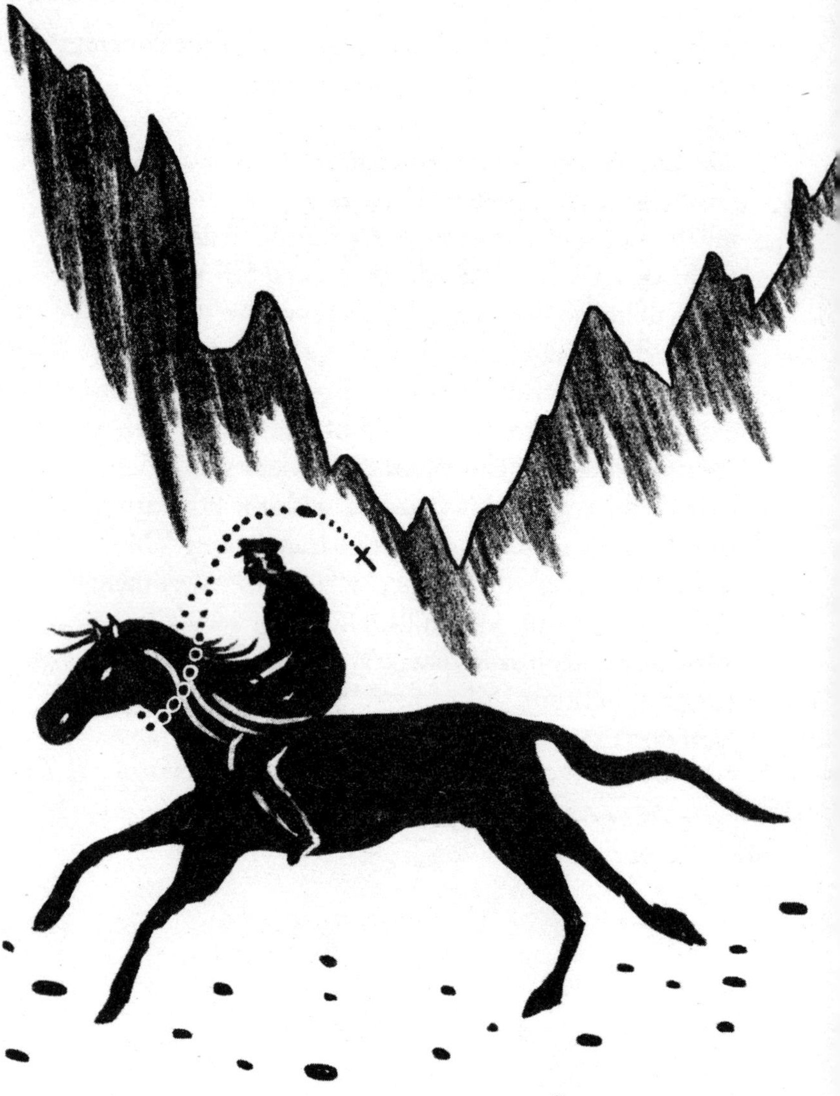

25 May – 1 June
Lannemezan – Ossès, Nouvelle-Aquitaine

Last night I dreamt I was on an ocean. When I woke, I realised this dream was in fact a memory. A memory that I have chosen to forget, until now. Exactly a year ago I crossed the Atlantic Ocean on a thirty-two-foot boat called *La Siesta*. It took twenty-three days. There were three of us on board. A seventy-year-old captain making the last voyage of his life and his two crew.

I remember now that, in my fatigue, hallucinations became so strong that I would spend hours looking out for birds, desperate for some corporeal reassurance. But the sky was like a desert. At night it was the worst: the sea reflected the stars that reflected in my eyes, and through that I only saw formations made by the diffracting glowing light from above and from below: metallic bodies hopping around the decks, flopping hair like strings of pearls; dogs with fish heads chasing each other across the lid of the ocean, and then snarling barks that would encircle the boat like the six or so porpoises we saw somewhere near the west coast of Africa.

As a boat we three united through the killing of fish. Beyond food, this exercise served two purposes: it filled up the captain's need for physical conquest, and it tied my body to a real time and place.

And now, as if it were in front of me, I can vividly picture the colours of its body. I can suddenly recall how empty I felt when the blooming honey, blue and verdant shimmers of one particular dorado silently screamed out its last echoes of life, writhing upon the deck in iridescent desperation, before extinguishing into a limp, cold shape of ash. Like a dying star.

How could I have forgotten about this killing until now? A creature with a stare that pierced me so deeply as to disallow me even to think. What else has my memory chosen to leave out?

Something is happening in the midst of this journey. At times it seems like a fog. Will experiences that I can't confront be conveniently forgotten? Perhaps it is only a matter of time. The gravity of killing the dorado was so clear in that moment, the creature in my hands; blood under fingernails, scales sticking to my bare feet, a dying star's unblinking eye glaring up at me. And then it became a scene submerged.

On this ride, as much as I try, I cannot see anything beyond what lies before us. There is no tangible consequence. What we do, how we think – me, Kiki and the horses – have no relevance outside of this time.

For three days we all sleep, eat and live in the quiet village of Seissan. The rooms of the house are pastel coloured and wooden floored, and in the attic a draft of cool air disseminates through so that clothes can hang and dry from the rafters. In the morning I hear Jen, our tall, silver-blonde host, walking out of the house and talking with the men and women in the market nearby. She comes back with vegetables for lunch. Kiki buys a linen dress from the village; the fabric is the colour of barley.

I lie in bed. The dust of these past days settles as the adrenaline dies. The physical pains come to light. Exhaustion. I hear footsteps climbing the wooden stairs of the house – the girls laughing outside in the garden – the footsteps softly ambling along the corridor.

My door opens and Kiki walks in. She lies down next to me and we don't say anything for what feels like an age. We then turn and look, closely, into each other's eyes. A pink peony sits behind her ear. We talk. Languid. She tells me that she is drawn to Scotland. That she can see herself living there one day, or England perhaps, somewhere close to the sea, is Devon nice? Norfolk? Somewhere where she can bring Istia. I tell her that I want to ride with her again, to explore other places.

'We could go east – to Romania. And then beyond – the Silk Road—'

'And down Portugal,' she interrupts, 'just us. No phones. No distractions.'

'Why stop there?'

She smiles and we bathe in the silence. The laugher of Mariella and Raffi drifts through the open window.

I reach out my hand so that it lies between us and she does the same, feeling, placing her hand inside mine. Slowly, I rise to get on top of her. My legs either side of her waist. I then stare down at her as she stares back, neither of us uttering a word; I follow the precious veins of her amber irises, amber breaking into bronze and then to a spectral, blue-pearl faded rim.

The veins stir. I feel her fingers grip the tops of my shoulders. I lean down, our noses almost touching, and plant my hands either side of her head upon the pillow, breaking my fall. At no point do I take my stare away from her swelling eyes. Now only the sound of her breath ties me to the rest of her.

Her fingers dig into the tops of my shoulders and, for a brief moment, it feels as if everything is going to burst and tear apart. But we manage to stay as we are, completely still; the breathing steadies, her fingers soften.

'When I get back – after Amsterdam – I think we shouldn't ride together.'

'OK,' I whisper.
'I will ride behind you... it's better if we stay apart.'

Once more we stand over a long table and mark out the route that will take us closer to the Atlantic Ocean. As far as I can tell, the most significant encounters between us and Finisterre are going to be the town of Lourdes and the Pyrenees mountains. Lourdes has been on my mind ever since we rode into the Occitanie region. I have never been but have heard so much about this religious metropolis. The concept of it is so foreign to what has become our structure of living – the continuum of rivers and hooves – that this town is almost alluring; the idea of all these human beings coagulating in one place, for one reason only, all that electricity and voice. I want to make sure that we absorb as much of it as we can.

As for crossing the Pyrenees, there are two options. The first is to ride towards Saint-Jean-Pied-De-Port and then over the border into the Spanish town of Roncesvalles, Navarre. From there we can continue along the Camino Frances, the most popular and straightforward path of the Camino de Santiago de Compostela, a collection of pilgrimage trails that all lead west, to the bones of St James. And then, just forty-eight miles further, to Cape Finisterre.

The second option, and perhaps the most challenging, is to ride over the mountains from the village of Sare, close to the Bay of Biscay, before joining the Camino del Norte, the lesser-travelled pilgrimage route that follows the Cantabrian coastline.

I have kindly been given an itinerary of the first option from a French baker who attempted the route a few years ago with two Lusitano horses. He has provided me with a complete list of stables to contact, people to call, farriers, vets, names and numbers of all the *albergues*. This amount of information makes me feel nauseous. We all agree on option number two.

First, though, we have to reach Basque Country.

Before taking the bus to the airport, Kiki left behind her collapsible bucket, her cocoon-shaped tent and a sleeping bag. Useless items to her in Amsterdam. I ride Sasha and take Istia alongside. At first she looks for Kiki but then, with Sasha near, and with all of our heads bowing to the western sun, we soon become one thing. All day we travel close to the slate-green Ardour river.

On the first night without Kiki, me, Mariella and Raffi find a *gîte* that sits proudly on a plateau, jutting out upon its sloping green field. A table stands in the shaded part of a courtyard and the horses roam free. From where we eat, we can all look up and inspect the low hills to the south, peppered in violet irises and pastel asphodels.

Above the wildflowers the shadowed mountains climb abruptly. Some of the summits are capped with snow. Others are crusted in rock. When the twilight moon rises, the sky remains blue for quite some time before it grows dark. We look up to the warm stars and I recall how in the Alps the rocks and the earth had felt so beaten and distant; the invisible tolling bells, the echoes of the cuckoo birds through the naked woods, the claustrophobia. Here, the mountains are close and young, mellow in the night. I find Sirius, burning above me. It has been a long time, my friend.

Just below the *gîte* there are five dun llamas and two rosy black Mérens ponies keeping Istia and Sasha company. The Mérens are prehistoric and powerful. Used in war by Caesar, Charlemagne and Napoleon, they have strong, short backs, enormous rumps and powerful, blooming chests. They are resilient and rustic animals, with their ancestors dating back 15,000 years. Where their breed truly stems from remains a mystery, but they are directly associated with the Pyrenees mountains and said to be native to the upper valley of Ariège, near Andorra. They remind me of Irelanda, the Highland pony I used to ride down the UK. I wonder if these Mérens could be the answer to a bigger journey. I have become fixated with the search for *the* horse to take me across the world. The mule remains leagues apart, however. Supreme.

The northern face of the Pyrenees is the backdrop. We pass underneath the Romanesque tower of Château fort des Angles. A young farmer stacks hay on his tractor and the land begins to flatten and become pale. Healthy young calves on the side of the tracks glow in coats of ginger and cream-white velour. A man with an arched back and a red-checked shirt swings a scythe back and forth, the tick of a fabric clock. He pauses and stands upright to gaze at me, Sasha and Istia as we come round the bend. The clang of hooves on the road lingers dully in the heat. Cut grass and sweat are sweet in the air.

Before long the spire of a far-off cathedral arrows up in the distance and the streams from which the horses drink fill the depths of the Ousse river. The outskirts to Lourdes are at first ugly and plain, but then very quickly they become striking. The seventy-metre-high spire of the Basilica, Notre Dame du Rosaire de Lourdes, shines into the seraphic sky like a defying message from the middle of the Gothic earth. We trot past the casino and over the bridge. The Ousse throws itself at the day, thrashing green and silver underneath us.

South American women hop around the streets like chickens and fat men grin and point at Sasha and Istia with swollen fingers clutching rosaries. Pizza cartons lie on pavements and neon-lit images of Jesus Christ beam red and blue. I ride past the New Orleans Café, the nightclubs, the dustbins and the bars; I peer into shops selling pocket knives, tea towels of Mary, paracetamol, apostolic fridge magnets and Pope-faced lighters. We have arrived at Roman Catholic Disneyland.

Behind tall black gates the Rosary Square (La Place du Rosaire) plains wide, a landing strip for the jets of God or, as I suspect Sasha and Istia may be thinking, a holy galloping ground. At the far end of the tract there is the Crypt (La Crypte de la basilique de L'immaculée-conception) and the Grotto (La Grotte de Massabielle). We approach the black gates. I reckon it would be a straight twenty-second gallop from the gates to the Basilica, waiting in the foreground. Two confused voices interrupt my imaginings and a woman emerges from inside a security box. She tells me to halt. Upon request, the officer then kindly calls her superior, who confirms that dogs and cats aren't allowed to enter La Place du Rosaire so therefore horses will have to stay out too. Apparently, it doesn't matter if they are 'holy horses' or not. We move on.

Sasha pauses outside a stall. Something has caught his eye. He turns his body into the shop and brings his nose close to a long, dangling rosary, the colour of mahogany. He sniffs a little closer and then attempts to eat it from where it hangs. It's a sign. I ask the wide-eyed shopkeeper how much this rosary will cost. Without uttering a word, she removes it from the metal hook and stretches out her arm. I am not sure who she expects to take it, me or Sasha. I jump off and, with the help of a dozen onlookers, I don Sasha with his first rosary.

With Istia alongside, we trot off to find a pint of Guinness. The sun sweats the rubbish-filled alleyways late into the afternoon.

Drunkenly, I ride out of Lourdes. The sounds and smells of the town wash over and through us and, eventually, we find our way to a stables three miles north. The owner has two small children and a collie dog that leaps onto her shoulders as she drives the quadbike. I ask her if it would be OK for Istia to stay on for one extra day, without me. I tell her that a girl called Kiki is coming to get her. I will travel with Sasha alone.

That night I go back to Lourdes. The energy is a drug. The protruding neon-blue cross overlooking Château fort de Lourdes beams from above. I make my way up onto the stone stairs of the Basilica where I can observe the hundreds of people below, praying, singing, grieving. Flags and candlelight fill up the night air. From where I watch and stand, I am hit with the transmissible power of total unity, cohesiveness; a healing power of a body of people all dreaming of a heartfelt thing. It's scintillating. Over six million people from all backgrounds, non-beliefs and beliefs visit Le Sanctuaire Notre-Dame de Lourdes each year. Processions and prayers are held each day. Everyone prays for miracles to happen.

The steeple wears a cloth of opal light. All the people hum on the cement ground, shuffling forwards in unison, chanting in their different languages, believing in hope. I wonder what Bernadette Soubrius, the fourteen-year-old girl who saw an apparition of Mary Magdalene, would think of what Lourdes has become. It was on 11 February 1858 that she witnessed her first vision of Mary. She was out gathering firewood with her sister. At the time, Soubrius and her family lived in a one-room basement, formerly used as a jail, called *le cachot*, the dungeon. Because of her, these people see God here.

*

The next day is Sunday. The sun climbs at 6.45 a.m. and I am awoken by church bells. I stand in the sun and I close my eyes. I say a prayer for my cousin Victoria, and for Sasha. I then pray for Kiki and her sister, Siu.

After feeding the horses I go to say goodbye to Istia in her paddock. I separated them in the night, hoping it would make departing with Sasha alone that bit easier. Istia whinnies at me from afar, settling upon seeing me, and then comes to the gate, observing as I approach. I open the gate and place my hand on her head. I then hug her neck and stay there for a while. She is a deeply gentle-hearted horse. She knows things that people and other animals don't. From the very start she has had an unnerving aura of calm that surrounds her. What she lacks in Sasha's determination, she makes up in sensitivity. I press my face into her neck and wonder what this is all going to lead to, this severing. Will we ever ride together again? Somehow the future doesn't seem so certain.

As I go to pull away, she places her face below my chin. Her eyes are dark bodies of water. And then, looking into the depth of her stare, I realise that I am saying goodbye to the only thing I have left of Kiki. I sit down on the grass next to her. She stands above me and I close my eyes to cry.

Sasha and I walk away and the horses call out to each other. Harrowing, longing calls. After almost a mile or so, I hear running and look behind to see the husband of the stable owner coming towards us. He catches his breath before handing me an address and a telephone number on a piece of paper with the name 'JOACHIM' scribbled above.

'For tonight. This man will help you,' he stutters.

We travel along the banks of the Gave de Pau, its waters brushing the dense woodland. The trees clear and the track takes us down towards a house. Cows are baking in the sun in fields either side. A woman with ragged brown hair and a joint in her hand comes out of the open front door. Wearing nothing but black boots and a thong, she listens to what I have to say. She leads me down the rest of the track, her track, she says, and takes me past her donkey that is as wild as a snake, she says, before sending us on our way. I tell her I'm grateful for the shortcut and she asks if I want to stay a little while longer. Sasha pulls me on.

The final five miles before Joachim's village is on a straight tarmac road. Lorries fly past. My head reels from the pressure of the heat and lack of water. I am exhausted.

The hard road ascends gradually – tormenting the balls of my feet – before descending into the village of Louvie-Juzon. Pigeon-grey buildings are nestled comfortably underneath a blue cone-shaped mountain that rears up to the west, blotted with pine trees. A broad-reaching valley engulfs the land south, as far as the eye can see.

There is a church tower in the middle of the village square. I ride down with Sasha, dazed and absent, my eyes as heavy as my boots. A young man calls out to me and I follow him. He has a gruff beard and wears pale shorts and a dirty blue shirt. An old white dog and two collies encircle him.

'I am Joachim,' he states. We shake hands. 'You are the one with the horse? You have come far today. More than forty kilometres.'

'I think so. It feels like it.'

He takes me beyond the square and over the village road. The dogs chase us onto the pavement and down an alleyway, and we all emerge into a long, lush paddock, shaped neatly upon the eastern bank of the Gave d'Ossau river. There is another Arabian horse there, chestnut in colour.

'I have twenty-six Arabian horses,' Joachim exclaims. 'I'm a hoarder. They are high up in the mountains at this time, near the Spanish frontier. They live with the sheep and the cows. Up there.' He points south to the valley that is now turning the colour of rosewood due to the setting sun.

'Do they ever get lost?' I ask.

'They only go so far. Tomorrow I must go and catch them. They've been disturbed by the motorbikes and the walkers.'

Joachim gives me some horse feed and I find a place to sit down at the foot of a tree and watch Sasha eat. It was Sasha who got me here today. The entire way my head beat in pain and my body was slow and heavy. Sasha looks in great condition. His coat shines, his muscles pulse. The mohican mane has been lost to thick, dark hair.

The Gave d'Ossau glistens black and silver from the sunlight and pappus of dandelions float past me in the air. Specks of dust drift above the water. I close my eyes and fall asleep.

Just off from the village square a cobbled alley takes me left. I find two wooden barn doors, facing me from within their stone wall. I push the broken handle and walk inside. It is hard to work out if it is a stable or a basement. Old clocks, bicycles, mirrors, chests of drawers, saddles and speckled sunlight are strewn across the scene. A bale of hay has fallen to pieces in an opening to a second room. The windows are coated in cobwebs and electric sockets hang out, mimicking lianas. There are stairs that line the side of the left wall, climbing up to the first floor. It reminds me of a scene from a Western.

I follow Joachim's voice up the stairs to discover a narrow kitchen with a wood-burning stove, a table, a bench against the right-hand wall, three chairs and four glass windows of which two are broken. The floor is patterned in red-and-white linoleum checks and from the windows you can climb out onto a grated roof where pots and pans lie out in the afternoon.

In the next room an ingot of sunlight is stretched across the grey-painted wooden floor from a hole in the ceiling, and an enormous square vinyl player stands in the corner. Hundreds of records are neatly piled up. I discover that the house of Joachim originated as a bar in 1884. By the turn of the century it had become a brothel. In the early 1920s desires changed and it transformed into a hospital, and then a hotel, a restaurant, and now a home.

My room looks out onto the square. A gigantic image of a young girl is graffitied onto the building opposite with the words 'CHILD OF THE MOUNTAIN' written in black paint upon her bottom lip. Standing underneath her chin there is a fountain with water that spurts out of a sculpted dog's mouth.

'You can use the toilet there,' says Joachim, pointing to the fountain. 'The loo does not work inside the house.'

My mattress lies on the floor and books are piled up all around me: Joseph Conrad, Albert Camus, Sartre, Kundera. I hang my socks out of the glassless window. At 10 p.m. Joachim's girlfriend arrives, Morgan. She has broad shoulders, a square jaw, bright eyes as round as marbles, flowing auburn hair and tanned skin from the mountains. She is young too, perhaps thirty, and she is strong. Like Joachim, Morgan is a freelance shepherd. It seems that both of them have discovered some shape of living that many spend their entire lives searching for. They glow.

Together we eat bread, olive oil, beef pate, anchovies, courgette, local sheep's cheese and sausages. We drink red wine and Morgan tells me of her winters and her summers spent as a shepherd. It is normal for her to spend up to six weeks at a time in a shepherd's hut in the mountains.

Thunder wakes me in the night. Rain falls like pebble drops onto the square and slides down the face of the graffiti girl. I have always been terrified of the clap of thunder. Unable to sleep, I reach out to read something from *Heart of Darkness* in a bid for comfort. It only makes things worse. Pangs of jealousy and angst reverberate around my body. I think of Kiki and I think of R. They will be together now. Lying together, skin together.

> It had become so pitch dark that we listeners could hardly see one another. For a long time already he, sitting apart, had been no more to us than a voice. There was not a word from anybody. The others might have been asleep, but I was awake. I listened, I listened on the watch for the sentence, for the word, that would give me the clue to the faint uneasiness inspired by this narrative that seemed to shape itself without human lips in the heavy night air of the river.

My head is aching but I am so covered in sweat that I know I must have eventually slept deeply. I think I've got a temperature. There's a burning behind my eyes. Frank has texted me. He says he wants to come out and join the ride. Soon.

The rain continues to pour. Down at the river the dandelions and the sifting dust have gone. I lead Sasha across the road and find a space for him underneath the stairs in Joachim's house where the saloon piano had once been. He dives into the broken bale of hay and I dry off his back. The chestnut horse was sad to see him leave the riverbank.

'This house can change shape,' says Joachim, standing at the top of the stairs. 'It's now a stable for Arabian horses and Scottish wanderers.'

In the kitchen he lights the wood burner and prepares coffee, bacon, bread, sausages and honey on the wooden table. We speak about his twenty-six Arabian horses that he keeps high up in the mountains. They are stronger, he insists, than anything down below. I'm sure he is right. Joachim's philosophy is one of self-determination; to allow the animals to grow and die and live as close to their nature as possible. They discover how to survive for themselves, to locate water, to find the right glades on which to graze and to understand how to protect one another.

'This way it is correct to break them in at four years old,' he states, 'no earlier. They grow slower, yes, but they are wiser and stronger for it. Putting a saddle on them is simple. They are not scared by people or by thunder. They are calm with themselves as they have known the greatest dangers that nature can give them. They become tame in their wild.'

He hands me a brown paper bag with some string and I make sandwiches for the day ahead. Outside the rain runs through the grass and over the trees of the blue mountain and it trickles softly down into Joachim's house. I don't want to leave, but I have to say goodbye. It feels like a place I have known a long time before, perhaps in the life where I knew Terra di Mezzo. I thank Joachim and tell him of a girl called Kiki who will soon be here with her horse. I don't know when exactly, but she should only be a day or two behind me.

'Please give her this.'

I hand him a necklace that I found in Lourdes. It has a small stone of malachite attached to a silver chain.

*

Sasha and I cross the bridge and follow the river to Ordiarp and to Ossès. Finally the rain ceases and the high morning sun swells in its own light. Silver-lit pappus float through the air once more.

My father calls. He tells me that my cousin's health is deteriorating fast. The chemotherapy isn't working. They will try again.

Unable to think, I bring Sasha to the side of the track and dismount. I sit down on the ground and look up at the sky. My eyes close.

My cousin is thirty-one years old and she has terminal cancer. What the hell am I doing here? This no longer makes any sense. The privilege of a journey – an exercise belonging only to the bored, the unsick and the unhindered. This is all wrong. Sasha grazes next to me. Kiki is somewhere behind. The only place I want to be is next to my cousin. In hospital.

In a panic, I take out my phone and call her. She picks up immediately. Her voice is light and clear. Different from before, softer. She wants to know every detail of each day. I do my best, taking her from the woods at Castello del Calcione and along the Via Francigena through Tuscany. We then go into the Ligurian snow and warily climb all those mountains that I still can't pronounce. Then there is Kiki. She wants to know all about Kiki.

My cousin makes me promise that I will take her on the next ride, one closer to home. She asks me if she thinks Leo is watching over me again and I say that he is and that Siu, Kiki's sister, is watching too.

'Well, you better keep them entertained,' she giggles.

In the evening I find Mariella and Raffi at a campsite. Raffi makes a delicious supper. But this is her last night. I will miss her. Although Mariella remains, our little family is breaking.

I wish I had appreciated it more when it was together.

1,107 miles, 70 days

Kiki's diary
26 May, Saint Gaudens
The realisation just kicked in how utterly mad this all is. It makes me smile. Indeed, I got on a train to London to meet a stranger because I couldn't make my mind up about whether to embark on this anomalous trip or not. And after a very unconvincing meeting I decided to do it – and so here I am, writing as I walk behind him, on a Monday morning, carrying hundreds and hundreds of kilometres in my feet.
Only one more day and a bit before I go home. One more day of walking, running, and all these other things we do. Just the other moment we entered an ancient empty church... From tropical dampness to a distinct Christian mustiness. I saw him rise up from this kneeling he does upon entering a church – every time, without exception. In the middle of the aisle his shadow looked grand, the light dim and old, just like a Rembrandt, tiles brown and a dark shade of white, a great spectacle and for a second my heart sank to my stomach. We sat down on the benches in different rows and prayed; him on his knees, me with my wrists resting on the bench in front of me. I looked for Siu there but couldn't find her. So I asked for guidance, a new thing, and then the bells chimed 10:30. I lit a little candle for less money than was asked for, but rebellion is her too.

30 May, Amsterdam

Here, in Amsterdam, the city is windless. Nothing moves, which makes every object seem unbearably heavy. A thick heavy blanket that leaves you tired and lethargic. The trees have stopped talking to me. Hopelessness and weariness of life hang over the streets like wallpaper. There, out there, is where the magic is and where life tingles like bubbling champagne water. Out there, my body awakes, my mind skips a beat, people look me in the eyes and I climax without touch. Ideas about an unseen future. At this moment, in this situation, I don't want to be anywhere else than back out there. Never before have I been this lost.

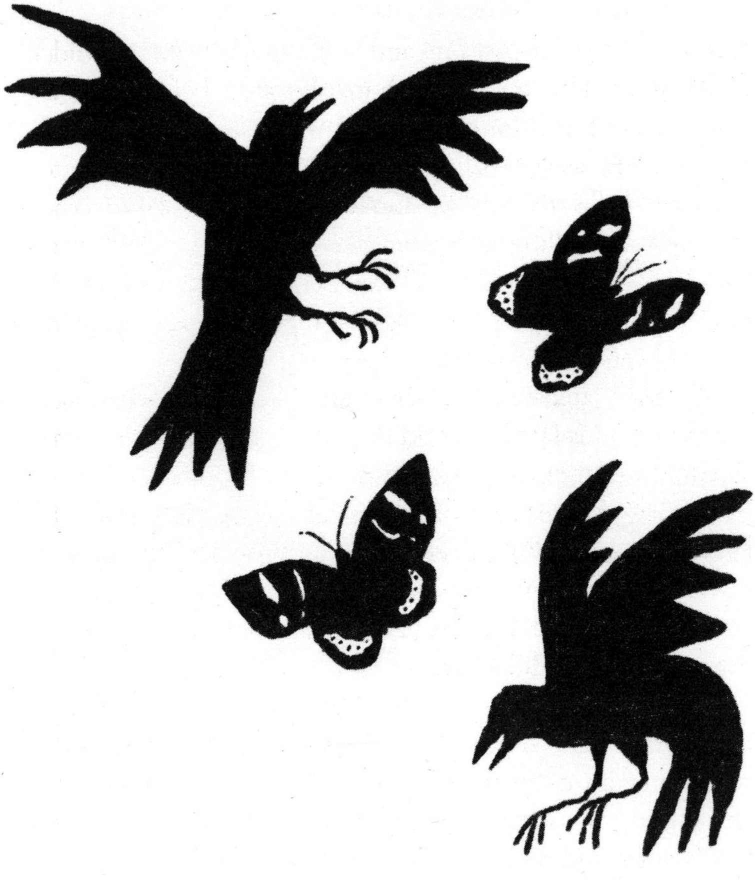

2–8 June
Ossès – Errenteria Gipuzkoa, Spain

It is cold. I wake at 5.30 a.m. and Sasha and I set off, shoulder to shoulder. The moon is high up above us. Before long we come across three donkeys eating grass upon the wet banks of a stream. Sasha brushes his nose in and out of the water and then walks towards the donkeys. They all stand together grazing and smelling each other's faces and necks. Ever since I have known him, Sasha has always been fond of donkeys. All of us are in a blueish kind of light as this side of the valley has not yet been seen by the sun.

An hour later we come across an old collie dog that takes me through his farm, beyond his farm, and doesn't leave my side for almost eight miles. It isn't until the village of Saint-Just-Ibarre that his furious owner comes swerving down the lane in his little white van. By this point the dog has come to be called Jack and we have made firm plans to go all the way to Cape Finisterre together. Perhaps beyond. Jack is a good listener and a candid leader.

To celebrate this brief encounter, I follow a painted sign that reads 'EZTIGAR CIDRE'. Sasha and I take a turn off-route into an open warehouse with the enormous letters hanging above us and six gigantic cider casks with empty bar stools surrounding them. We pause near one of the casks, a little dazed from the sudden change in light. It is almost midday.

The Basques have been making cider since the Neolithic period. The cider they produce today has evolved from *pitarra*, a fermented drink resulting from the maceration of sliced and dried apples. It first became popular as a substitute for water. Ships leaving from the Bay of Biscay would be piled high with enough bottles to ensure each sailor had three litres a day. I made a journey here on foot some years ago, and I remember the *cidre* (or *sagardo* in Basque) to be non-carbonated, bone-dry and to taste a bit like kombucha. It was also blasted directly into my mouth from a tap that spouted from the side of a gigantic barrel.

Sasha and I wait for the curative liquid to arrive, thirsty on our own voyage under the scorching sky. A man with a shaved head and a missing tooth emerges through sliding glass doors like an apparition. He notices us coolly, his eyes like blooms of talc in the haze. He then passes into another glass room, before reappearing with three low-shouldered Riesling-shaped bottles of organic cider.

The man sips the liquid as if it is sacred. I follow suit. He has lived on this cider mill his entire life. So did his father. I try a glass of all three and decide to buy four bottles of the Sigarno Idorra, a specific 'apple wine' that usually accompanies a board of charcuterie, a plate of fresh fish or a hearty dish of red meat. It can also complement a can of tinned peas. Sasha and I march on into the afternoon, a little braver than before.

How long have we been in Basque Country without knowing? We are riding against a current that never stops flowing through us. I remember so vividly, as if the memory hovers behind me, when I was awoken by the *kaark* of a purple heron and then disturbed by the sight of a bull approaching a horse in the silver tops of the Camargue grass. We are now only days away from Spain. Already there are glimpses of this fertile land changing, knuckles of rock reappearing. From a scape of dewy life, we will soon be tumbling into the prehistoric.

Today the heat is suffocating. There is no escape. The sun hangs on us. We descend steeply into the village of Ossès. My hand bleeds and throbs at my side from opening a second can of tinned peas too rashly.

A church bell chimes for six o'clock and a man in a blue tractor wearing an old shirt and a pair of faded cotton trousers motors past. I see the cream whites of his eyes that circle the silver-blue. His body is dark from the sun. We greet each other and he approaches Sasha. He touches him gently on his neck, as if they have known each other from before, and then leads us to a field. His name is Eugene.

Nothing but verdant colours surround the village. Beyond Sasha's paddock, to the south, the Pyrenean mountains curve and launch darkly. I am told that you can reach the Spanish frontier in less than a day if you ride directly into those hills.

Eugene puts an arm around Sasha's neck and rolls his fingers down his mane. With movements that seem as soft as a breath of air, he makes his way around him, Sasha mellow all this time, before placing his cheek on his back.

'This horse belongs to you,' he remarks sincerely. 'I think he will find it difficult when you have to leave.'

We turn and wander through the village. Each *baserri* building is held together by russet-coloured wooden beams. The tracks underneath us are covered in dust from the seed heads of hay and in some places are flecked with mud and straw. Eugene inherited the entire village from his father and uses the land to feed the animals.

The land in these parts of Basque Country pours up from the earth – the grass appears wet and heavy. The rivers run deeply and the trees decant over the earth, indecipherable in their masses. The living spirit shared between beings and nature was once a fierce component of Basque folklore. Before the introduction of Christianity, Mari served as their one true goddess (all divine beings in Basque mythology are goddesses). Mari represents the earth, *lurra*, and she can take on any form or shape as she pleases.

Over time Eugene has carefully and surely bought and raised sixteen horses. I meet each one. Spanish, Mérens, Lusitano, Arab; he has never bought a horse for more than 500 euros and I cannot remember the last time I met such a pacific, familial herd of animals. They are troubadours in a curated world and Eugene their silent, clay-like master. Or perhaps it is the other way round. Eugene is root-like. He cradles his dark hands over the tops of their necks and lightly they curve down and press their faces against him.

Later we look over a map in his kitchen, which has an old ceiling as high as a church. Paint flecks from the walls like petals. He explains to me the possible routes for the next day, my penultimate day in France, and, of course, for the crossing itself.

Eugene has been riding this land since he was four years old. I am told that I need to make a choice between the border villages of Sare or Ainhoa. Sare is twenty-seven miles from Ossès and Ainhoa is twenty-four. Eugene says it usually takes him two days to make the journey to Sare and, if we make it there, we can rest for the night and cross over the Pyrenees the following day. I explain to him our usual mile count and he looks up at me and nods.

'Maybe you can make it to Sare in one day, then. You have come far... either way, it'll be best for you to use the ridge trail along the Errebi mountain. That's the best way to go west.'

Later he shows me to a barn full of clean straw, and I am asleep by ten o'clock. I wake in a pool of sweat just before midnight. My body is beyond tired. There are layers and layers of exhaustion and I am suffused by them all, breathing and blinking somewhere beneath. I go outside to lie down upon the cool of the dust and the stones. I picture myself on a raft drifting aimlessly, and then shuffle my body to get more comfortable and remember that I am on land. Alone on my back in the middle of the night. There are no stars in the sky. Kiki is close. Coming closer. She has returned from Amsterdam and is with Istia again. We are only a day apart. If I were to stay here, just for one day more, she would find me.

With no stars above, I close my eyes and begin to build a house. I don't know how many rooms it has or how big it is but the entrance is tall enough for a horse to make its way inside. Looking out, standing at the front door, there are several hills surrounding it, a valley curving away in the distance, and two or three mountains steeped somewhere behind, each with differing rock formations and with their own glacial-green pools. The rooms must be equipped with different coloured ceilings and in their corners are depicted scenes that never get old when you look at them, mostly in the colour of almond tree blossom – it's a pretty colour. I would like the corridors to shimmer like streams that I have passed over, never straight, alluring but not hypnotic, and all the floors to be carpeted with sands and earths that Sasha and I have trodden. The stairs should be smooth but compact like the pebbles from the edge of a lake. The electricity and wiring of any house is vital, as is the plumbing: the lamps and lights will be ones that resemble marigolds, like Sirius and the Pole Star. The front door is never closed and people can walk in whenever they like, dead and alive. At two o'clock in the morning the house owl will whistle in each room, on the dot, and only those who wish to see the sunrise will continue to move and converse. Starlight from the ceilings will reflect upon the dirty floors, flaming glow worms, so no one can get lost. When I lie in my bed made from hay, I will recognise the shuffling of boars and wolves, the bray of the velvet donkey and the murmuring of the foreign dialects, coming and going, and we will sleep with magnificent ash in our hair, smoke in our eyes, forgetting, reinventing like larks, fit for tomorrow. It is Kiki that lies with me. And then I will reach for the clock that ticks like fire crackle on my bedside table and there will be nothing there except the shadow of my hand from the light of the moon. In the morning I wash my face in a deep sink of cold water that I share with Mithra, who circles the house through the night, finally sleeping at dawn, and I will have no true idea where I am but will always know that I am home. My curtains are made of rain loom. Did we find a shelter just beyond the village, asks Kiki, or was it just before? Did we ever find out the name of that crooked tree? We are so near to the sky yet feel the ground so close upon our bodies to the point where it would be no different to be flesh or to have decomposed, once and for all.

The sun burns at the rims of the horizon. I get up and see Sasha roving next to an oak tree in the distance. My mind and body are totally drained. There is no way I can travel all the way to Sare or Ainhoa today. After saying goodbye to Eugene, I leave Ossès and walk with Sasha to a nearby village called Biddaray, seven miles west.

Mariella finds me and tracks down a *gîte* set deep into the side of a bowl-shaped valley. It is owned by a man with a gammy leg. Sasha runs in the pasture below, relentlessly chasing the farmer's six donkeys. He is acting peculiar.

True to his word, Frank arrives that afternoon from Ireland. The last time we travelled together like this was on my journey down the UK. He arrived when I was stooped deep somewhere in the Pennines of England. The weather was miserable, and my Highland pony was losing patience. For a brief moment I remember wondering how on earth I was going to get to Land's End. Frank came, we walked on, and then he left. I have known him since I was twelve years old. He had more hair then, wild, blond and curly. He is now tall, broad-shouldered, intensely intelligent, and could probably run across Europe without breaking a sweat. His willpower is contagious.

We cook up some sausages on a fire outside the *gîte* and the wind picks up and the rain begins to fall. The sky around bruises fast. A storm sets in. I think of Kiki. She will be somewhere in the bare open hills above Eugene's farm by now, seven miles east.

The wind shakes the windows. The rain taps at the glass and taps into my ears. Through the blur, I make out Sasha running madly in the field. The donkeys have taken shelter under a cluster of hackberry trees. Kiki will be drenched. She will be close.

There is no longer a choice. I can't stay here. Without telling Mariella or Frank I jump into the Freelander and drive back to Ossès. I don't know what to expect, or what I will do once I see her, but there is no way that I can watch this storm from behind the glass, knowing where she is. Seeing her so clearly in my mind. On a journey across countries, seven miles is the reach of a hand.

I park the car just before the village. The rain continues to fall, softer now, and I walk quickly between the yellow stone *baserris*, their walls now disfigured with the stains of water. I pause by the side of one of Eugene's barns and peer round the corner. The wind has calmed. The rain tempers to drizzle.

There – standing in the field where Eugene had rolled his arms down Sasha's neck – I see Istia. I can't see Kiki. Where is she? Without thinking, I approach.

Istia's head jolts up in alarm. Her ears then prick forward in recognition. Hastily, I open the gate into the field, wondering where Kiki could possibly be. Perhaps she has found somewhere else to stay.

My hand strokes Istia's neck. My heart racing in confusion.

'I had a feeling that you might come.'

I glance up to find Kiki, emerging from behind the tree. Her eyes smile at me from underneath the hood of her red poncho.

The next morning it is the Queen's Platinum Jubilee. The French president, Emmanuel Macron, gifts her a grey mare called Fabuleu. We all wake early and Mariella drives Kiki and Frank back to Eugene's. They feed Istia and then retrace my walk from Ossès to Biddaray, making up for the seven miles that had separated us.

The reunion between Sasha and Istia is made known for the entire Basque farm and valley to hear through their homesick calls. Istia jostles around the curve of the road and Sasha runs up to her from the pasture, frantic to reach her through the barbed wire fences and the stone. The moment they see each other their ears cup forwards and their velvet nostrils flare. Sasha winces as Istia bites his neck. They touch each other's bodies with their faces, recalling the smells and the feelings that they had left behind.

By ten o'clock, Frank, Kiki and I are off. We begin on foot, the horses by our side. We aim to meet Mariella in Sare, twenty-one miles away, for our final night in France.

*

It is clear to see why animism was once the religion of the Basque people. The land is rich and teeming. Foxgloves and orchids droop onto the path and a mist reluctantly clears for our bodies before reconvening behind us. Slowly we climb a track that traverses a mountain dense with bracken. The mist has risen enough for us to see how the track curves round to the west and that the drop is steep to the south. Semi-wild Mérens and Castillonnais horses peer down above us, bells around their necks. These horses are smaller, finer, than the Mérens from the Nava valley. Better suited to this buckling and turbulent landscape. The path begins to narrow so that we are forced to move in single file: the drop below has now become a bottomless depth.

Two hikers approach us from around the bend of the mountain, a man and a woman. As they come close, I observe that they are fit and well equipped. Their legs and arms are brown and strong. Sweat drips from their temples. After making way for us, shunting themselves into the shrub, they ask if we have done this route before. We answer that we haven't. They pause before moving on, glancing back in the direction from which they came, and then they look at each other, concerned.

'It gets steep,' the man says.

'Are we close to Mont Errebi?' I ask, remembering the route that Eugene had advised. They both shake their heads.

'Have you seen any wild horses up there?' asks Kiki.

'No. There's nothing. It's too steep.'

'Vultures,' interrupts the woman. 'We've seen lots of vultures.'

By now it's almost too narrow for the horses to turn. One slip and they will fall. We all lean into the mountain, deliberating what to do. Frank runs ahead to check the way, and walks back shaking his head. It's too dangerous.

Carefully we move the horses. We retrace our steps and try to find another way to reach Errebi. It seems close on the map, but the route to get there is apparently non-existent. For hours we circle the northerly face of the wrong mountain, the land grows hostile and the heat becomes stifling. A swamping, unshakeable heat. The flies swarm amongst us.

We walk round a bend and stumble upon a griffon vulture about to take flight. We halt. The creature has its back to us, unaware of our presence. Its bald head surveys the wild impervious land that reaches out below. Commandingly, it stretches out its wings from its body, the arms of a feathered overcoat, neither fully fledged nor enclosed, while its talons grip the rock. The bird then faces the view, straightens, crunches down – coiling like a spring – before leaping from its rock, its tawny wings engulfing the air.

It isn't until two o'clock in the afternoon that we manage to find Eugene's route. Guilt runs through me as I silently acknowledge that Kiki isn't supposed to be here: that I have driven to her and have brought her to me. I have forced this. Her presence is all that I wanted and now I regret bringing her to me. But there was no way I could have stayed away. I had no choice. The whole day is loud with only insects and our footsteps.

On we move. Eugene's trail takes us south up to the border of Spain, 'the smuggler's route'. Frank runs ahead, and Kiki and I mount the horses and canter along the pass. We then ride north along the narrow ridge of Mont Errebi. Despite the mist, the visibility is enough to know that the drop either side is severe. Slowly we travel beyond, as if the ridge were a path leading us into a sea, before making our way down the other side.

*

Ainhoa lies like a handmade town at the bottom of the mountain. The sun is setting, casting a cornsilk light on the land. Broad, flat plains unfurl themselves far beyond the houses. We come across three wooden crucifixes with sculptures of Gestas, Christ and Dismas nailed to the cross. The wooden structures are tall, stretching at least ten metres into the sky, and the bodies are life-size. The young faces of the three men show expressions of agony, and the dried blood could have been real. Beyond the crucifixes there is a graveyard with stones that appear Celtic and a small white chapel, La chapelle de Notre Dame de l'Aubépine. More Mérens and Castillonais horses stray amongst the grassland, bells around their necks, taking little notice of Istia and Sasha, drifting through their graveyard, across their Basque lands.

The buildings in Ainhoa are the colour of red brick and cream. The architecture has unmistakeably changed since Louvie-Juzon. The half-timbered *baserri* homes coat the streets, each one with their characteristic sloping roof, patterned by the mesh of white stone and dark wood.

Near the centre of the town there is an open space, like a *plaza mayor*, circumnavigated by low-lying stands and an imposing salmon-pink concrete wall at the far end. Slaps of skin against leather and then leather against stone salvo through the air. A game of *pelota* is on, a child of handball. Men and boys run madly around the court, closely pursuing the flight of the fast-flying ball, before one of them smacks it against the salmon concrete in the hope that it will be impossible to return. It's said that the legendary Basque giants, the *jentilak*, used to play *pelota* upon the Pyrenean and Cantabrian glades using boulders left unclaimed from the ice age.

Six miles beyond Ainhoa we find our stables. All the way we are watched by another herd of Mérens and Castillonais horses, pencilling themselves into the skyline.

In the morning we travel on to the town of Sare. Scarlet gables protrude above us like the pointed hats of giants, and locals flitter through the cobbled square. We find four wicker seats underneath the stone archway of Hôtel Arraya and we let the horses roam freely by the entrance of the seventeenth-century Église Saint-Martin. I make out an inscription written on the stone wall: '*Oren guziek dute gizona kolpatzen azkenekoak of the hobirat egortzen.* Every hour hurts the man, the last one sends him to the grave.'

The owner of an *okindegia* (bakery) appears and kindly hands us a giant flour bag full of stale baguettes and the horses pick them out themselves. They have developed a curious skill in allowing their teeth to project further than their lips in order to nip on to the heel of the bread sticks.

Wherever we stop I like to witness how people react to the horses, who are so loose and calm in an urban setting. For 5,500 years this interaction would have been second nature, and now, only in the last 100, it has become foreign. Some people react to this primal sight instinctively. Like an unthinking child, they are drawn magnetically to the horses with an outstretched hand, beaming in fascination, unable to walk by without making contact. Others start to approach and then stop in their tracks. They hit a glass wall, it seems. Cautiously they then go close or, as if knowing their own limits, change course. And then there are those who are truly lost. Their shoulders hunch up like wary cats and they twist their necks and glance around at the other strangers. They are searching for reason, for provided answers, confirmation that it is all legal and permitted. They must replicate the human consensus of their environment.

These past forty days in France have been a fast and warm rush. The locals have been kind and accommodating, practical in their treatment of the horses. This is exactly what we needed. But there have been days too when it has felt like we exist in a sort of limbo. Too wild for civilisation and too civilised to be wild. It seems that motions against the grain can be deeply unsettling for people. Like the sight of two horses eating baguettes outside a church, many are fearful of evidence that displays alternative ways in which to operate. It doesn't fit into the man-made box.

The mountain of La Rhune towers high above Sare, and as soon as we leave the square it is the only thing we can see. I learn from the owner of the *okindegia* that upon the summit of La Rhune we will be in Spain. 'You climb up La Rhune and you limp down Larrun.'

The peak pierces the south-east, concealed in cirrus, and our mountain pass weaves through a stream and then gradually climbs, closer and closer to the frontier. The pass is well trodden and on either side there is bracken mixed with lilac foxgloves, stooping under the weight of their tubular flowers. Before long we stop and twist round to gaze down upon Sare and France below. Sasha stares into the distance. I wonder if he ever recounts the places he has been. We stand together above another country, ready for it to be washed away from us into the past, another invisible border waiting to be crossed.

I feel a sudden urge to be still and to never move again.

Sasha's eyes dart to the east face of La Rhune. Coming down the ridge is an old maroon tram retrieving hikers from the summit. We travel into a cluster of pine trees and emerge the other side to find the tram's metal tracks intersecting our route. It is close. I can feel it underfoot. We wait as the tram trudges down and sleepily approaches. The metal tracks rattle and smoke gushes out from the belly of the old wooden beast. Passengers point and wave in delight, flashing phones and cameras, and Istia and Sasha freeze and go to dart away in mistrust. Kiki and I hold the horses tight, keeping them close to us, stroking their necks.

A herd of Castillonais tear at the grass beyond the trams and walkers now gather at the base of the final ascent. We have two options. A choice. We can either take the longer, gentler way that circumnavigates the top of the mountain, curving round the neck upon the north side of La Rhune into the view of the Bay of Biscay, before bending back into Spain; or we head straight up the north face upon a steep, rocky track that zigzags all the way to the summit. We are told that there are two restaurants at the top. We choose the summit track.

As Kiki and I begin the climb, it becomes evident how fit we have become. Practised, hardy-looking hikers pause at the sides of the zigzag track and rest upon boulders, gasping for breath, peering back down the French face of La Rhune. We find it easier to climb vertically. Our legs bound us from rock to rock and the horses climb and stride with us. They have become mountain horses, adept and in control over how to tackle the awkward ground. They no longer need to be guided. They know from experience.

We find the summit of La Rhune with the horses and travel into the lofty mist. Emotions and adrenaline pump through our bodies and eyes. Mariella and Frank reach us and we all travel together across a boulder plateau. Ahead there are the two restaurants, a shop and the tram station. A triangular cairn rests in the middle of a clearing, the centrepiece of this surreal summit resort, and after we touch it with our hands, we go to the restaurant that looks out into Spain.

Sasha and Istia stand together and snooze by our table. Kiki buys us all small silver spoons with the green and red *ikurriña* flag on the handles and says that she feels like things are going to change. I drink my beer and say that things always change when we cross the invisible borders. The strangers and the sounds of the horses are the only things that ever stay the same. After saying goodbye, Mariella makes her way back to the car, all the way to Sare, and Frank, Kiki and I march on into Spain.

Last week I was contacted by a newspaper asking me if I could record a short clip, reading something aloud in order to remember the dead by. The idea is to celebrate those who have died who affect us while we still live. I readily agreed. Death touches the ride every day. I would not be here had I not made the ride down the UK for Leo. He dragged me out of sink holes and bogs, walked beside me at the beginning and end of each day. After seeing Kiki upon the summit of Mont Férion, I have sensed her sister's presence. Sui is with Kiki. The presence of the horses too reveals something far beyond flesh and bone. By their very nature, the horse sees through us. They are animals of the spirit.

As we cross into Spain, I find a bluff high on the south side of Larrun that faces the land we are about to cover. Spain draws itself out before us like a collection of jade and cayenne stamps, pressed down upon folding hills. Frank films with his phone as I sit upon Sasha and read an extract from *Winnie the Pooh*.

> ... Christopher gathered all of his friends together and began walking back down the hill. They were all busy

discussing the memories they had had with each other.

'Christopher?' Pooh said, looking up at Christopher as they walked hand in hand. 'You aren't coming back, are you?'

Christopher looked down at the ground and took a moment before he responded.

'No Pooh. I won't be coming back this time.'

They walked in silence, listening to the sound of the crunching leaves underneath their feet.

Pooh suddenly stopped and looked intently into the ground.

'I believe I am going to miss you Christopher,' he said with a soft, broken voice.

Christopher leaned down and took his lifelong friend into his arms.

'I will miss you too Pooh. I will miss you very, very much.'

As I finish, I look up to see Kiki crying in front of me. She then turns and walks away. Not wanting to disturb her, I follow silently behind.

Beyond the bluff, the way down into Spain is shown bright and plain to see in the shape of a long, smooth concrete road, almost fit for a car. It shoots down Larrun at a near forty-five-degree angle.

Due to her sensitive, intelligent nature, Istia rarely takes the lead down these steep passes or when traversing awkward crossings. Usually, it is Sasha that goes first, thinking less and doing more.

But Kiki's mind is elsewhere and Istia senses this. She is close to her, next to her. Together they both leave the safe clutch of the grass and step onto the shining concrete. And then, without warning, as if the path had turned to ice, Istia's back legs give way.

I hear the manic scrape of her metal front shoes as she tries to correct herself, clambering to get back up. But it doesn't work, there is nothing on the bare concrete for her hooves to grasp. Her neck rears up to the sky in desperation and then, as if in slow motion, I watch half a tonne of animal slide down the hard, smooth road. Kiki let's go of the reins. There is nothing she can do. She leaps out of the way to avoid being crushed.

After almost thirty metres, Istia's body finally grinds to a halt. A shocked silence hangs in the air like after a gun shot. I watch from far above, Sasha next to me, unsure of what I have just seen, waiting for this amorphous mass to reassemble. Trembling, Istia then starts to haul herself up, back onto four legs. The afternoon stops, waits, and Larrun seems absurd in its vista and sunlight. The poor horse tries to shake off the fall, but she is hurt. Her body has twisted 180 degrees. She looks up at us. Kiki stands rigid in shock.

Using the thin strip of grass at the side, Sasha and I pick our way down to meet Istia. The hair on her back legs has been shredded to raw skin. The back left is worse than the right, with skin torn above, upon and below the hock. Blood oozes from the wounds. Kiki pours water over the legs to inspect the damage and then disinfects them. Istia seems unfazed by the pain but Arabs are not to be trusted in this – their instincts for endurance can often override their discomfort. As far as we can see, however, the damage done is superficial. Skin burn.

With the sense of the day entirely shaken, it soon becomes apparent that we have a long way to go. Sixteen miles. We should have left earlier; we shouldn't have lingered for so long at the summit. This was my fault.

Kiki is utterly silent. Her sadness has now turned to stone and her whole body seems immovable in its disbelief. Istia travels close behind her, her eyes wide and her steps tentative.

After an hour of carefully weaving down the tarmac road, our first Spanish town appears in the near distance, Bera. It is then that Istia slips again. Her back legs buckle on the concrete but, this time, her front legs remain standing. I hear a thud. Her rump makes contact with the track.

In a hurried scramble Istia props herself back onto her four legs. She then walks on, as if nothing has happened. From the side and the front, she appears a completely normal horse: dark bay coat, black mane, 150-something centimetres, a placed and elegant gait. Yet from behind, blood now covers the backs of her legs.

Kiki walks her on. Frank and I rush inside a bar to find water. Together we clean and disinfect the wounds, before looking closely for any new signs of harm. At first it seems the same, bloody but superficial. But then, as we glance deeper, we find raw flesh, an exposed tendon. Raw, pale flesh, like the flanks of a dead fish.

We are miles away from anywhere and anyone we know. We think to call Mariella but there is very little she could do. This is a new place entirely. We grab three plastic chairs outside the bar and sit down to consider the situation. And then Istia stirs. She points herself away from us and starts to walk on. Sasha follows. We all get up, watching her from behind as she stands tall, defiant it seems. Her back-right leg holds a limp, but it seems less awkward than before. Her ears are pointing forwards. Together, we keep going.

Beyond Bera we move back into grassland. We travel carefully, keeping each other close. Istia's rhythm is slow but constant, her beat leads the way. With the concrete behind us we pause and lie down upon the shoulder of a hill that leans over a reservoir called San Anton. The horses graze and we make sure to disinfect the wound once more, adding cool water to it whenever we can. Now that the sun is less high in the sky, the air is coated with a distinct purple and blue hue.

Our route traverses the hillside before descending to the reservoir and onto a low-lying mountain pass. I make sure not to look at the time but it must be well beyond seven in the evening. The rocky scarp of Erroiarri Monte sits high above us to the right, and to the left flows a shallow stream. Our path has turned to a soft gravel-and-mud mix and it is clear to see where it will take us. It will follow the water and haul its way up the mountain ahead.

Kiki moves silently. She is sombre. She travels close to Istia, keeping watch on any wavering step. Slowly but surely Istia travels forward, a limped march it seems. Frank points out the mouth-like shape of the caves beyond the stream, with rivulets and waterfalls trickling over them, and we all feel the cooler air. Kiki agrees that there is a new violet haze in this dying light, and that this valley is a calm one, unthreatening. As our path winds up, the Erroiarri rock watches on.

By 10.30 p.m. it begins to get too dark to see. After summitting the far valley side, we emerge from a wooded ridge to find Mariella. She is waiting at the side of the mountain road with feed, food, water and beer. We eat, drink and, once more, clean Istia's wound.

The lights of Irun shine amber and ruby. The black sea of Biscay forms a cloth with the sky. Mariella drives to the stables and we keep moving, the night air cold now, but Istia walking well, it seems. With our headtorches on, me at the front and Frank at the back, we descend down a road that snakes into the town of Oiartzun. Stark traffic lights and chrome-yellow streetlamps fizz with electricity. Beyond the old, watchful eye of Erroiarri rock, I feel exposed. The calm of the violet valley has gone. I begin to think about how it is we got here. If we had chosen to take the gentler, curving path up Le Rhune then none of this would have happened; if I had remembered to ask the farrier to put on the correct shoes; if we hadn't stopped for lunch at the summit; if Sasha had led the way down the tarmac road; if I hadn't driven from Biddaray to Ossès to collect Kiki and to bring her to me, then none of this would have happened.

Later, in the dark, at 2.20 a.m., we reach our stables in the town of Errenteria, somewhere in the Basque province of Gipuzkoa.

Everything is going to change.

1,218 miles, 77 days

Kiki's diary
8 June, Errenteria
Izzy has been injured and what first looked like something manageable now seems to be serious. The tendon of her back-left leg has most probably been torn or perforated. The wind was still. The night was as heavy as home. I felt Siu very close to me. It stops here: if Izzy can't go on, neither will I.

III

The Dark Sun

'All other creatures look down toward the earth, but man was given a face so that he might turn his eyes towards the stars and his gaze upon the sky.'
from Metamorphoses *by Ovid*

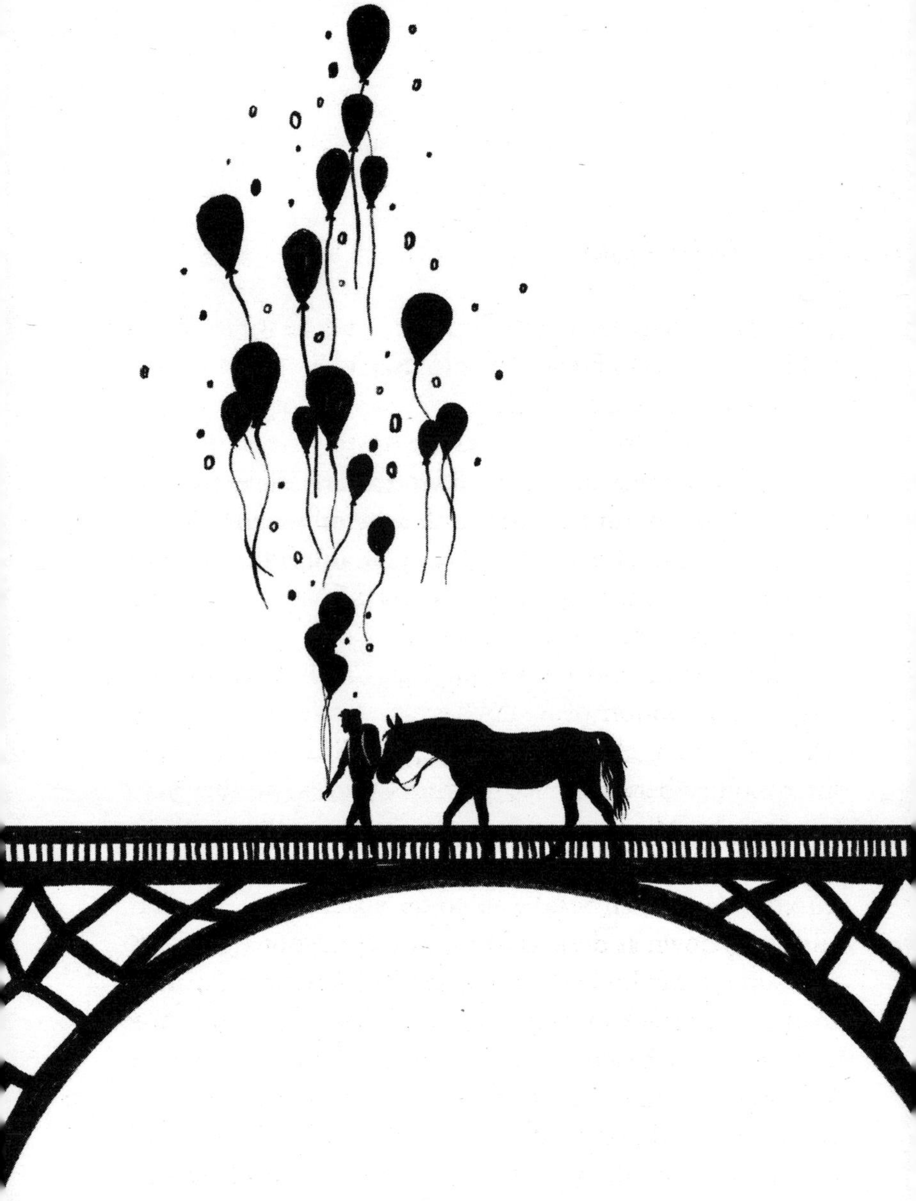

9–14 June
Zestoa – Cudón, Cantabria

A vet comes to see Istia in the morning, and we speak French to him as he speaks French back to us, and he says it is either going to be a five-day problem or a six-week one. It doesn't look good. Amidst the heat and the dust of the morning, it is agreed that Sasha and I should keep moving. Kiki will stay with Istia to wait for the prognosis. Tomorrow, Mariella will travel to Scotland for a funeral. Frank has already left. Once more he joined me at a journey's most difficult point. He is either a blessing or a curse.

Alone, Sasha and I turn our backs and travel into the elegant commotion of San Sebastián. Strangers hover and demand if I am allowed to be there, oscillating like trepid metronomes between their instincts and what they have been taught. My mood is dark. We reach Ondarreta Beach, where there is a patch of grass for Sasha and a sand slipway into the Cantabrian Sea. I walk to the water's edge. I wade in and swim down as deep as I can, half of me not wanting to ever surface. My body needs the salt. My muscles hurt more than I care to acknowledge. After drying off, I take Sasha down onto the beach so that he can roll around on his back. He loves the sand. Two police officers then approach us. I expect to be admonished; it is illegal to bring horses onto Ondarreta. Instead, they ask how far it is we have come, how far we are going.

'*¿Cabo Finistere?*' the woman responds.
'*Si, Finistere,*' I repeat.

'*¿Y luego?* And then?'
'Who else is with you? Are you alone?' interjects the man.
'No. There is someone else. There's a girl but ...'
'You have lost her?' A wry smile develops at the corner of his lips.
'Yes. It seems that way.' I answer.

Beyond San Sebastián there are the Basque mountains. Sasha and I travel at an average of twenty-four miles a day. Unearthed by what has happened and what might be, my body responds with a mechanical sort of energy. Something has been triggered by the magic being taken away. We have to keep going. Sasha reacts too. His speed becomes quick and consistent and, now that we are the only ones, he listens and communicates to me with a sharper focus. We are the herd again. I spend most of my time on foot, next to him.

With the added weight of Kiki's cocoon-shaped tent and sleeping bag, my rucksack now weighs nineteen kilograms and it rubs on my skin with the sweat.

I wake up on the side of a hill, pack up the tent and find Sasha close by, waiting to go. I have become nervous about these mountains. At times this landscape resembles a hinterland. Water sources have become infrequent and the unexpected concrete and tarmac descents are like nothing I have come across before. I still haven't found a farrier to change Sasha's shoes. One slip and that could be it. Just like Istia. I sit on the ground before the sun has time to rise. The surging voice of a motorway softly tears. The dawn haze distorts the distance. I try and look close, hear what is in front of me, around me. There's a bird. There are two. I see the cracks upon my boots and then the roots of grass twisting from the sand-coloured earth. There is dew on the dark green grass. Sasha looks out and his breath steams. I take a sip of wine from the *bota*.

We head north over a mountain before descending down into the town of Deba. I find a bar called Izenbe and have *pinxtos* of meat and a tall *garagardoa*. Sasha ambles around the square and is befriended by a kind homeless man, much to the amusement of the locals. Beyond the town we ascend the hills of the Urkiolako natural park: Aldoskako gaina, Urkarregi, Erribaso, Onuntzezabal. Each ascent is as rich as the last: bottle-green pine wood, foxgloves, flowing streams, bracken, ancient holm oak woods; a tribe of mountains with all its living bodies. The air is sweet with the bark. That night I find my way to the hamlet of Markina. A young man and a woman are waiting for me. They let me wash Sasha using an outside sink and then lead us through a gate and into a 25,000-hectare field.

The sun loses shape, clutching at the slope of the hill before me with fierce terracotta-red hands, sliding and dripping. Sasha wanders back and forth in the open space. He never ventures too far. Together, we have now travelled over 1,200 miles. It is the furthest I have ever travelled with a horse. When the sun goes the pine-green land softens, melts, and a dark crinoline cloth covers the earth and the air. Sirius emerges before midnight.

By noon the following day I find a stable in a town called Mungia. It is further north than I need but the people on the phone seem kind and I don't have another option. Foreign eucalyptus trees dominate the primal land, expelling the local trees. The young ones shine timidly through the gorse, standing in schools with hard, narrow trunks the colour of unripe bananas. The shades of their leaves waver between saffron and a cider green. The older ones rise tall, shaking with the wind upon the vertebrae of ridges. In the fields there are often ibises resting on the backs of ochre cows. Far out of reach but so close in sight, there are power stations and smokestacks. A constant struggle between what is natural and what is not. Just south of Guernika there are wonky sycamore trees with bark that peels like paint, and noble-looking oak trees too: the symbol of Guernika and of the soul. We trudge south of the main cities, keeping into the hills and out of sight, using the Camino Del Norte as our rough trammel. In the forest of Billakaio hill there is a menagerie of birch trees, Monterey pine trees and firs with trunks the colour of sunstone copper. I am seeing things that I have not seen before. We are not as alone as I thought. Even on the worst of days there is always something, darkly shining.

In the afternoon we are chased by a bull and his herd of cows. I jump onto Sasha and we gallop as fast as we possibly can. As we approach a gate, I dismount with a leap and then sprint up the road. I have to ignore the screaming woman and the barking dogs. Somehow the bull escapes through the fence line and attempts to follow us. He is furious. We keep on moving until we lose him.

On we travel through the town of Gamiz-Fika, where there is an Athletic Bilbao football match being watched in two bars: one for the men and one for the boys. We reach Mungia in the evening. There are over thirty boxes for horses and at the far end a clubhouse overlooking a smart, sand-coated manège. After giving Sasha a wash I sit down to write at a table on the clubhouse terrace. An awkward-looking man comes over to me.

'Excuse me.'

'Yes?'

'I am to tell you that the owner says that everything is free for you, whatever you want.'

A beer is served to me at the bar by a woman named Gloria and I am joined by the owner of the yard. He is a showjumper with sunburnt lines on his cheeks and forehead. We speak French. I thank him for his generosity. He orders me a rum and Coke before heading home. Romaine, a tall, middle-aged man with a limp, a thick bottom lip, eyebrows the colour of soil and a rough, good-looking face, comes over to introduce himself. He says he is the other owner of the yard. There is a girl of about twenty years old hanging off his left arm. Gloria throws a stern glance across at the girl and then curls her lip as she stares at Romaine.

The night turns into a smoke-fuelled concert. The legendary Spanish rock band Fito & Fitipaldis are performing a comeback show in Bilbao and the clubhouse television is turned on full blast. The lights are extinguished. Cigarettes, whisky and rum and Cokes flow. When the evening is done, or at least when it becomes too much of a mess to understand, I notice Romaine leave with Gloria, his wife. The young girl is his lover. I pass out on the floor of the tack room.

The next day is 12 June and I wake up drunk. Sasha and I leave while everyone sleeps. Kiki has contacted me. My heart quickens and I stop at a café to read the message properly. For a moment, the world feels lighter. Up to this point I haven't allowed myself to contemplate her, distracting myself with nothing but moving. She tells me that Istia is recovering. The wound remains open, but with gentle exercise, water, antibiotics and anti-inflammatories, she seems to be getting better.

'Everything is so slow here,' she says.
'Yes, I can imagine. Slower than slow.'
'I can't bear it. I can't bear not moving.'

'You've been moving so fast for so long and now you've come to a halt—'

'Slower than slow. I'm in reverse. Everything is so stale and dead. I can't believe what I've done to her.'

I try to console her but nothing seems to work. In fact, I think I make it worse.

She sends me the directions. The plan is to cross a bridge that breaches the Bilbao estuary. On the other side of the Río Nervión we should find a fourteenth-century town called Portugalete. And then we will continue up to Muskiz, a Biscay community on the coast. On we move.

The air thickens, the concrete way staggers on and the sun rips down upon our bodies. Eventually the industrial town of Leioa forms itself below me, the estuary beyond, and then Portugalete sitting established upon the far banks of the water. Today is Portugalete's 700th anniversary.

The Policia Local wave me on and people touch Sasha with pointed fingers and stretched-out arms and children scream with balloons in their hands. The sun swells. I teem with alcohol, sweat and anxiety. My nose fills with the smell of tarmac. I ride along the Las Aranas promenade of the Nervión. The river is wide, but I can almost touch the festivities on the Portugalete side of the water, the trumpets and fireworks pour into the weekend air, underneath the sandstone watch of Basílica de Santa María. According to Kiki's route, the crossing point is further along the promenade.

Sure enough, in the distance, I see an enormous structure reaching high up into the blue sky, crossing the water, and descending down onto the Portugalete side. It is the 164-metre-long Vizcaya Bridge. Built in 1893, the iron masterpiece is the world's oldest transporter bridge. The architect, Alberto de Palacio, saw it partially destroyed during the Spanish Civil War, shortly before his death.

As the hanging bridge looms closer, I begin to wonder how you cross it... surely not on the top track, 50 metres up? How do you get up there? A queue of people stand by one of the support pillars. A hanging platform – the gondola – crosses underneath, suspended above the water with two cars on deck.

It is then that the penny drops. There are two ways to cross the bridge. You either walk on foot along the barricaded track above, after being shot up into the air by a lift, or, for cars, motorbikes, cyclists and stragglers with a fear of heights, you travel on the gondola that floats above the water. Desperately I search the map in an attempt to decipher another way for me and Sasha to cross, but the next accessible bridge is along one of the busiest motorways in Spain, six miles south. For that bridge we would legally require a horse trailer.

There is no other way to cross the water except over de Palacio's masterpiece. I hover around the entrance of this vast structure wondering what the hell I am going to do and wishing that I was invisible. Families with small children pose at Sasha's flank and take pictures. They utter words to me and don't expect responses. Two brothers with matching checked shirts and haircuts approach me with the permission of their mother. As they near Sasha's muzzle, they each reach up and hand me a one euro coin.

I inspect the bridge. There are two lifts built into the red iron pillars, left and right, and a wide space in between for the gondola. There is also a gigantic decorative rubber duck hovering above us in the air, the size of a small house, which, fortunately, Sasha hasn't quite noticed. He must be too distracted with the opening and closing of the gates, the sliding doors, the rising lifts, the faraway trumpets, the water, the boats, the balloons and the moving floors. But with all things considered, he remains calm. He is trying to work it all out, just like me.

The crossing seems impossible. The only option I can think of is to call the hungover stable hands from Mungia to send out a horse trailer. Since leaving Castello del Calcione, I haven't used transport once for Sasha. Breaking this course would mean severing the natural way. One more flicker of magic extinguished.

Patting Sasha on the neck, I turn and mount. We ride back down the promenade, away from the crowds.

The alcohol desperately escapes my pores. Sweat slides from my temples as the fat sun shrieks above. I want to jump into the dirty water. Swim across. Anything but go back. I dismount and peer over the edge of the promenade to see how far the drop is. At least three metres. I don't think Sasha would ever forgive me. Besides, there is no slipway on the other side. I look to the bridge, the lifts, the colossal duck... there *must* be a way.

Without thinking I take Sasha's reins and defiantly we walk back towards the crowds. We stop at the ticket office, ten metres from the first rising lift. Automatically the doors to the gondola slide open and close and Sasha notices our reflection on the glass. A short-haired man with crystal-blue eyes walks hurriedly towards us and asks where it is we have come from and where it is that we are trying to go, and then another man approaches and then a kind-looking woman. The first man is fascinated, the second man is practical and the woman desperately wants to help.

The practical man tells me he works for the water-taxi company and has just finished his shift. After hearing our story, he promptly asks the officer on duty if I can take Sasha across on the gondola: 'They need to get to Cape Finisterre.'

The response is one of reason. The officer shakes his head.

Once more the gates swing open and close and the floating deck departs the promenade with another load of humans and machines, rolling its way across the water towards the revelries of Portugalete – the way to Finisterre.

After some time, the practical man manages to contact his superior on the telephone. Artfully, he explains the situation, adding tones of enthusiasm and empathy when needed, catching eyes with me as he manoeuvres his words, and then waits for a response. There is silence. The practical man remains expressionless. I start to lose hope. Finally, the superior speaks, hand-picking his words, it seems, one by one. The practical man hangs up the phone.

'What did he say?'

'He said: a horse on a gondola is not the most improbable thing there is. It has most likely been achieved someplace before.'

I cannot believe it. I clench my fists in relief and lean my face into Sasha's neck.

'But there are ground rules,' continues the practical man, now with an officious tone.

'Ground rules?'

'No vehicles except you and your horse must be on the transport grate.'

'OK.' I nod quickly, in agreement.

'And if the horse shits, you pick it up.' I nod again, a little slower this time.

A frantic rush of sound and steps pour into the side galleries of the gondola, onlookers keen to witness the approaching traveller and his horse. The queue of cars and motorbikes has been instructed to halt. A woman in a high-vis jacket nods for me to go. It is time. Sasha and I make our way gingerly over the threshold and onto the bare metal grate. The water ripples three metres below us. With his rear legs safely off the promenade and onto the gondola, I turn quickly to thank the practical man and, before the swinging gates have time to close, the kind woman rushes to the front of the onlooking crowd and hurls a bottle of water at me that bounces on the grate, startling Sasha. With better aim, she then throws a sandwich, securely wrapped up in tinfoil.

Passengers and their cameras glare behind the acrylic glass of the galleries. We are animals in a zoo. Or perhaps a circus. With a jolt the gondola leaves its mooring. An applause erupts from the Las Arenas promenade as all those children, parents, bystanders, operators and officers witness the result of the afternoon's diplomatic struggle. The floor moves. Sasha dances on the metal in confusion. I close my eyes in disbelief. I could dive into the water with happiness! I kiss my horse and run around the deck, our life-raft, yelping as I leap up into the air. Don Quixote would be proud. The magic hasn't died. Leo is here. Siu is here. With the kindness of strangers, Sasha and I are flying on water.

After six minutes the gondola moors up on the Portugalete side. We are greeted with a cheer of Spaniards drunk with the secrets and clamours of a town's anniversary. The gates swing open and the passengers empty out from the galleries. I take hold of the reins and begin to follow but, just as I approach the concrete of the promenade, Sasha stops. He looks at me sternly, clenches, and then proceeds to relieve himself upon the grate. With difficulty, I pick up the manure using the foil from the uneaten sandwich. The driver then presents his hand, waiting for payment.

'How much is it?' I ask.

'Two euros. The same as everyone else.'

I reach into my pocket to find the coins donated to me by the matching brothers.

That night we approach Muskiz. I am more exhausted than words can describe. My body aches. Nothing but concrete ensues after the cobbles of Portugalete. A vast power-plant roves below us like an Orwellian vision, a ghost town of metal and burning amidst these tender mountains. Smokestacks pour black into the sky. We reach the top of the road and Aiert, a vet, and Idols, a showjumper, lead me into their yard and provide Sasha with a cool, shaded stable full of straw and hay.

The young couple lead me to a poppy-coloured hut that rests on the side of the mountain, looking down at the sultry-looking Cantabrian Sea. There is a bed and a semi-circular view of the open water. A storm is coming in on the horizon. Rain and coal tremble through the air. I lie down and sleep, my body drowsing between smokestacks and the waves.

In the morning Aiert checks Sasha over. This is the fifth vet I have met and the fifth time a vet has been impressed with his condition. I explain to him why I have not been riding much and he tells me that I am being overly cautious. He hands me a cream that he states should work as a mask for the saddle sore.

'Ride on,' he utters. 'You are almost there.'

We travel through the town of Laredo, with palm trees that straddle the wide roads like a scene from *Miami Vice*. The air is thick with salt from the sea and the sunlight wanes to apricot. People stroll along the pavements with no shoes, sand tracing the concrete from nearby Playa de Laredo O de Salvé. We pause at a set of traffic lights and I take out my phone to look for directions. A moment later a siren erupts behind me and I am gestured to the side by two officers from the Guardia Civil. They get out of their car and inspect Sasha from the pavement.

'*¿Es tuyo?* Is it yours?' one asks, his aviator sunglasses a little squint on his round face.

'*¿El caballo,* The horse?' I answer, confused.

'*Si, el caballo,*' he repeats.

'Yes. I mean... I hope so.'

'You are in control of a vehicle,' butts in the other officer. He is shorter than his colleague, his black leather boots reaching rather high up his legs.

'A vehicle?' I answer.

'*Si, un vehículo.* You cannot use your phone when you are in control of a vehicle.'

'This is true,' I answer. The round-faced officer produces a notepad and jots down what I say. His colleague nods in approval.

'Where have you come from?'

'Siena.'

'*¿Siena?*'

'*Nosotras vamos al Cabo Finisterre.* We are going to Cape Finisterre.'

The officers look at each other in disbelief.

'*¿Por qué?*'

'*Estoy empezando una revolución.* I am starting a revolution,' I answer.

The light goes green and a car full of girls start shouting and whistling at the officers from behind, their giggling faces poking out the windows.

The officer with the notepad thrusts it into his pocket. He turns on the spot and marches over to the offenders. The man with the long black boots gestures me on. I wave him goodbye.

We turn down a road and then arrive at a flat expanse of shrub and sand, divided up with round pens, square paddocks and pretty horses. A man with a rider's limp and dirty jeans comes out of the stable office.

'You are the boy from Italy?'

'Yes. *De Escocia y Italia*, from Scotland and Italy.'

'My name is Enrique.' He shakes my hand. 'Luis Salvador is coming to shoe your horse.'

'Yes. Thank you. I need studs on the shoes, if that's OK.'

'*Claro*. We are in Spain.'

After being taken to a Bancomat to withdraw 70 euros for Luis Salvador, Enrique then calls three women to come to the stables. Berlin, Roxy and Anna.

That evening we all go out for dinner and then on to a bar. The girls spend most of the time comparing their sexual encounters from the yard. From what I gather, one particular Venezuelan stable boy hasn't slept for two years.

At the bar, men are playing *Mus* on the tops of sherry casks. I join a game with two locals while a gaunt waiter with black slicked-back hair serves us negronis. The girls drink and smoke and, somehow, we all make our way back to the stables. In the morning I wake up in a field wearing nothing but a jacket and my boxer shorts. I have no idea where I am. My cap and rucksack have formed my pillow and my phone and empty wallet are lying on the grass. I follow the smell of horses and eventually come across the sand paddocks of the yard. No one is to be seen. Sasha is lingering impatiently in a round pen. I am late.

After making some ground I look at my phone and discover a picture of me stripped down to my boxer shorts on top of the bar with the slicked-back barman coolly making a drink next to my left ankle. Roxy, the larger of the three girls, is standing at the side of the frame. She appears possessed. Her right fist is raised in the air as if in defiance, and strands of blonde hair cover her face. And then it all comes back to me. As one of the girls drove back, the other two tied me up in the back with the seatbelts. In my excited state I remember becoming convinced that I was being kidnapped for a foursome. Whether I was right or not is hard to say, but in a bid to escape from the impending danger I managed to untie myself from the belts and force them to stop the car. I must have then leapt out in the name of freedom. There remains a plum-coloured hickey on the left side of my neck.

With Sasha's new studded shoes, we make our way to the town of Entramabasgues and then onto Cudón. Hen harriers drop down into rounded cow fields guarded by sleepy Basque sheepdogs.

Kiki strays in and out of my mind. Thoughts of guilt interrupt the beat of the day. I shouldn't have taken her from Ossès to Biddaray. I shouldn't have kissed her neck in St-Guilhem-le-Désert. None of this would have happened if I had let her be. I miss her. I miss Mariella, I miss Raffi. I miss when we were all together. A family. I am only travelling on so I don't have to stop. Sasha has become my only purpose.

We walk over a red-barriered bridge that hangs high above a reeling motorway, a concrete spiderweb below. The last time I walked through these towns and along these paths I was making the lone journey to Santiago de Compostela in some form of escape. It was six years ago to the day. I was nineteen years old. Ido met me in a park in Bristol and I asked him why he had done what he had done, and he told me that none of it mattered and that we were above it all. Sex means nothing, he said, and what happened between me and her doesn't touch what we have. 'She's just a girlfriend. We are brothers, remember?'

I wanted to hurt and hug him at the same time and for everything to somehow be back to how it was. By the lake. Since leaving Mongolia Ido's mind had become unstable. He was on a lot of medication and had an altered sense of right and wrong. He had been diagnosed with a psychotic disorder. But I hated him with all my heart. He slept with my girlfriend and claimed insanity. We said goodbye and I walked away across the grass and knew, very strongly, that I wanted to die. Two weeks later I arrived into San Sebastián with 110 euros and I didn't stop walking.

The salvo of cars underneath the bridge goes mute and the bright grey light suddenly dulls. I stop walking and peer over the edge of the barricade. The world drags to a halt. It is then that I realise: I am as guilty as Ido.

Sasha disappears and I am back where I was, six years ago. But this time, it is me carrying out Ido's work. It has all come full circle. Without any excuse, I have passed on the betrayal inflicted on me to R.

After managing to stay south of Santander, Sasha and I reach our designated yard, an old warehouse. The man in charge shows me where the water is and gives me some hay. He is covered in dirt and sweat from a day of riding, and walks with a crooked back. The first of his horses that I see had been found in a scrapyard and brought to him on a crane. Its hip bone is visible, it has raw pink flesh showing on its flanks, cuts like a boxer on its face and is skeleton thin. The living doppelganger of Rocinante, Don Quixote's horse. The man has set about to save it. The other horses are healthy. He has two grey Andalusian stallions that march free in converted cow stalls once used as dungeons. Black metal-barred gates shut them off to the outside world. Several times the man in charge reiterates that I shouldn't take his generosity for granted. Despite his abrupt style, I trust him because it is clear to see that he considers a horse's welfare more important than his own and, despite the aesthetics of the yard, he has done a loving thing by converting this old warehouse into stalls and stables.

◆

In Basque *'aupa'* means 'hello'. People say this as I pass, and sometimes they say *'augur'* too, which means 'goodbye'. My vocabulary is growing. The Spanish Basques have a rugged appearance. The sun is hotter on this side of the border. So obscure and ancient is their ancestry that it seems they are closer related to rock than they are people.

I notice integral differences between the Spanish and French Basques: the words and pace of the language; the use and shape of the land; the birds; the stories; the animals. After crossing into Spain, the intoxicating greens of Pays Basque no longer coat the views. Instead, the shades turned a beaten copper, moss and dark gold – sweating in an iridescent light due to the fiercer sun. Geraniums are the colour of blood.

It seems the weather makes people tough here and it shapes the land starkly too: the sharp cliffs of the Gipuzkoa coastline; the wide-reaching San Sebastián sands; the beaches of Deba, Mundaka, Cudón, with waves crashing onto the shore; orchids that look like lungs.

At a bar I discover the meaning of three letters that I keep on seeing spray-painted in black letters onto road signs: ETA. The Euskadi Ta Askatasuna (Basque Country and Freedom) is a Basque separatist group founded in Spain in 1959 from a student magazine. The group developed into a nationalist terrorist organisation that killed 829 people between 1980 and 2010 and resulted in the last use of capital punishment ever carried out on Spanish soil: the 1975 execution of Ángel Otaegui and Juan Paredes in 1975. Almost every death that the ETA was responsible for was carried out in Spain.

My feet are getting worse and worse. The balls of them being ground down by the hot, black tarmac. Just as I begin to understand the seductive, rock-faced spirit of Spanish Basque Country, I have to leave it behind. On we move.

1,354 miles, 83 days

Kiki's diary
13 June, San Sebastián
The city is making me depressed, tired and manic all at the same time. Filled with self-hatred which in turns fuels the self-hatred because of the perverse self-indulgence it requires. I can't seem to get rid of it. I feel petty and superficial and ugly and here there are so many beautiful people, so many people. When all senses are wide open it is rather overwhelming. The little bit of life I had I have thrown away.

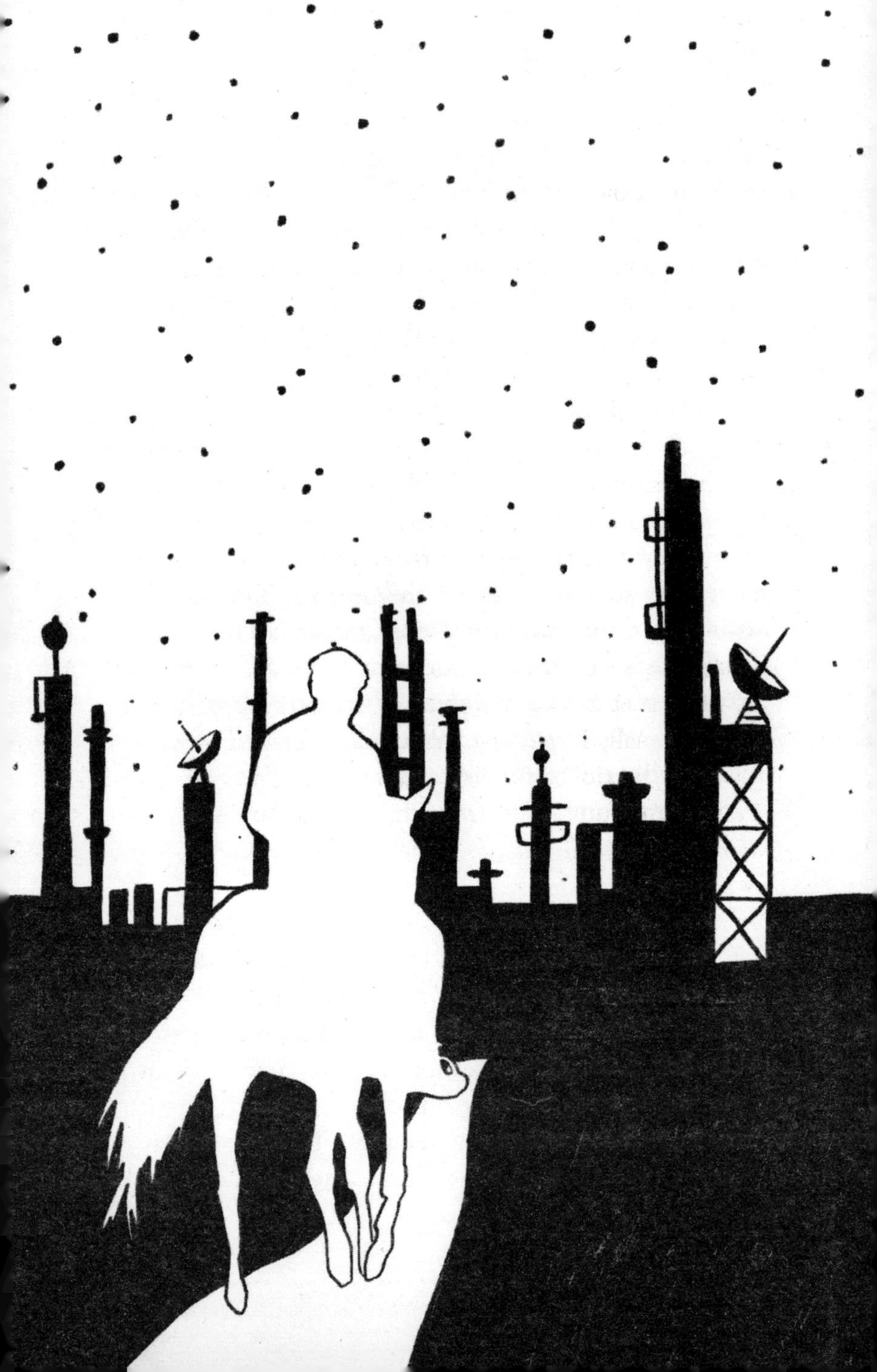

15–25 June
Cudón – La Espina, Asturias

Restaurante Venta de Tramalón, somewhere near the Cantabrian towns of Sierra and Trasierra. The sun scorches most when we stand still. After finding him water, I leave Sasha free to roam underneath the dappled shade of a tired tree in the middle of the car park. The sea is near and the air smells of tar. I walk into salted shadows of sweat, calamari and *croquetas*. Inside I have entered the depths of an old wine cask. Hunched up men with smart black shoes stick to the insides. So do the paintings of flamenco dancers and bull fights. I now stick too. We are the innards. The building is made up of three sections, separated by saloon doors. Everywhere it is wooden.

   I sit down at a table across from the bar. I need to eat something small; I want to ride on and keep moving so that we can be rid of this inexorable heat. The owner of the restaurant stumbles in from the outside and cries out, '*¿Quien es el dueño del caballo?* Who owns the horse?'

   No one stirs.

   '*Él es mío*,' I reply.

   The exchange is interrupted by a man coming through the saloon doors leading to the next-door room. His belly enters first and his white shirt is open at the chest. A space like a bullet hole holds a half-smoked cigarette in his mouth and his head is shaped by strands of hair that trickle with sweat upon his forehead and temples. The doors swing behind him and he plants himself up at the bar where a pair of silver-mounted bull's horns dully reflect his movements upon the pale red wall.

Since leaving San Sebastián alone, a numbness has kept me going. As it was when I exchanged the disarming comforts of Tuscany for the mountains of Liguria, a steely adrenaline fills me up like a motor. Sasha has it too. When I wane in the daze of the Spanish afternoons, I feel him stir and push us on; he fuels that silent, unstoppable animal of six legs and two hearts. Inhaling and passing, nothing and all, leaving only our ephemeral tracks. The companion-machine.

Over the last few days, as the beat of the machine ticks over, I have allowed myself to think more about Kiki. The livid shame I felt for bringing her to me on that stormy night in Ossès, and the consequences of all the things I have or have not done – the force of this shame has begun to withdraw. I am coming to see that the nebulous and ever-changing state of the journey is beyond my control. Perhaps there is a place of resolve in the iris of the chaos. When I lie down in twilight and when I watch Sasha roving in the near darkness of the early morning, I try to think deeply about the body and being of Kiki, and then of her silently communicating with her sister. It is a meditation that puts everything into place.

For the first time, when I picture Finisterre, I can see a horizon. Not just a desert ocean.

Time clicks to the metronome of footsteps and hooves. We are already in the province of Asturias. Beyond the sounds and smells of the sea our route takes us south. We travel into the falling sun and, to the left, the blue ridge of Sierra de Cuerra striates the afternoon sky. Sasha and I wash and drink from the waters of the Río Cabra before arriving at the bed of a valley, in a hamlet called Boquerizo.

A man named Danny, a vet and part-time chef, waits for us with a beer in hand, leaning on the doorframe of his late grandmother's farmhouse.

A storm harasses the night. The lightning and the thunder fight together, and the rain slashes down upon windowpanes and onto the rooftops of the quiet community. I peer out from my bedroom into the coal-grey darkness and see Sasha standing silhouetted at the crest of the hill, as dark and unmoving as a rock. He has no doubt witnessed this wildness before. He stands still. The wind stampedes. The land flashes emerald green, before being swallowed into the luminous black and rain once more.

The night has rearranged the shapes of the land. Estranged water welts within newly sunken gulfs. Deeper they go. The bedraggled rims of the hills and spines of the trees are now iridescent in new skin. After a breakfast of *huevos revueltos, queso, jamón, tostardes y café*, I thank Danny and ride on with the waters of the Río Cabra as our guide. The bustling town of Llanes is our first port of call. It is a Sunday.

We find a bar called La Barrica Blanca beyond the Plaza Barqueras bridge and, opposite my table, there is a narrow alleyway with yellow, blue and red crates of Mahou Beer stacked up against the wall. I take water for Sasha from the restaurant using the collapsible bucket and he dozes in the shade of the alley, out of the way of the Sunday people.

That evening my head spins as I sit down upon the wooden chair in a *sideria* called Muros. I write as much as I possibly can to combat the motion. I collapsed by a stone wall earlier in the day. I do not know why. A man named Francisco helped me to my feet as Sasha stood by me. He then took me to a house belonging to an English family that haven't returned for months on account of the UK leaving the European Union. Francisco has begun to adopt the house as his own, inhabiting the stone turret that faces the sea. I pitched a tent in the garden and Sasha rolled in the tussocks of unkempt grass, relieved to catch up on sleep lost to the storm.

I walk back to the tent from Muros before midnight. My head feels better. I must have been dehydrated. Tired too. Stars shoal the sky and I fall into a deep, unbroken sleep, accompanied by the song of Sasha cropping the grass.

A drop of rain upon my face wakes me in the morning. My face and my torso haven't managed to make it undercover. I decide that it is not enough rain to make me get up nor enough rain to force me to close the cover of the tent. I sleep for another hour with faint drops falling and I dream that I am trying to cross a wide river made up of tyres and black water, and that it is essential that I reach an archipelago in the middle of the current, its islands slowly being prised down by seaweed. Kiki waits upon a rock. The seaweed appears like wild electric cabling.

The going is coastal but low-lying. The tracks are sandy and meander and rise unexpectedly. Sasha races along. We make good ground until the medieval town of Ribadasella. The sky has been ugly all morning and the cold rain comes and goes. We ride into a square with four chestnut trees standing as pillars in each corner. Boxed flowerbeds sit underneath each one, not a weed in sight within the dark soil, adorned only with meticulously planted flowers. The rain pours hard.

To our right I see a boy and a girl huddled underneath the undrawn veranda of a closed-up tobacconist. They have been caught out: the boy is wearing crisp white shorts and the girl a t-shirt and a skirt. The weather is a surprise to everyone, it seems.

I gesture for the boy to come over to me. The girl's face lights up and she pushes him out towards us from under the cover. As soon as he gets close, I collect up the reins and hand them to him.

'*Toma,*' I say. Take. I don't give him time to respond.

First, I go into the *frutería* to get some apples, a banana and a kiwi, and then I walk next door into Cafe Bergantin and ask for a *café con leche* and a *jamón* sandwich. Water streams down from the hems of my German poncho. I sit in the warmth of the café and close my eyes just for a second. I glance up and see myself in the reflective glass placed inside the wooden panelling behind the bar and I stare at my face and then look at the reflection of the other customers. Some are reading the papers and others are gazing onto the square. It is a beautiful bar.

The boy has unsuccessfully managed to contain Sasha. Like the awkward admonishing of someone else's child, he pulls at the reins with the force of a small cat as Sasha stands unfazed with a mouthful of delicate flowers. The girl laughs in hysterics. I thank them and ride over the Puente del Sella, a Roman bridge built upon the Río Sella.

For an hour the rain stops. With the looms of water now gone, I can begin to see the untouched coastline that we travel astride. It is Jurassic: through the town of Colunga, along the Cantabrian sands, through dripping eucalyptus woods, back onto the wielding coastal tracks before heading south once more. On we haul towards the town of La Vega.

For the rest of the afternoon there exists an architectural style different to anything I have come across before. We travel into villages languidly copsed around churches, and within these communities there emerge wide-based, isolated wooden structures, each propped up by four stone pillars. Uniform throughout, the stone steps lead neatly up to a narrow door on the first level of these floating huts. The rooftops are gabled like chapels. These are the chestnut-wood *horreos*. The structures are elevated upon the two-metre pillars to prevent flooding or rodents getting at the grain or hay. In the open space underneath, tractors and debris are kept out from the rain.

Along the narrow lanes that connect the villages like a string of wooden beads, cattle come through and saunter by. We stop at one of these beads, Priesca, and Sasha grazes on the grass of the San Salvador de Priesca church. I lie down and fall asleep. We have travelled forty-nine miles in two days.

In Asturias, the grass is not like other grass. It is encompassing and sublime. It intoxicates the environment like an addiction of the land, spreading its gleam wherever possible. The Cantabrian mountains and rivers of concrete have finally been consumed and revulsed by the evergreen hills. Poppies and milk thistles arch and shelter under the webbed limbs of emerald grass. This land is Celtic. A density has altered in the air.

With this change, I consider the end. I wonder to what extent curiosity overrode the fear for the sailors of the *Niña*, the *Pinta* and the *Santa Maria* as Christopher Columbus sailed to the edge of the earth. The fact that there *will* be a drop, that the land *is* going to fall away and there will be no further place to go, makes me feel uneasy. All things will come to light. The consequence of my actions. My guilt. I recall spotting the first rock of land for the very first time after twenty-three days when crossing the Atlantic upon *La Siesta*. The sight of it made me suspicious. I hadn't considered that we would have to leave the boat. Anything but the end. The unrelenting motion of the ocean had replaced the need for terra firma.

Istia won't be able to re-join. That much is clear now. And where will Kiki be when I finish? With R. She will do what is right. The dream of riding together again is drifting out of reach.

Sasha and I take refuge at a *sideria* called Carcabada. As is the tradition, I pour the cider bottle from well above my head and watch half of the golden liquid splatter onto the floor as the other half finds its way into the glass. I am better on the second bottle. It is an efficient way of getting rid of awful alcohol.

We trudge into a quiet and withered town called La Pola Siero. I want to push on and keep going through to a parish named Tiñana for that night, but Sasha pauses outside a bar and isn't for moving. This is unusual. Something seems wrong – perhaps he is just tired. I unclip his reins to make sure he doesn't trip should he wander, fetch some water for him using the collapsible bucket and then order a beer from the bar. I rest underneath the veranda discussing the temperament of horses with a man from Seville who is smoking a cigar the colour of demerara sugar. His wife next to him asks where it is I intend to sleep that night. I tell her that I hope very much for a good field, possibly even a stable.

We travel through an oak wood beyond El Berrón village and then we hear the sound of horses and there are paddocks either side. The biggest mule I have ever seen approaches us from within a field thick with grass. There are horses scattered about. We ride up to a tall, deserted building dragged out of a gothic fairy tale. The mawkish green-and-teal-tiled walls are half standing, its singular tower has a warped tree sprouting out from the open roof, and the windows are housing the branches. Paddocks surround the ossuary.

Melissa, a friend of Danny's, greets me, and together we pick out a spot for Sasha. I massage his back and feel for anything new or old along his spine, down his legs, and around where the saddle and bridle have been. His body is fine. I can't work out why he appeared so exhausted today.

I am shown where I am sleeping. In the middle of the stable floor a mattress has been laid neatly upon a steel bed frame. Finally, a real bed! A deep, spring-held sleep. A cream-coloured goat named Dolores is standing on the mattress staring at me, and Juan, a collie dog with one blue and one black eye, eagerly wags his tail where my imaginary pillow will lie. That night we feast upon *huevos, patatas y jamón*.

When I lie down I can hear the rocking sound of Dolores snoring. I close my eyes and remember the velvet donkey from La Brigue, all those weeks ago, with his face shaped like a crescent moon. I am sad when I wake up because I register that it is a memory and not a dream, and that this journey is now moving so fast that memories like these are becoming untraceable. Step by step with Sasha by my side, I am detaching myself from yesterday and the days before. Kiki's eyes are no longer as clear. The amber from the bronze is no longer separable. The last I heard from her she was thinking about trying to come and find me. And she spoke about what might happen after the end. That ride down Portugal. 'Just us.' But her voice did not sound the same. It was fainter. More monotone. So much further away than just a phone call.

Dolores and Juan continue to sleep as I go to give Sasha his breakfast.

We ride into the ancient town of Oviedo, the capital of Asturias and once the capital of Spain. The mysterious and fertile vistas of the countryside, the giant mules, the olive-shaped horses and the cows and all the milk, are violently replaced with motorways, metal and concrete. We clamber up the steps of an old bridge and cross over a nightmarish scene. Lorries and cars charge underneath us. Sasha plods on. He is now noticeably slower than usual. Occasionally, he even stops in his tracks and refuses to move. People take pictures and touch him, and I find myself having to shift him from left to right to get him going again.

I ride him straight through the centre of the city. It's the quickest way out. We travel on the stone steps and upon the well-manicured banks of Campus de Llamaquique Universidad de Oviedo; bewildered students and professors and amused security guards. We are stopped by police. I plead ignorance. In the suburb of L'Argañosa I find a little bar to give Sasha water. Children gather round and the mothers and fathers guide them through the different parts of the horse, and they ask me if he is safe and how far he has come and to where it is we are going.

'You are travelling backwards,' remarks an old man. 'Backwards in time.'

Emerging beyond the urban metropolis we head south, far away now from the coast. We descend a long track dripping with chestnut and birch trees either side. The way appears ancient. I see an oyster shell engraved into a rock. We have now left the Camino del Norte and have joined the Camino Primitivo. It is along this route that King Alfonso II first travelled in the ninth century upon hearing that the remains of St James had been discovered in Compostela.

A friend of Melissa's has kindly agreed to house Sasha for two nights. It is time for a rest. Sasha's field is watched over by a distinguished farmhouse that has a valley to itself. There are other horses in the paddocks and our host is very sweet. I ask her to feed him well and to watch over him when I am not there. I tell her how tired he is.

Kiki calls me. Her parents have joined her in San Sebastián. She tells me that, as a three, they will come meet me tomorrow. Istia is walking without a limp now, but is a long way from being ridden. She is safe at the stables. Kiki then mentions that she is considering walking with me. Perhaps for a day or two.

Mariella has returned to Spain. I have missed her. Sometimes these days feel half-empty without her. I miss knowing that I will see her when I least expect it. An image of obdurate love. And always when I need it most.

The troupe arrive and we find two converted *horreos* to stay in. I have discovered that these floating granaries differ depending on where they were established and, in Asturias, they often feature wooden balconies encompassing the first level. In the evening we watch the shape of the sun plunge between the balustrades of the balcony and onto the chestnut wood, and then the sky turns amethyst upon the olive-black and beryl-blue hills that surround us. Kiki and I speak about what will happen to the horses when we finish.

'I can't ride down Portugal anymore,' she says. 'Istia isn't going anywhere... you can though.'

The idea of riding down Portugal without her doesn't make any sense to me.

'We need to find a place for the horses to be together,' I reply, after thinking for a while. 'We could ride them home.'

'Home?' she asks.

'Yes, home. We could ride them back to Scotland.'

'Is that home?'

'It could be. Either that or we sell them, together—'

'I'm not selling Istia.'

'I know. I'm not selling Sasha. I'm just trying to think. I don't know what to do.'

The next morning Mariella takes me and Kiki to Sasha's paddock. He looks exhausted. Vacant. His coat has waned to a sickly shade. Kiki approaches him and opens up his lips to see the colour of his gums. They are pale.

'Call a vet.'

'A vet?'

'We need to find a vet. This isn't good.'

With the help of Melissa's friend, I manage to get hold of seven telephone numbers. None of them are able to come out to us but one of them tells me to keep going, there is a vet on my route. Kiki agrees to come with me.

Throughout the day Sasha's fatigue worsens. Slower and slower he moves. Still no vet returns my calls. I am nauseous with worry. I am scared. Kiki insists that we stop and I insist that we keep going. As ever, I cannot see any other option but to move. To journey. To flee the moment.

We fight. Kiki takes her lunch from my rucksack and marches off. I travel solo with Sasha along the Río Nanaya and through the villages of Cornellana and Casazorrina. *Horreos* sprout like wooden mushrooms in the distance.

'Pilgrims' are gathered and drinking from bars in the medieval square of Salas. Drizzle faintly falls. I tether Sasha to a tree off Avenue de Galicia and order a beer in a quiet corner. After coming back from the bathroom, I see a figure writing furiously at the far side of the bar. I touch her on the shoulder and she looks up at me as if it was planned all along. Kiki. We hug. She tells me that she is sorry and I say that am sorry too and we discuss what we are going to do about Sasha.

A contact from the seven numbers has returned my call. A man named Gumer. We ask him to meet us in the small town of La Espina.

As a three we amble beyond Salas and into the falling afternoon. We break through a current of cows that flows around us and past working farms. Sasha seems happier now that Kiki is with us again. His ears point forward and he presses his nose into us as we walk next to him.

You could drive through La Espina and not see a thing. Our destined paddock is on the side of a roundabout and has been offered to us through another friend of Melissa's. From a stranger to a string of friends. After leaving Kiki to find us a room for the night, I stand at the side of the road with Sasha. Cars whirl round the concrete bend of the roundabout and blurred faces gawk out from the car windows. My phone rings. Gumer is close.

He parks up in an unmarked white van on the grass. He gets out, walks towards me and presents a bear-like hand. His forehead is furrowed. His big face is kind but sincere.

'It is funny that you arrive in La Espina,' he says with a deep, smooth voice. He is a big man, and looks down at me.

'Why so?'

'Well... I work all around Europe – Holland, France and Germany. But here, here in La Espina... this is where my laboratory happens to be.'

He pats me on the shoulder and then turns his attention to Sasha. I tell him my concerns as he inspects his gums. There is a change in his expression. We both look at the horse in silence.

Sasha is weak. His coat has turned a brassy chrome colour and his eyes stare like the ends of burnt-out matchsticks. Gumer stabs a needle into Sasha's neck and slowly extracts blood. He offers no resistance.

I wait under the bright lights of Gumer's laboratory. Dried sweat lines my spine, my shoulders ache, and I can see a toe protruding at the end of my boot. I feel cracked. Forced to stop and sit with myself in this room, the situation dawns on me: whether the ride can go on entirely depends on these results.

'Do you think it is bad?' I ask without thinking. 'Do you think he will be able to keep going?' I can feel myself panicking. Everything is going to fall to pieces once more. No control. Every step will have been for nothing. 'We don't have that much longer to go... until Finisterre...'

'Whether or not Sasha reaches the end is not so important, young man,' replies Gumer gently, his back to me as he stands over his computer. 'Whether or not he is alive tomorrow is what we must think about now.'

1,514 miles, 94 days

Kiki's diary
17 June, San Sebastián
  My family is breaking down in front of my eyes and perhaps this is the way it should be. To nothing – nada. To one day come back together in a different life.

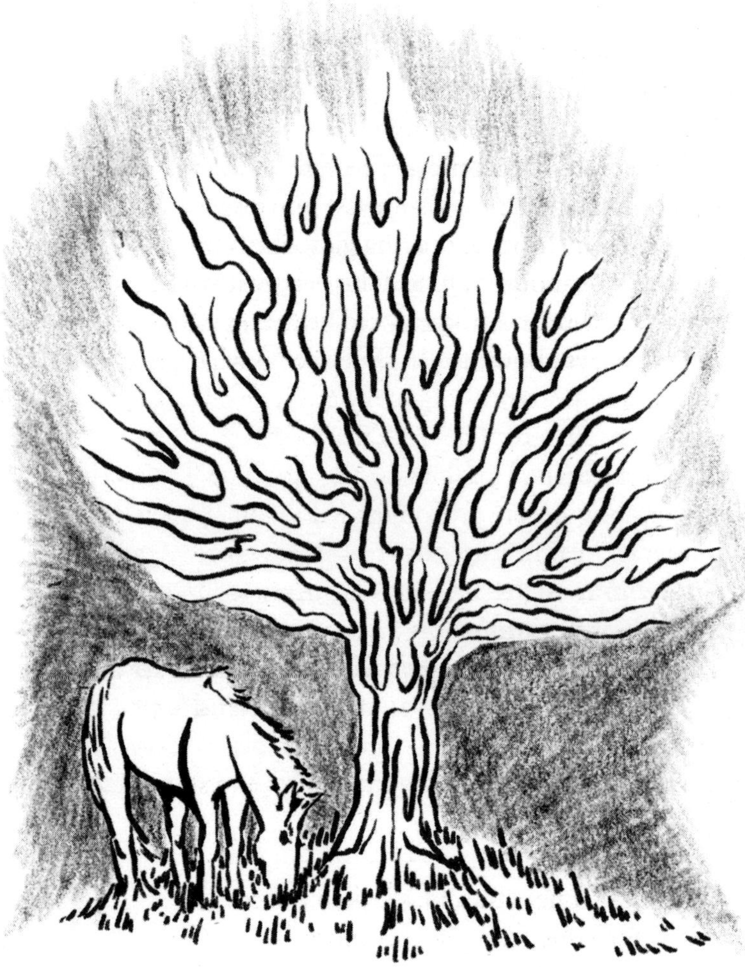

26 June – 7 July
La Espina – Fazai, Galicia

The printer jolts into action. The fate of Sasha ejects itself from the plastic box. I close my eyes. The pristine white walls stare. The lights from the ceiling glower. So this is what the journey was all about? Failing. This is how it is going to end; the star being burnt out, the dorado turning to stone. There are no two ways about it. I have neglected what has come to be the most important thing in my life. The only reason I am here – we are all here. The steed that bears us.

Whatever Sasha's prognosis, the situation he is now in was sewn long before I brought Kiki from Eugene's farm to Biddaray. I cannot use that reason anymore. Beyond the Pyrenees, that night in Saint-Guilhem-le-Désert; before Van Gogh's Arles and before Liguria too. The problem lies with me. I am the thing that wounds. The anatomy of a horse is perilously fragile. I open my eyes and wait for the worst.

Gumer rips the paper from the printer and stands tall. He sighs. I glance up at him.

'Sasha is suffering.'

I am silent. I hear the clock tick in the corner.

'He is suffering from piroplasmosis.'

'Piroplasmosis?'

'Yes. It's a condition that produces an iron deficiency. It was probably transmitted to him through a tic. It is common here. I see it a lot with the cows. The incubation period is between eight and ten days so the bastard could have infected

Sasha as far back as... well, wherever you were ten days ago. Somewhere in Cantabria, I guess.'

'How bad is it?'

'You have seen for yourself. He does not look well.'

I exhale and bring my hand to my head; my fingers dig into my legs.

'But,' he continues, 'there's a chance that we can make him better.'

'Better?' I ask, unsure if I heard him correctly.

'Yes,' nods Gumer. 'If we are careful, I think Sasha will be OK.'

The walls loosen their grip on the room. I breathe deeply, timid in hope.

'Come,' says Gumer, walking to the door. 'Let's go to him.'

We return to the makeshift paddock by the roundabout. Sasha stands motionless as Gumer gives him three injections in the dark: Catosol, Banamine and Imidocarb.

'Will they work?' I ask.

'I hope so. We will know by the morning.'

'And if they don't?'

'If they don't? If they don't he will be lying on his side. And that will be that.'

I stay silent.

'You know it's good that you came to La Espina,' he continues, patting Sasha's neck. 'I don't think your horse would have lived had you not found this place. Yes... you are very lucky that you came here. Very lucky indeed.'

I nod.

'Tomorrow, if these injections do what they're supposed to, you must make your way to the village of Campiello. There you will meet a dairy farmer. His name is Adrian. Follow him to where his cows are. Sasha can rest there.'

'Are you sure it is safe to walk him?'

'Yes. Take him slowly to the cows. And then he must be still for at least four days. I will come to you in the nights with the medicine. He must eat and sleep like the cows. If he rests well, then maybe he can keep going. Until tomorrow.'

'Until tomorrow.'

Gumer shakes my hand and leaves. It is almost midnight. The occasional car swings lifelessly round the roundabout, greasy headlights passing over us and then leaving us in darkness again. I rub my hands down Sasha's mane and stand close to him. I rest my head on his back and look up at the sky.

The dotted stars quiver. The night does not have the energy to turn black.

The journey to the dairy farm is heavy and fragmented. Sasha stumbles, continues on, grinds to a halt, looks behind him, around him, and then looks at me, through me, with such tired, sad eyes. He takes a step and goes again.

When we arrive we are greeted by Adrian, the young manager, along with Tammara, his girlfriend, his parents and Ivan, his older brother. We speak in a hearty Spanish, made clearer for me to understand. They show us to our apartment, the milker's lodge, which sits up in a corner of the dairy barn, overlooking the cattle below. There are two bedrooms, each with one window. Drowsy sunlight slants in as the day comes to an end. The burning scent of cows and manure lines the walls, the pillows. As promised, Gumer comes.

In the morning I sit at the kitchen table with a cup of tea. The cows stir below me. It is hard not to feel in awe at how we got here. I feel hollowed out through disbelief when I think of finding Gumer, the forgotten town of La Espina, this farm – Kiki's presence.

I force open a window – the miasmic smell already somewhat comforting. One hundred dairy cows are beginning their day. Some are lying down on their raised canvas beds while others amble over to the robot milking machine. They speak to each other occasionally, and move about, tranquil and inquisitive, coarsely licking the sides of their grey lips with sandpaper tongues. I lean out of the apartment window and can almost touch the wet nose of Paula, a smooth lilac-grey cow who stands below me. Her eyelashes are like moth wings. I catch sight of Sasha eating some hay in his makeshift stall with two cows either side. I whistle and he calls back to me with a whinny and then stares at me in disbelief at the sight of half of my body hanging out from the window. He is getting on well with his new friends. They are teaching him how to eat. How to be still. Little does he know that the dairy farm not only exports the finest Asturian milk to the rest of the Iberian Peninsula, but the finest horse meat to the rest of Europe.

I have discovered that Gumer is one of the most respected vets and bovine scientists in all of Spain. On top of his credentials, he also happens to be one of the nicest men I have ever met. His heart is as big as the sea. He is a hero. Another hero.

Over the coming days we are careful to survey Sasha's condition closely – his gums, his coat, his stool. Is he drinking water? How much is he eating? Tentatively, a shimmer of colour begins to return to his body, the jaundice sheen dissipating. On the second day his ribs and the bones of his hindquarters are less pronounced. His eyes are growing deep once more, the seas refilling. Each morning Adrian clambers up the metal stairs in his wellies and presents me, Kiki and Mariella with a glass jug of fresh milk. The kindness of these strangers is bringing Sasha back to life.

In the afternoons, when the sun is shining, I take Sasha out to a field so that he can feed on the lush grass. I sit and watch him and lie back on the ground. The thick air is replaced by something cool and unknown. I acknowledge how lucky I am. Leo watched over me as my pony and I made our way down the UK. Someone is watching us now. If Kiki hadn't been there to insist that we get him checked, and if we hadn't found Gumer, Sasha's condition would have deteriorated too fast to stop. It is a stark reminder of how frail this all is and how little I know.

Kiki seems quieter than before. There are moments when I find her sitting alone, wanting to speak to no one. Since joining me in Terra di Mezzo, now seventy-six days ago, this is the first time she has had to make this journey without Istia. But I think her sorrow runs far deeper than the absence of her horse. I think it is a pain that has very little to do with horses at all. This I can only sense. I cannot say for sure. She is torn up by the fact that the journey she was making with her sister in her heart had been cut short by the accident on the mountain of Larrun. She is angry at herself. I can imagine that her time spent in San Sebastián was testing. She was static while the ride kept moving, further and further away. The journey she was threading was being severed. While she nursed Istia, opinions and judgements were being put upon her: friends and family reaching out to console, and then to inform her that she must now walk on alone; or that now is the opportunity to stop; give in, it's a sign, you have done enough.

When she grows so alone that it causes her to cry, I try to hold and reassure her. There are moments, I think, when my lightness and my burn for survival is a comfort to her, and there are times when I recognise that all she needs is Mariella. All anyone ever needs sometimes is Mariella. She and Kiki have become as close as sisters.

*

On the third morning we all drive off to the fishing town of Luarca. On the way the land is shocking and archaic. Burrowing crevasses with wooded realms lie submerged below; blackened ravines, the staunch shapes of hills that dissect the skyline. There is nothing subtle in this part of Asturias. It feels like we are traversing above thousands of Celtic years.

Kiki and I find a restaurant that overlooks the lemon-yellow and blue fishing boats that rock in the waters of Biscay. We have fish soup and white wine and speak again about what we are going to do with the horses. I am running out of ideas and the cliffs of Finisterre are only coming closer. As far as I can tell, once we reach the end, the best thing is to somehow bring the two horses back together again. At least then they will have each other. They cannot be separated.

'We ride them home or we sell them as a pair. That's all I can see happening. What the hell are we going to do—'

'Joachim has contacted me,' interrupts Kiki.

'Joachim?'

'The shepherd from the Pyrenees. He messaged me out of the blue. He says he can look after Istia. I think he wants her foal... I don't know why he wants to help me so much.'

'Well, that's something, I suppose.'

'Yes. It's something.'

Sasha is not back to full strength, that much remains clear. If we were to walk on soon, I worry that he may somehow relapse or be wearied further, irreparably, by the exertion of the journey. But that night, after the three injections, Gumer tells us that we can start again in the morning.

'Make the days shorter,' he says, stroking Sasha's neck.

'And then slowly build them up. Don't ride him. Travel by his side.'

I thank him for what he has done. He replies with a monstrous hug, lifting my feet off the ground.

'You won't need to worry about where to sleep,' he says, stooping down into his unmarked white van. 'I know everyone from here to Finisterre.'

The next day Mariella, Kiki and I say goodbye to Adrian and Tammara and thank them for everything they have done. There is nothing that we can give them or say that can surmount their generosity. Nothing ever could. Not even the bottle of Laphroaig that I managed to find them in Luarca. They are kind because they wanted to be kind. Mariella jumps into the Freelander and, with Sasha between us, Kiki and I walk on west.

Matted bracken and lone Carbayera trees are strewn along the trail, and a single grassy path meanders over the hilltops, cutting up the soft, rolling land for us to wander. Tough semi-wild horses become a frequent feature. Kiki travels behind me. She is silent. Horseless. She could leave the journey at any moment. She can go anywhere she wants. There is no reason for her to still be here other than the reasons that she has decided for herself. She owes me nothing.

I drag my fingertips along the walls of old houses and Sasha treads carefully over sunken cobbles that supersede the earthen track. A chapel is shrouded in its slated tiles at the top of the village, Capilla de Santiago de Montefurado. It appears indomitable to time, fulfilling its purpose only by not falling.

The route curves up and round a steep mountain that is scarred with the limbs of sawn-up pine trees. The sounds of chainsaws ring around the desolation. The crack of splitting wood shoots through the air and Sasha's body tenses in fear, spotting the surreal sight of a falling tree somewhere in the distance above. Suddenly sawdust is the only thing I can smell.

The vast Salime reservoir surfaces below. The shapes and the colours around us have become shocking. Bare trees erect like daggers. Crooked limbs coursing the wasteland. With Kiki now somewhere ahead, we descend the far flank of the shredded mountain and the enormity of the concrete dam wallows before us.

Abandoned houses are dispersed upon the banks of the reservoir. I peer through the broken windows and inside there are signs of a sudden desertion. Creepers have taken hold of the floorboards and the walls. Broken table legs and window frames have been resurrected as apocalyptic weeds. The 1940s houses had once belonged to the workers of the dam.

Sasha and I cross a wide concrete bridge. The immense body of water holds itself to our left, gleaming in the heat of the afternoon, and on the right side there is nothing but the precipice, and the incredible drop. We follow Kiki's footsteps until we reach Grandas de Salime, a village with one leg in the province of Asturias and the other in Galicia.

Gumer calls me to say that he is confident I will find a place for Sasha to stay overnight.

'The people in Grandas de Salime are good people. Some even have cows.'

A man named Riccardo lets Sasha roam in the garden of his *albergue*. A stream runs through the middle of it and thirty-odd white sheep are dotted in the shade of apple trees. I lie back in the grass and watch Sasha move in another new home. We have now been travelling one hundred days together.

*

I think Sasha's coat is beginning to shine. His energy grows. Autumn hawkbit, Himalayan blackberry, bell heather and common gorse watch us walk by. The sun sears down on top of us. Kiki and I travel closer now.

'Let's find a way to get Sasha back to Istia and, once he is there, we can take them both to the Pyrenees.'

'To Joachim's?' I ask.

'Yes. They should be together.'

I hesitate before speaking, expecting her enthusiasm to diffuse.

'And then we can ride them north,' she concludes.

There is a newfound frankness to her voice. I have not heard this note yet. Have thoughts of the future returned to our conversation? The separation of the horses has become blurred up with what happens to me and Kiki. If we can reach the end – if Sasha keeps going, if the horses can be near – then perhaps so can we.

'North? But he needs to rest,' I reply cautiously, checking myself, remembering my mistakes. 'After the end he will need time to be still. He will need to recover.'

'OK... well... we can ride them north in six months' time.'

'Six months' time?'

'Yes. To Paris,' she exclaims.

'To Paris?'

'To Paris and to anywhere else we like.'

'Romania,' I state.

'Romania. From Paris to Romania. Wherever you like. The horses will be together.'

We cross into Galicia. Sasha and I have now travelled over 1,600 miles together. The heat is becoming implacable. I miss the snow and the cold. We have started setting off earlier in the mornings, by eight o'clock at the very latest. We aim to get as far as we can by noon. In the latter hours of the day, we manage to cling to the shadows of the giant eucalyptus and alder trees that throw their forms down onto the dusty tracks. We move slowly, dousing ourselves in water wherever we can.

Cafe A Casa do Acebo lives on its own at the side of the road. The familiar torrents of tussocky grass and hazel trees surround it. Kiki and I stop for some water and coffee while Sasha drinks and then snoozes in the shade. A man with a coal-coloured waistcoat and silver hair stands behind the counter. His eyebrows are like slugs. Newspaper cuttings, stickers, pictures, pewter tankards and brass mugs hang from the stained tawny walls. Upon crossing the threshold, I get the immediate sense that lives have been lived in this room: the nights and the stories. The man in the waistcoat describes to me a fountain for Sasha that isn't too far from the café. And then, just at the moment he raises his arm up to point me in the right direction, the sound of motorbikes shrieks through the air.

Quickly, I go outside to check the clamours of the engines haven't scared Sasha. He looks alert but unmoved. Six riders come to a uniformed halt on the gravel. They are wearing matching outfits. The force of their motorbikes is difficult to comprehend. The speed, the noise. It scares and fascinates me at the same time. I ask them how powerful the engines are.

'Eight hundred and sixty-nine horsepower,' replies one of the riders.

The scenes south and north of us are far-reaching and intangible. They appear like sketches, imitations. Oak, alder, hazel and sweet chestnut trees surround us. Gold and pale green grass sways in the foreground wherever we look and, in the cooling pockets of woods, moss and lichen clutch onto trees. Kiki has begun to talk again, gradually, and something has started to emerge, or remerge between us. We talk about luck and misfortune, and how strange it is, in all of this, that we have met.

On the top of a mountain pass we find a bar called Bar Xestoa. The air is cool and misty. Old farmers hover and Kiki has a coffee and some orange juice. She watches them.

'Look at those men there, all together. They have such beautiful eyes,' she remarks, transfixed. I look over to them. Their eyes sparkle darkly. Glasses of sherry in their hands.

'They appear as young as boys,' I reply.

'That's right. They're still boys; you can see it in their eyes.'

We travel through the hills of Alto da Legúa and Alto das Penas. Whenever we stop to rest we are quiet, listening only to the birds and to Sasha, cropping the grass. If there are no birds, then we listen to the wind. After crossing into France we started to sit next to each other, and later on we would lie down as if on a bed of grass, and weeks later we would pull each other close and Kiki would lie on my chest. We then made a rule to have our stops only in public places, to avoid pushing it too far. Even if we weren't moving, we were never still.

But things have changed now. There is a serenity that was not there before. A respect and a care. We feel the undergrowth beneath us, and we look out at new scenes together; the smells, the birdsong, the change in the trees.

Beyond a forest we find the village of Castroverde. An *albergue* is situated in a field with a shallow river running by. We stop and drink water.

Despite the bucolic setting, the interior of the *albergue* is overpopulated with metal beds, printed signs, fire doors and white electric lights. Oyster shells hang from rucksacks in the sweaty shade of the long rooms. The 'pilgrims' have caught up with us. Endless cables spring out from charging points on the walls like invading tendrils from the forest, turned white from the lack of sunlight in the room. Stuck onto the electric glass doors is a sheet of laminated paper stating that there is a curfew of ten o'clock. There is no one to check us in, just a touchscreen registering us upon entry.

In the night I can't sleep. The groans of snoring travellers and the clinking of metal beds sound like someone is trying to fix a train. I begin to feel claustrophobic, boxed up in a metallic carriage. Sasha is outside, wandering in the grass somewhere with the moon and the tumbling body of the river as his company. Perhaps there are cicadas too, I wonder. Are there any stars?

Adding to the mechanical soundscape, I make my way down the metal ladder from the top bunk and find a fire exit in a room where all the boots and coats are kept. Holding my breath, I push the lever. Immediately I feel the pull of a midnight breeze wash over me, and relief that I haven't disturbed the sleeping train.

The grass isn't too cold under my feet. The stars are faint, unsure whether they are gold or silver, and the moon is an eye of bronze. I travel closer to the sound of the river, the cold scent of water, and then spot Sasha on the other side, lowering his neck to the grass. He doesn't notice me. I observe and listen. The night is so still. It fills my ears and mouth. Covers my naked shoulders like cloth. The quivers of the water, the form of the animal beyond the trees, and the sky just light enough to allow for it all to be witnessed as one thing, threaded together. No separation.

Something stirs from behind me. I turn, but it's too dark to see. Only the square mass of the *albergue* is beyond. I survey the darkness.

'Who's there?' I whisper.

'Who's there?' a voice replies.

It is Kiki. I follow her words. They lead me further down the river. I find her lying on the grass, watching the stars.

'I don't want to sleep in there,' she says. 'It seems strange not to be out here.'

My head rests on the ground and we stay there for a while. She then puts her head upon my chest as the air becomes a little colder. I hug her, and we don't let go.

Somewhere from within La Espina, Gumer is unlocking a secret way for us. He contacts me to say that he knows a good friend who might be able to host us for the night beyond Castroverde. Another vet. His friend isn't sure if he is going to be home but has kindly opened up his spare field for us, just next to his house.

The field is vast and perfectly square. There is long grass in the middle and on the sides it becomes dense with brambles. Sasha travels to each corner of his Galician home, inspecting the space. Kiki and I do the same. There is one open side of the square that isn't covered with shrub or stone. We find some branches from a forest opposite in order to build a makeshift fence line, hoping that Sasha won't try and escape. His spirit and his energy have now almost fully returned; his explorer's curiosity has been restored too, which is always dangerous.

I fall asleep in the grass as the sun softens in the sky. In the early evening Mariella finds us in the Freelander and so too does a local farrier, Miguel, who drives up the dusty track in a maroon pick-up truck. Miguel's ten-year-old son jumps down from the passenger seat and becomes his father's apprentice, assisting him with everything he can: holding the hammer while his father goes to hoist one of Sasha's legs, displaying the nails in the palm of his little hands for fastening the shoe to the hoof and even reaching up and stroking Sasha's neck to make sure the client is at ease. The white-hot shoe is fresh from the heat of the kiln. The boy is fixated by the hiss it makes when it is plunged into a bucket of water. After it is done, Miguel hands me Sasha's four old shoes and I put them in a box under a seat in the Freelander, where I have been storing the rest of them. The only set I haven't kept are the ones without nails. The ones that caused Istia to fall. I don't believe in superstition much, but I have an inkling that they may attract some bad luck.

After Miguel and his son leave, our host, Juan, returns home and invites us all for dinner. We walk across the long grass to a table laid underneath the veranda of a barn. His three daughters sit at one end, talking over each other about horses, and I can't think of anything other than how delicious the tortillas are. Juan speaks sincerely about the rising demands that the growing population of Spain and Europe will inflict upon the land, farming and animals. He reports about the lack of rights for farmers in the Netherlands, pushed outside by the city. The urbanisation of Spain – over 90 per cent of all votes come from urban environments, he states – and the low yield that farmers receive from their crop once it reaches the consumer. He then goes inside and brings out a newspaper from that day:

FROM MOROCCOO TO CROATIA, THE CENTRE OF THE WORLD BURNS Intense mix of drought, soaring temperatures and wind gusts have caused outbreak upon outbreak of forest and live fires in Europe and beyond.

We gather round to read the front page together and I then sit back down, jarred by the outside world. I glance away and search for Sasha's silhouette in the distance. Everything feels uncertain except for his cropping of the grass. Voices of the table morph into one.

'That's right... 74,000 acres have already been devasted...'
'Rare birds die in the desperate Dadia National Park of Greece...'
'Yesterday it reached fifty degrees...'
'The fires are now less than sixty kilometres away. They come closer each day.'

Images of horses on fire flash through my head and I regret reading the news.

'This isn't my idea,' she shouts, not looking me in the eye. 'None of this is mine and I am just walking next to you, behind you, always behind you, walking your little adventure. Not living mine.'

'What's yours, then?' I reply, trying to remain calm.

'I don't know. But none of this is mine. My horse is miles away.'

I attempt to comfort Kiki but know that there is a lot of truth in what she says. At times it is plain that she doesn't want to be anywhere near me or Sasha, that we are dragging her along to an invented destination, away from the places she remembers. And then there are other times when she asks nothing more than to go with us, forever it seems. To Portugal and beyond. Selfishly, of course, I am glad that she remains. But I am scared about what might come. What shape the cracks might take.

There is an unrelenting wind all through the night that shakes the grass and shrills along the stone walls. Sasha stands proudly with his mane, windswept in the morning. He is weathered and he is strong.

1,607 miles, 106 days

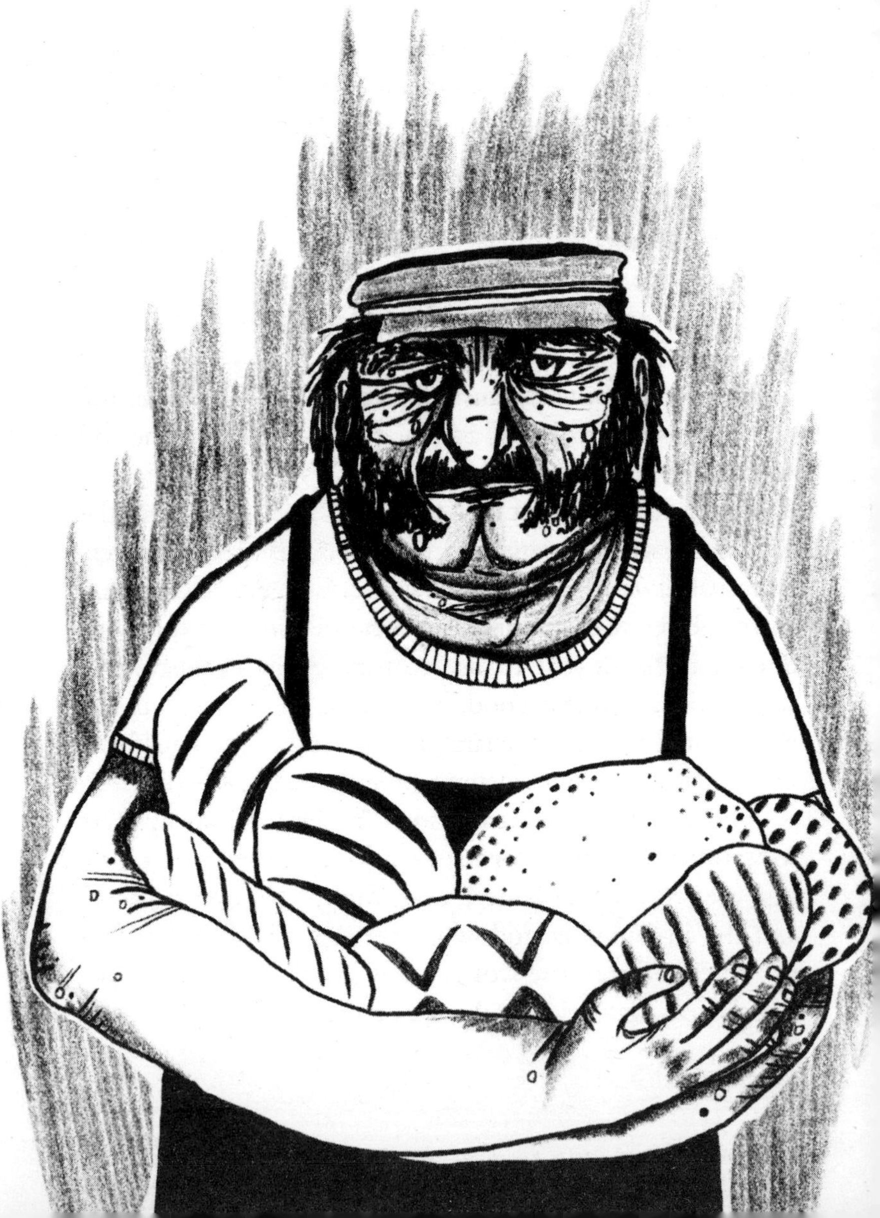

8–11 July
Fazai – Negreira, Galicia

The Camino Frances, Camino del Norte and the Camino Primitivo all converge at the town of Melide: the pilgrim's confluence. We have been told to expect change. In order to receive the coveted Compostela certificate confirming a pilgrim's completion of the journey, walkers must travel the final 100 kilometres (or cycle the last 200 kilometres) of any of the (281) Camino routes, with stamps on their Camino passports to prove it. It is therefore at Melide that the Camino swells into its most ugly form. The river of sweat, braids and broken trainers runs exhaustedly for exactly 100 kilometres, to the Catedral Basilica de Santiago de Compostela: the end of the road for pilgrims.

Rosy, plump calves can now be observed roasting in the heat as the more experienced mahogany-coloured travellers roam in between. By the time we reach Melide, the culture surrounding the Camino has become so fraught with desperate clichés that I want to turn south and leave this well-trodden trail for good. We have done well to put up with it since spotting the first premonitory oyster shell back in Arles. I preferred it when we were alpine cartographers.

The 'true pilgrims' can be identified right away by their suntanned hue, well-worn rucksacks, a toe or two poking out the front of a trainer, an eroding stick in one hand and the all-knowing nod whenever they pass another one of their brethren, the words *'buen Camino'* ready to slip from their cracked lips. For a handful of travellers, the walk is a pilgrimage to the bones of St James the apostle, entombed in the Catedral Basilica. For most, however, the Camino de Santiago de Compostela is a pilgrimage for alcohol and sex. This I well understand, but what I can't work out are those that pretend it isn't. When they sit and drink in the pilgrim bars, meeting and rediscovering fellow travellers from the days and nights before, often the words spoken at each other are as vague and pretentious as their own understandings of what the way of St James actually signifies, or, indeed, what it has become: a train of passengers. I make attempts to portray detachment from the queue as I walk on by or conspicuously tie up Sasha under a tree in the square or at the side of a bar. We are not lost like you, I tell myself, we have purpose – Sasha is the true explorer. You don't know how far we have come or where we are going.

But we are all identical. Travelling with my back to a reality I do not have the courage to compete with – a disillusioned actor with no direction known – muttering that the horizon holds the answers. At least, though, I am close to the horse. Sasha ensures that whoever is near him is taken somewhere simpler, somewhere new and ancient. The present.

Raffi has returned and brought her dad with her, Nat. He is full of life. A booming voice and a great hug. Our own confluence is emerging, it seems. Beyond Melide, Kiki and I find a paddock in Arzúa for the night. It belongs to a man named Roberto. Along with two fat horses, Roberto owns a prolific *panaderia* in the centre of the Galician town.

We go to tack up Sasha early in the morning, keen to beat the human traffic. Roberto embraces us with an old t-shirt and drooped blackberry eyes; he has been awake since 2.30 a.m. He shows us to the room where the bread is made.

A stout woman with strong shoulders and a man with weathered hands machine the oven. The woman throws down flour from a pale amphora that changes colour when the bread oven is opened, the light of the embers reddening the clay; another man – who has a face scattered with shadows from fire flames and soot – is stationed alone in a room that resembles a cave. I stand upon the threshold. Dust and flour hover in the air before mixing up with each other and falling around the stone floor. His body buckles down as he spades more coal, stoking the fire.

'Between 200 and 250 degrees Celsius,' coughs Roberto, 'this is the perfect temperature for the bread oven.'

The heat and the fatigue written on the faces of these people is almost as crushing as Roberto's hugs. The scraping of the bread pan upon the ash and the stone; the clink of the bread-oven door, the slap of the rolling pin, the sliding lift and flip of the dough. The motions of the *panaderia* are both machine and human. Within the joints and the hinges there is a latent pull towards another time, and yet an inescapable coarseness of the here and now; the scorched face of a craft, glaring with carmine eyes.

As well as baguettes, Roberto produces bread shaped like a Mexican calendar stone. It is the colour of dark sand. A man with purple cheeks gives me and Kiki enough baguettes for a week. This is fortunate as that is all the time we have left.

The incandescent weather is unstoppable. From Arzúa onwards, herds of travellers coagulate with their identical outfits and destinations printed like barcodes upon lips. In the afternoon, the rounded shadows of the oak trees and the tall svelte shape of eucalyptus provide just enough shade for us to get by. We soak and drink, horses and humans, at every fountain.

'We can't go on like this,' says Kiki, concerned. We both sit, water dripping, under the shade of an ash tree.

'We won't,' I respond. 'It's all about to end.'

The scene of the *panaderia* remains playing in my head. There was something strangely alluring about the mundanity of it all. The timelessness. We are now in the endgame. The cathedral will come. Another milestone. Another step closer to Finisterre. For a moment a ball of excitement grows inside my stomach, but I am quick to ignore it. Nothing good ever lasts. A roll of string being held at the top of a hill – everything about to unravel. Sasha's health remains recovered, but this could change in an instant. We are always only one second away from disaster.

The others find their way into the suburbs of Santiago de Compostela while I remain with Sasha. A man named Toni arrives to meet me once the sun begins to set. He drives into a paddock that I have sourced from a man named Joseph, a five-acre forest kept hidden from the outside by a rusty metal wall-gate that had to be prised open with the full force of my body. Joseph lives close by. He has a confident, darting expression. He knows of me, he claims, from a newspaper article. A fellow taste for exploration, Joseph created the first maritime Camino de Santiago de Compostela, a route that begins in La Rochelle.

Toni clambers down from the door of his French 1980s red-faded *camión* and shakes my hand, looking me up and down. His cheeks and eyes are young, but his body is noticeably worn; he has a hunched back due to time spent on the saddle.

'I can no longer do what I once did,' he exclaims, self-consciously. He limps to the back of the long vehicle like a man broken down by doing it a thousand times.

Toni is the fabled horseman of Oviedo. I heard of his existence long before I discovered that he had horses to rent. I have spent almost three weeks tracking him down, desperate to find two extra horses for the last days of the ride. It only seems right that Kiki makes the final steps to Finisterre on horseback. Raffi has helped me fund the other horse as a surprise for her father, Nat, a keen rider.

After unlocking the bolts, two big, round-bellied horses march down the wooden ramp of the *camión*: Bermuda, a black Breton-Arab mare, and Carbonarro, a grey Hispano-Arab gelding.

Toni, Joseph and I watch as the three horses wander about the shadows of the pine trees and then Toni and I set out some feed and hay for them. I pitch my tent on the soft pine floor. The others are sleeping in an *albergue* in town. I want to make sure that the horses are tacked up early in the morning so that we can get into Santiago de Compostela before the torrents of walkers. Most of all, I want to be alone. To hold this night as tightly as I can.

Morning shakes and trembles and I find Sasha standing by my tent. The other horses are resting in a shaft of light that has made its way through the tree cover. I find a hose and spurt cold water on my face and brush my teeth. Toni emerges from the *camión* and together we feed and tack up the horses. For Bermuda and Carbonarro, Toni uses heavy Western saddles and provides them with deep saddle bags. Sasha appears lean next to their round, full statures. With the horses ready to go, the others arrive from their *albergue*.

The flagstones are still wet from the water that was used to clean them in the night. The sun is blurred and the sky smooth and bright, shimmering, not white, and is laced with a barely detectable lilac. For a short time, nothing but the beats of hooves accompany us through the waking streets; Bermuda, Carbonarro and Sasha calmly take us into the old city. Joseph and Toni made sure to tell me that it is best we don't hang about: usually, in order to bring horses into Praza do Obradoiro, the main square of Santiago de Compostela, it is customary to ask the police for permission. In typical Spanish style, this process can take up to six months.

Step by step the walls either side of us turn back in time upon the Rúa de San Pedro. The bricks darken, revealing their story and their age. I glance back to see that we have been joined by the white, black and scarlet Galician players on their way to perform for the tourists in the square. The *mantilla* shawls of the women and the *faixa* cloth belts of the men trail in their movements, the frills of the midnight-black *vasquiña* skirts rustle.

A chill of air brushes over me as we enter the vast open square, the Praza do Obradoiro. To our relief, it is empty. We have beaten the police and the pilgrims. The cathedral façade stands colossal to the left, reaching wide and high up into the blue morning. Only the very peak of the Romanesque Torre de la Carraca is lit by the sun. All else remains in a cool shade. A ticking of hooves and the players' wooden-soled *zocos* (or *chancas*) echoes around the walls. I don't know what I expected but it certainly wasn't this. It's so light and still. Not even a bird in the sky. Weightlessness. The *praza* a theatre in limbo with no one here to watch.

A thin veil has been drawn behind us. The previous days have been crushing: organising the new horses, maintaining Sasha's recovery, swathes of travellers, faces, voices; joining the frenzied train. Now sitting upon Sasha in the shade of this ageless building, the pressure finally dissolves. The morning is still ours.

I look round to see Nat's face. His whole body, it seems, takes in the structure of the cathedral as he sits tall upon Carbonarro. Kiki places her hand upon the long bay neck of Bermuda. I see Mariella and Raffi talk with the Galician players, but the words that they say are indecipherable from where I am. Only bodies and their mouths. We are hovering. Somewhere between matter and air, unfixed in form, sifting limbless between past, present and whatever is to come.

Then the players prepare their *tamboril*, snare-drums that hang from belts, their *bombo*, bass drums, and their *gaita*, bagpipes, and where we are and what we are doing floods back to me. Sasha stirs. Words and sounds begin to tick once more. We wander upon the *praza* cobbles.

The life that has gone before us on this ground is difficult to comprehend. The *praza* has been a centre of music, art and religion for over 800 years. Once upon a time it was regarded as the arcadia for travellers, pilgrims, street musicians, street sellers and craftsmen and women from all over Europe. Praza do Obradoiro translates as square of the workshop. I feel a rigidity and a rooting on these cobbles now, a physical comfort within the clasp of the never-changing walls, the arcane embrace of the cathedral. We are part of something far bigger than anything we can touch or understand.

The police arrive and ask us to move on.

We travel towards the exit on the west side of the *praza*. Before turning down an alley, I look back one final time. Pockets of exhausted travellers are now beginning to creep into the arena from the shadows of the Rúa de San Francisco entrance. I see a woman fall to her knees. She hangs her head and kisses the cobbles underneath her. She stays there, speaking to the ground, her palms outstretched on the stone, before hauling herself up and rising to the cathedral above. Her dirty fingers are stretched, her face twisted with crying, and her mouth grows round, the shape of the moon, as if her body is speaking one long word. This must be one of the few who make this pilgrimage for the bones of St James.

Behind her, the Parador hotel has begun to rouse. One of the oldest hotels in Spain. Scatterings of twos and threes emerge from the single glass door, watching the travellers and players with cups of coffee in their hands, before strolling back inside for breakfast.

We move wordlessly. Bewildered faces of tourists watch us travel down Rúa do Franco. At the bottom of the street a small square opens up with two cafés. We tie the horses in the shade of some sycamore trees.

An old man with a crimson beret and a large, pimpled nose is selling ink pens with feathers, photographs from the Spanish Civil War and large, rusty keys. I see Kiki coming down the steps of the church. I follow her through the crowd. She walks down an alley and then turns left. She stops by a shop selling portraits of galleons. I approach her from behind and put my hands on her bare shoulders

'Did you manage to light a candle?' I ask. She turns to me and nods blankly.

'Is everything OK?'

Her eyes are vacant. For a second, she brings her face to mine, and then I reach out to hold her waist in my hands. Her eyes remain open, glassy. She doesn't hold me back.

'There are only five days left,' she utters, turning away.

1,689 miles, 110 days

Kiki's diary
11 July, Negreira
    I feel utterly useless, lazy and shallow. Trying to smile and laugh my way through the day, merry, merry merrily, head up, or down when out of sight, this churning blob in my stomach – it is nauseating. Disappointment rises up from the soil like morning dew, it reeks and reels and deeply penetrates the pores of the skin. A hollow vessel with nothing to say, a pain buried so big and dark that no one wants to lay their eyes on it. And so we hide in plain sight, deeply unhappy – hollow – useless, lazy, shallow.
    It will be a nightmare as I lose touch
with whatever I thought I had found
    Utterly restless, spiders crawling up my back up to
my shoulders
good old spiders, how you
    cover me like a thick black mantle always crawling, crawling, crawling pain well deserved nevertheless
    so bring it on more
let the blob grow and nauseate
until it makes you puke spit vomit
vomit black spiders and let the thick
sticky disappointment pouring out of every hole of
your body
I swallow
I smile.

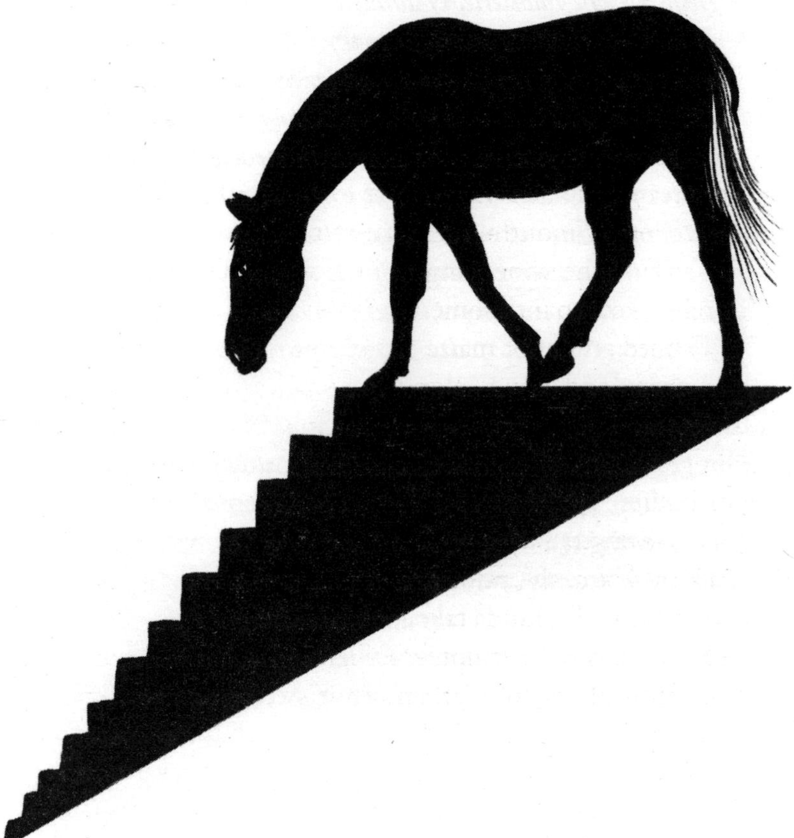

12 July
Negreira – Cape Finisterre, Galicia

We pass round the *bota*, which swells like a black leather rabbit in the heat of the day. Kiki raises it above her, the neon-blue sky behind her head. Wine pours down in a strong red stream. She licks her lips and passes it back to me. The corners of my mouth have begun to crack with the sunlight and at first the wine stings, but after the second pour the pain is licked up into something else.

Cloned armies of maize quiver in the breeze as we canter past them and down along the shades of a dusty track towards the hamlet of Santa Marina. Twice we halt and plunge our heads into fountains, dousing the horses and our bodies. The three horses are becoming a herd, a unity. Kiki is sitting tall upon Bermuda. She makes her mammoth black neck arc, the power of her body shifting to the rear, and suddenly Bermuda takes on the appearance of a god-like creature ready to be sculpted, a mighty epitome of mankind's most faithful friend. Carbanarro is sweet-natured. Gentle, large and biddable. Nat is devoted to him. Sasha soldiers on, the wisest of the cavalcade. His energy and colour are getting better each day. Honey no longer drips from his legs. His wounds have healed.

Santa Marina is quiet. There is a small, open square with an obelisk and a fountain in the middle. Here Toni meets us. We let the horses roam free in a paddock hidden in shade beyond the hamlet, and we find an *albergue* run by a mother, her daughter, a black cat called Lupo and Paco, the son.

I walk in under the veranda. Paco is being whipped by his mother with a tea towel. Despite being a large man, he is exceptionally nimble through the plastic chairs of the restaurant. In the evening the barely coloured moon rises high and Nat bellows into the sky with a deep, theatrical voice, much to Toni's delight.

In the morning I wake early. Paco is slumped on the same chair I left him in six hours ago. His hands are propped smartly on his belly and his young bald head rests on his left shoulder. Lupo is fast asleep on his lap, sprawled out, head and legs hanging. Like many when they sleep, Paco has been taken back in time, to the exhausted child on the chair.

In a flash he jumps up upon hearing my footsteps. Lupo falls off his lap and hits the ground, not quite fast enough to land on his feet. Paco rubs his palms upon his red t-shirt as if to wipe away the sleep.

'*¿Zumo de naranja? ¿Toastadas? ¿Café?*'

I tell him not to worry about anything and quietly make my way outside to feed the horses. Apparently hearing a different answer, his body jerks into action and he hurries behind the bar. Paco, devoted barman of Casa Pepe, grits his teeth and begins squeezing oranges.

I am relieved to discover that what I thought was the ocean staring back at me directly west is in fact a blur of hills. There is still time. There is still land that we have to cover. It is not over yet.

Gently, Kiki, Nat and I ride up Monte do Sino. Down below, the Río Xallas gapes its gloomy mouth and lays its tongue upon the land, a river that leads to the sea. The landscape is mutating faster than I can keep up with.

'Do you think we will reach Finisterre?'
'Yes, I think I do.'
'It's close now, isn't it?'
'Yes. Everything is racing to the sea.'
'Like us. Pass me the *bota*.'

The black leather sack of wine is hanging loosely from my saddle. I untie the yellow-and-red string and throw it to Kiki, on top of Bermuda. She tilts her head back before squeezing, the currant-coloured liquid flows into her mouth.

'Follow me.'

Kiki throws the *bota* back to me and urges her horse on. Her legs don't move but somehow Bermuda knows what she wants. By now, they understand each other well. Sasha follows suit and before long we are cantering abreast of each other along the flat mountain track that cuts neatly into the dry shrub land. Purple campanile flowers lean back into the slope above. Somewhere behind, Nat is in pursuit on Carbanarro.

For a brief moment, Kiki glances at me. She then rises up in her stirrups and out of her saddle. Bermuda's power rumbles underneath her. I feel Sasha stretching his legs, matching his comrade's growing speed.

The track curves round to the right, tracing the nose of the mountain. My eyes water. Dust pursues the horses' tails, shrouding our shapes. Kiki yelps in the air like a coyote. Bermuda responds. Faster and faster. The wine and blood power. The timeless creatures carry us. We stand up and hover upon their striding bodies.

It is then that I look ahead, just quick enough to see. There is a sharp kink in the track, leading over a narrow, stone bridge. I ready myself to balance the turn, but there is no way that we can both cross the bridge at the same time. At the speed we are galloping, one of us is bound to slip on the bend, down into the ravine below.

'Kiki,' I whisper almost to myself, my voice inaudible above the stampede. 'Kiki!'

I look at her next to me, her body poised above the saddle, her quartz eyes shooting directly ahead, flying a plane, seconds from taking off for the very first time.

'Kiki!'

At the last moment I yank the reins right and pull Sasha away. I veer off and gallop up a goat track into the undergrowth above. Sasha slows in the shrub. We catch our breath.

Nat and I cross the bridge upon Bermuda's hoofprints. A fog of dust roams in the distance.

The fleshing tongue of the river shrinks away as our trail leads us upon a path flanked by old stone walls, each stone a different shape and colour, and we approach the village of O Logoso.

Cushioned into the side of the valley, the cobbled community lies beyond a wide, slanted field that reveals itself to our left. Tree cover shrouds the view to our right. Planted in the middle of the field is a vast round rock, at least five metres tall, the big bald head of a Galician giant. There is an old, spindly *horreo* at the edge of the field, once acting as the sole granary for the village.

Ahead I notice a fork in the road. Go right and the track will lead us down to the river, de Hospital. Go left and we continue traversing the upper valley, our heads pointing towards the Atlantic Ocean.

It is then that I finally accept that tonight will be the last night of the ride.

Toni appears from around the corner; the *camión* is parked further into the village. We untack the horses, pour buckets of water over their backs and lie the soaked saddle cloths flat out to dry in the firm heat of the sun. I then haul the saddles up the ladder into the cool space of the rickety *horreo*. Carbanarro and Bermuda's Western saddles weigh far more than Sasha's Prestige – the lucky Ligurian saddle discovered the night before France.

We release the horses into the slanted field. Nat and Kiki summit the globular rock and stand together, watching the horses roll and stretch in their brimming green sea. It is Sasha's 110th home since we left Castello del Calcione.

After a late lunch we say goodbye to Nat. He has to return for work. As the taxi draws away upon the tracks written with hoofprints, I feel a hollow. My stomach is the seabed for a retreating wave. I remember this feeling from when we entered the confluence of Melide, when all the walkers, tourists and pilgrims coalesced together upon one road going west. This feeling forewarns change.

I sit down in the cool of the *albergue*. The news is being shown on the television screen. There are images of black smoke and fire engulfing forests somewhere in Europe.

Kiki books a room in the *albergue* for Bernadette, her mother, and then showers and sleeps. Mariella and Raffi reach us on foot after their long walk. Their faces are sun-worn and satisfied. Together we amble down to find the river at the basin of the valley.

We spot an opening at the side of the track. We follow it and, quickly, it evolves into a green-lit path, enclosed by the saplings of chestnut trees. A stillness and a coolness intermingle with the dry, hot air of late afternoon, and the sound of flowing water makes everything suddenly lighter. Oak trees crouch, acting as a curtain behind the chestnuts, a window of cold light.

Towards the end of the path we see a dark pool. The water is translucent. Rocks fleck like moonstone and calcite gems underneath the surface. A continuous stream flows over smooth boulders that hem the sides of the pool to form a bath. We jump in.

Emerging from the water, I look back to where we have come in from and notice how the light of the path appears bronze and blue, lambent with the uneven shapes of branches. We decide it is the perfect place to camp for the last night. The hollowing feeling has gone.

After supper at the *albergue*, one by one we make our way down to our emerald riverbed. I am the last to go, staying up with Toni, debating the best horse for a journey across the world. He is insistent on an Appaloosa. I am not sure, but I know the horse should be small, strong, intelligent, and not have the coat of an Arab. Honey is not so easy to find in some corners of the world. It should surely be a cross of some sort, hot- and cold-blooded: Sasha's mind upon a brute's body. Perhaps a Berber or a Mérens. I also point out that I know nothing.

'Napoleon used an Arab,' remarks Toni.

'In the paintings, yes,' I answer.

'The paintings?'

'He crossed the Alps on a mule.'

The stars are faint and dotted. I find my way in the dark, the air gently warm, and then lie down, keeping half of my body outside of the tent. Everyone is asleep, their breathing and the flowing river the only sounds. For a moment I decide that I could be anywhere, my body on the ground and the sky above me, with the sound of any dark river. It could be the sea too.

But then Kiki stirs in the tent. I feel her reach out for my chest. She places her head upon my shoulder. Now there is the heat of her body. The cool grass underneath me. I hold her in my arms.

In over a hundred days and nights there has been no place that could ever compare to the side of this river. Living has led us here. My restlessness has driven, her lostness navigated, and now we lie still, together. Finally removed from source and destination. I would be lucky to sleep now and to never wake up. To sink further and further into the earth. Holding Kiki.

Folds of gossamer carpet the moss floor and the water from the stream is fresh on my face. I feed the horses before six. The last day. The day I dread most of all. I pat Sasha's neck, massage his back, and then do the same to Bermuda and Carbonarro in the shade of the *horreo*. I want the day to be over and for us to return, somehow, to the days before, and the weeks before that.

Late at night my mother arrived from the airport of Santiago de Compostela. She took a taxi to O Logoso and stayed in a room at the *albergue*. Along with Bernadette, as a team of eight we have our final breakfast. Toni waves goodbye and drives on in the *camión*. With any luck we will see him tonight, somewhere near Finisterre. Hushed up at the side of the *albergue*, Kiki and Bernadette are fighting. I hear my name and the name of R. Soon the ride will turn inside out, entrails and all.

After breakfast we take the horses down to the emerald river. They glance and sniff around at the shadows that the saplings cast and drink water from the pool. I produce two corked bottles of *cidre* that I kept in the river overnight. Today is Kiki's birthday. As is so often the case, it seems, her joy is mixed with sorrow; it is the first birthday Kiki has spent without her sister being alive. The *cidre* makes its way around. The heat slowly creeps. The hot sun bleeds its way through the sea of oak trees. It is time to move.

*

More armies of Veronese-green maize and now eucalyptus trees bring the mystique of our riverbed to an end. After some time in blazing light, we find water for the horses from a fountain near Figueiroa and, after this, the route begins to veer decidedly west. Transformation is happening before me. Everything slowly slipping. Down to the sea. One hundred and eleven days are being garrotted into one. I want desperately to slow everything down, to call out to Kiki and to sit upon the ground, just us. To break this speeding river.

At 11.49 a.m., 12 July 2022, I see the sea. Unmistakable, dead ahead. Nothing more. Kiki and I pause. The others disappear down to the paradisical scenes below, walking fast into the sight of the Atlantic Ocean.

'Stand still,' I say. 'Stand very, very still. Take my hands.'

'OK.'

'Close your eyes.'

In a bid to somehow take back control, we try hard to truly consider what it is we have almost achieved. We breathe deeply in unison. In. And out. For a moment it seems to work. I can feel the ground present under my heels, the weight of air in my lungs. My mind blank.

We open our eyes and something has shifted, lightened perhaps. Together, we wander down the track and look out to sea.

With sand replacing earth, we flow down into the town of Corcubión. We tie the three horses to the mammoth trunks of two old palm trees. Kiki and I remove their saddles and pour water over their backs and bodies from a round stone fountain at the side of the road. They snooze in the shade.

Never on this journey have I put any importance on lunch. Almost every day it has come and gone at unchecked times, whenever we are tired or hungry, or if we come across a canal bank or a tree that can't be ignored. But today, under the shade of the Cafetería Pazo, I worry that it's the wrong place and the wrong time; the food isn't quite right, the table is too small. I could have chosen somewhere better. We are so far away from the streams and from the shade of an oak tree; long grass and a single orange being shared between the two of us. The juice dripping. No one else.

Without Kiki's knowledge, I have managed to organise a small cake and some glasses of Orujo for everyone. The waiter comes through the portiere with a thin smile and sweat pouring from his brow. In his hand he cradles the flame of a single candle burning brightly, wedged deep inside the centre of an almond croissant.

I go into the bar and ask for three more shots. I drink them in quick succession. My head gets hot, but my mind is focused, released from the past. Eye sockets brimming. Mariella comes in to get me. It's time to go. My mum asks if I am OK.

On we travel round the coast, the sun pounding up at us from the asphalt. The heat, the day, is becoming unbearable. The cider and the Orujo swirl in my head. I take a left turn – anything to get off the burning road, out from the fire of the white light – and a narrow lane guides us down into a neat little bay: Sendero Playa de Talón. I feel Sasha quicken his step in a nervy excitement. The road morphs into earth which then slips away into sand. He trots onto the beach and we approach the water. The gentle tide crashes down. He backs away. I bring him close to the precipice once more, his hooves sinking into the damp sand, and step by step we make our way into the low tide.

I sit upon him as he takes me as far as he can go, his head like a snorkel above the overlapping waves. From my waist down I am submerged. The cool of the ocean is glorious. Sasha the seahorse! Once upon a time he was scared to cross a stream. The horses all swim together.

A shrill noise erupts from the corner of the beach. A woman with leathery skin materialises like a sea creature from behind a rock, her naked breasts swinging in fury, her hair wild like Medusa. She believes that the horses are dangerous. She barks that her time on the beach is being disrupted.

I smile sarcastically and ask her to calm down. It is an antagonising move. In response, her voice reaches new stratospheres, her look is demonic and her hands rise up to the sky. She marches in her wrath, her nakedness bounding in the air. We bow out and slip away. We return refreshed upon the sandy lane and back on the road to Finisterre.

The weight of the day lifts and our footsteps start to match the patterns and the rhythms of the hooves. I breathe in and out deeply, trying to regain the peace of that archipelago moment earlier in the day, when we saw the sea. Something close to presence. Soon, the cape will begin to rise up and form. And then there will be rocks, a lighthouse I am told, and then only the endless view of the ocean.

The twelfth-century igrexa de Santa María das Areas de Fisterra appears at the side of the road and we stop to rest at the foot of Monte Cabo. The granite church became popularised by pilgrims in the fourteenth century: the next stop after the tomb of St James in Santiago de Compostela. After praying in this coastal silence, the pilgrims would then go on to see the ocean, many for the first time in their lives.

We follow in their footsteps after we fill ourselves with water. I look around and there are more people. Mum,

Bernadette, Raffi, Mariella, Kiki's aunt, three young strangers fascinated by the horses, and more – stragglers, tourists, lone travellers – begin to join us. The many roads morph into one. Our way climbs and bends. Around the corner appears the heartening sight of the red-faded *camión*.

Toni is pleased to see us. I take a breath and look ahead to see how the road narrows. Cars and buses full of tourists groan by, making their way towards the cape, eager to catch the sunset before returning to the town. I want to be alone. Alone as our team, our family. Me, Kiki, Sasha, Mariella and Raffi. Nothing else; no sound nor sight of motors, people or, even, other horses. I want to feel the wind. Just us; our breath and our steps. Alone with the beat of the hooves. I remove Sasha's saddle and leave Carbonarro and Bermuda with Toni.

The sun sinks in the sky and our own shadows are being drawn beside and in front of us from the steep hill to the right. The final ascent begins. Others, travellers and family, trickle behind us or ahead and fall away, talking and moving in the background.

Sasha travels by my side, not knowing where we are headed, but going, always going forwards. He moves between all, carrying us along – Kiki travels behind him, Mariella to his left, Raffi behind her – and we march, silent and together. My dread has gone. The sight of the reddening sun prevents thought. This is Us, one final time.

As we approach the cape there appears a man playing an instrument at the side of the road. He is sitting on a chair. We travel closer and, in the lowering light of dusk, I make out a small harp placed in front of him. His fingers pick the strings. The end is now close. Behind the harpist looms the broad white face of the working lighthouse, Faro de Finisterre. We are noiseless. An old boat coming into shore.

I put my hand on Sasha's neck. For the first and final time, there is no way forward. We are forced to stop.

Forty metres below, dark boulders of the cape ink themselves into the sea. A wooden cross stands solitary in memory of dead sailors, planted deep into the stoned earth, raised up to face the storms. We cannot go on. The cement steps that lead down to the cape are too steep. They are not for horses.

I turn to face Sasha and place my forehead against his and I put my hand on his neck. He is tired now. I stroke his face, softly, over and over, and slowly he begins to close his eyes. Two warm tears fall down my cheeks. Everything around is muted. Blurred. We are only this. Kiki rests her head against his neck. The only thing that we revolve around is this horse.

We all stand where we are. Holding him. I close my burning eyes firmly shut and try hard to create slides of time in my head, an artificial exhibition, desperate to suddenly remember it all, to hold on to it. I picture the silver colours of ice at the foot of a pine tree, rocks underneath me with spots of blood; dripping honey; white paths that never end; the mark of a hoof etched into mud; little footsteps ahead of me; Kiki's eyes in the snow; deep beds of straw and hay. The hands of the breeze upon my back.

When I imagined Cape Finisterre in my head, it was empty. No concrete anywhere, no buildings, no cars and no lighthouse. I am as ill-prepared for the end as I was for the beginning. The sky reverberates like a reluctant child going to bed.

Eventually the sun slinks away underneath the water. Aimless, Kiki and I walk back to the *camión* with Sasha between us. We walk away from the destination, the place that has been at the centre of my eyes for so long. It's now midnight. The stars are bright. The sky is black. We thank Toni for all that he has done and aim to see him soon, in Oviedo. We load Sasha up to be with Bermuda and Carbanarro, close the heavy tailgate, fasten the bolts and watch the red-faded *camión* drift away down the road.

In the town of Finisterre, we find food and wine at a place starkly lit in electric light. We move along the stretching sands of the Playa de Llagosteira, cold underneath our bare feet. Everyone has separated, running or moving alone. Some of them are swimming naked in the low waves. At last, it seems, we have all been deposited into the sea. Like everything else. I pick my way along the moving water's edge.

1,733 miles, III days

IV

This House of Us

'Remember, all of man's happiness is in the little valleys. Tiny little ones. Small enough to call from one side to another.'
From Blue Boy *by Jean Giono*

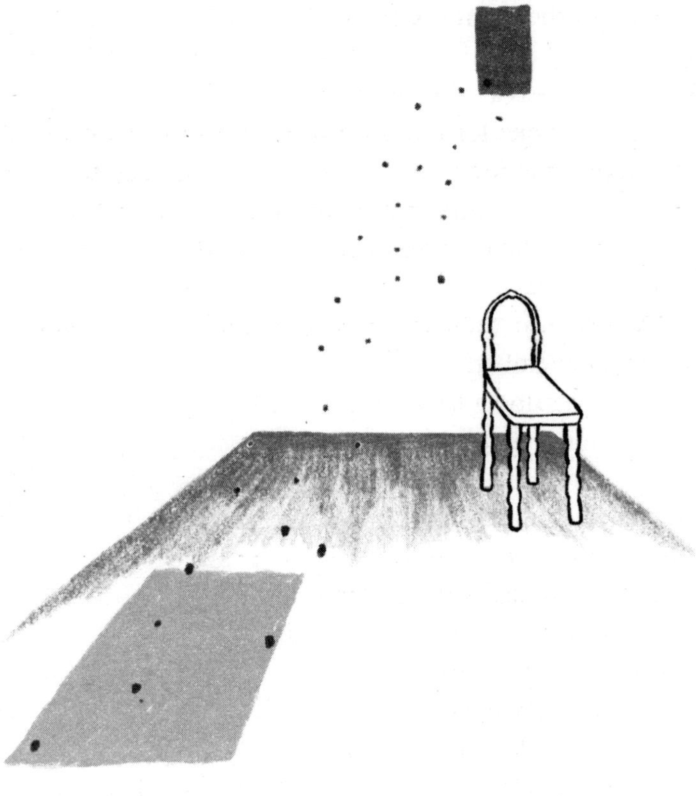

13–22 July
Finisterre – Lesaka, Navarre

A dark tall wardrobe stood in the shadows of the far corner. The rest of the room was faintly lit, blood-orange, distorting the air. I couldn't fully make sense of the ceiling and the walls. There was a figure, lying opposite me.

When I woke for the third or fourth time, it was much later. I sat up in my bed. A small window acted as the clock. Coppery light, chants of evening cicadas. Kiki was sleeping on the other bed. It was her and we were together. She opened her eyes.

'We are near the river that we never had the chance to swim in, remember?'

'The river under that bridge?'

'Yes, under that bridge.'

The night and the day held little difference; I was asleep and awake for equal measures of time. We drove east. With Sasha, we travelled *with* the land, thickening into a realm of our own. Not over or beyond it. Time was a different shape. Warmth, water and food. But here we cleaved right through the body, eighty miles per hour in a violent machine out of control. Crash landing onto earth.

Everyone left the day after we reached Finisterre. It was then just the two of us. Kiki was trying hard to ensure everything was still being held together. But it all felt bare. We couldn't hide behind movement anymore. I tried to make our world small. Like it was before, the lives of the horses became my sole focus. Getting Sasha to Istia, this was all I could think about. Once they were together, I believed that everything else would become clear again. I didn't know what Kiki believed.

'Are you not scared?'
'Scared?'
'Everything is about to change.'
'Change? But I thought—'
'Everything is about to change, Lu. Nothing will be the same when we go back. And I *need* to go back. I can't stay out here or disappear someplace else. There are people waiting for me. I'll need to speak – I'll need to explain what has happened. They will ask... I need to go to R.'

I pushed my hand through the pool of a fountain in silence, holding on to her fingers underneath the surface of the water.

'I need to be with my parents... soon it will be the first anniversary of Siu's death.'

That night we lay in bed in an Asturian hamlet called Llugarrón and the rain fell. The rest of Europe was in flames but for some reason, where we were, the rain wouldn't stop. We kissed. Our lips went deeper than they should have, in search of bone. We held each other tight, the nearest way to be moored to something permanent.

The reunion. It had been over a month since Istia limped into the stables in Gipuzkoa.

Sasha bundled out of the back of the truck, ears pricked, nostrils flared. His couple of days at Toni's yard had done him good. His belly looking full again, his coat glowing.

The first thing he heard was the call of Istia who shuddered alone in her box. Sasha called back and then stamped his front-right hoof and leapt in a circle on the dust. We walked him round to the corridor of boxes. Istia's head protruded like a reaching flower from her red-painted wooden stall, desperate to touch him before he touched her. Sasha's trembling walk jolted into a trot and a lurch and then a soft quiver as their noses approached. They were placed in neighbouring boxes so as not to cause them any distress. Their stretching necks were just long enough for them to reach out from the tops of their stable doors, their noses to be close.

With the horses together, we found a place to stay in Hendaye, a surfing town across the French border. We climbed the narrow staircase to the fifth floor and turned the key into our studio apartment. There were two windows. One faced the gothic gable of L'Hôtel de Paris across the street. The other looked south, into Spain. The sea was behind us.

In the middle of the night, Kiki rose from the bed and walked across the room. I woke from the feeling that she was no longer next to me. I watched her. In one motion she placed herself upon the windowsill. She hugged her knees. The shadows of her shoulder blades. The Spanish window, with the five-storey drop below. The grip upon her knees loosened, her body relaxed like a doll, her head lulled and swayed towards the open air and my stomach rolled in fear at what she might do. I sat up in bed. Coolly, her left hand reached into the room. She found a cigarette on the windowsill and began to smoke. Noiselessly.

'Can't you sleep?' I asked.

She looked at me through the dark. Her eyes reflected the lone streetlamp from the square.

'No.'

'We'll be fine,' I answered. 'All we do is get to Joachim and then we can—'

'I am not here. I have not been here for some time now.'

We lay far away from each other in the bed. I reached out for her shoulder.

The bustling tones of a market. I went downstairs to walk amongst the stalls and buy a bracelet for Kiki, Mariella, Raffi and for Victoria, my cousin. I found Kiki on the beach. She was wearing the long unbleached linen dress. Her shoulder straps slipped off and she made her way towards the water. Naked but for lavender-coloured underwear. I ran up to her and she chased me into the sea; the waves were powerful. I let my limbs be taken. Dragged out and pulled back towards the shore, tumbled in the throes and then dumped upon the sand.

Beyond the swell, Kiki lay back in the water, her breasts pointing up to heaven.

It was as if we were waiting for an answer to appear in front of us. Where do we go now? Kiki seemed more in control than I did. She still had reasons to go home. Her work wanted her back, her houseboat still there, R. It was her car that we were travelling in, left by her mum at Finisterre. She had a plan. I was adrift. Disillusioned. No revelations had been found. Only an edge and a drop.

We took a room in the town of Lesaska. The Basque community was hungover from the recent San Fermín celebrations, a sixteenth-century festival made famous for the running of the bulls, *encierro*. Although originating in Pamplona, other parts of the country have adopted their own versions. This year three people have died so far, in Valencia. I ran with the bulls a few years ago. A man was trampled and gorged. I tripped on the cobbles of the 825-metre stretch of street as two of the six bulls came charging towards the scrambling crowd. A veteran in the game, a seventy-year-old *hasierak*, picked me up by my collar and threw me against the door of a boarded-up shoe shop. He had been attending the medieval festival since he was fourteen years old. I had as much hope as an antelope calf before a pride of lions. I held my breath as the bulls stormed past me, into a sea of men and boys dressed in white shirts and trousers, red scarfs and berets. If I were to do it again, I would wear trainers (not riding boots), and would definitely consider sleeping the night before.

Scarlet geraniums draped themselves from windows above us. We found lunch at Kasino Lesaka, a restaurant hidden away on Plaza Zahara. The lamb *chilindrón* was rich and I looked out from the arched doorway that we came in from. Elderly men walking together, their pressed dark trousers held up smartly with brown-and-grey-striped braces, smooth opal hands held loosely behind their backs, black berets. Women met at the round wooden tables. There were others that swayed and talked.

'I got another message from Joachim.'

'What did he say?'

'He says that there may be space for Istia and Sasha – together. He says that he can help, at least until the spring.'

'But what's in it for him? Does he still want a foal?'

'I don't know. I don't care, Lu. We are running out of options.'

'So... Sasha and Istia to the Pyrenees.'

'Yes, for now anyway.'

A church called San Martin Tourskoaren Eliza was tucked away at the top of the hill, staring down at the medieval maze below. Pale pink mimosa trees accompanied its tableland. I began to spot these delicate trees in the town too.

Inside the church there were three gothic confessional booths either side of the nave. Kiki walked beyond the crossing and into the darkness of the left transept. She lit a candle. The altar vast, veiled in a covert shadow. The plain stone walls were high around us. I heard a sound. Two men scuttling above the nave, painting or restoring, mumbling to each other in overalls. I knelt down and prayed for Victoria and her mother, for Kiki and her sister, Sasha and Istia, my parents and my siblings. Shamefully I prayed for help. To know what to do. What did I think I would find at Cape Finisterre? What can't I see?

In the cobbles of the town we came across a house with an overgrown garden. Three floors, a terrace and two fig trees. A wooden stable door posed as the entrance. Number 15. The door was unlocked. We glanced inside.

'This is where we would live,' said Kiki.

I told Kiki that I loved her. She went quiet. She then held my hand and said that she loved me too and we headed to a bar called Arrano Ostatua. One final drink in Lesaka. Above the arched frame of the doorway, I saw these words written in red paint: '*Hizkuntza bat ez da galtzen ez dakitenek ikasten ez dutelako dakitenek hitzegiten ez dutelako baizik.* A language is not lost because those who don't know it don't learn it, but because those who know it don't speak it.'

Ten days since we reached Finisterre. In Plaza Beheko, between the thick pillars and geraniums, I wrote a letter for number 15. The house of the figs. I left my address and promised to care for the house and the garden as if it were living. After placing it underneath the front door, we went to the bank: 300 euros for the Gipuzkoa stabling fee, 300 euros for a man to transport the horses to the Pyrenees. To the house of Joachim. The final leg of the journey.

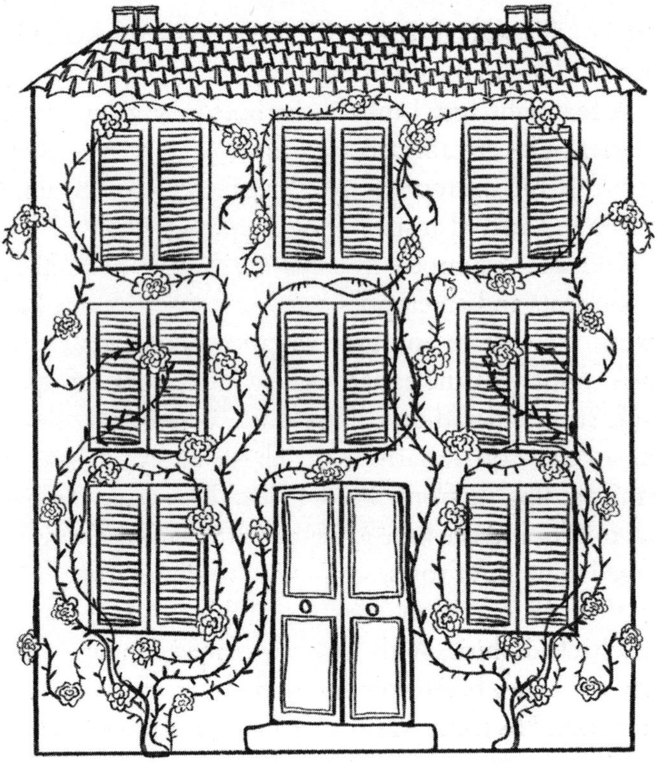

23–25 July
Lesaka – Louvie-Juzon, Nouvelle-Aquitaine

Joachim. He was far darker than how I remembered. He had been working in the mountains.

'A fortnight ago, I moved the horses from one valley to another. The streams became too low. I moved them by night to avoid the tourists that drive fast towards Spain. I left at nine and arrived at six o'clock in the morning.'

Kiki and I jumped into his old blue van. It had soft cotton seats and an empty boot. We drove through Louvie-Juzon, the austere and grey elegance unchanged, into the open country of the eastern valley. He turned off up a dirt track. It meandered up a hillside. Stationed at the top there was a small square farmhouse, three storeys high, a short man standing in front. He was leaning upon a stone wall that overlooked the lime-green pastures below. The wall was draped in limbs of roses, scrambling wildly down.

Wide blue cotton trousers, a blue cotton jacket, a red checked shirt. With tobacco-stained fingers the man removed a navy beret from his head and reached out to shake our hands. His name was André. Hair scruffy and ashen. His eyes lifted his face when he smiled. André lived alone.

'This is where the horses will stay,' said Joachim. 'Where my horses are is too difficult for them. They are not used to that way of life. André has offered to help.'

We walked to the fields André had in mind. String was tied around his waist to stop his trousers from falling down.

'How do you know him?' asked Kiki.

'I don't,' answered Joachim. 'Somehow, he discovered that I have many horses in the mountains, and that they will need good grass in the winter, lower down in the valley. He came to my house in the village and said he might be able to find somewhere for me.'

'He came to you?'

'Yes. I'd never met him before. I have since given him some chickens and some chicken feed. Each time I drive here, I see him watching them walk around in front of his house and into the deserted pig house opposite. He was very happy when I said I know two people who may need his help.'

What André had in mind was a wide five-acre space on the side of the hill. Not overgrown, but enough for a while. The upper half was strewn with trees and bracken. A river ran at the bottom.

We found fifty pickets in one of André's barns and hammered them into the soft ground, attaching 400 metres of electrical tape as we went. We got soaked in the grass. The sun was warm and the air was clear.

The truck crawled up the track and we helped the man unload the horses into their new home.

That night Kiki and I found a restaurant for dinner, L'Auberge du Caviste. The menu – the choice – overwhelming. We agreed that we preferred the life when there was no comparison and no premonition; people were only what you found them to be, no context; the land only as it felt and appeared at that moment. Nothing sweeter than a bed, a bowl of food, a glass of wine, water; the horses safe. With so little we were so full.

Joachim's empty house was dark. We felt our way up the staircase, across the linoleum floor of the kitchen. Lighting a candle, we found a room with bare floorboards. A mattress in the middle.

'This is where I slept when I was here last.'

'This is where I slept too,' replied Kiki.

We woke up still holding each other, just as we were when we fell asleep.

The horses were weathered and rich with the mud and grass they had been rolling in overnight. Their heads rose up sharply when they heard us whistle.

André was resting by the corner of the stone farmhouse. His beret at an unruly slant, his trousers slipping down his waist. Somewhere between wonder and curiosity, he smoked his unfiltered cigarette and followed the movements of the horses. We all walked over to the wall draped with roses. A chicken picked its way up a wooden beam that formed a bridge to the deserted pig-cote. Two dogs lay at André's feet. A big polar-bear sheepdog, like the ones I had come to know in Liguria. The other, a heavily pregnant tawny Pyrenean collie. I asked where all the other animals had gone.

André answered that he no longer even had cows. Other farmers rented his land for the winter. There was a time when he had his own animals though, he insisted. There were pigs and cattle and many more dogs. He had horses too.

'*Une fois, il y avait douze chevaux ici, puis il y en avait six, puis deux et puis aucun.* Once there were twelve horses here, and then there were six, and then two and then none.'

As if it were a well-known fact, he said that all of his animals had gone and all of his friends had died.

'*Avez-vous des montagnes en Ecosse?*' He asked.

'*Oui, nous avons des montagnes,*' I answered.

André inhaled his cigarette with a slow breath, looked out to the other side of the valley, the side unlit by the sun.

'*En Ecosse, y a-t-il des vaches?* In Scotland, do you have cows?'
'*Oui, nous avons des vaches.*'
'*Lait et viande?*'
'*Lait et viande.*'
He turned to me, squinting his eyes. His voice became quiet and intense. '*Y a-t-il des vaches dans les montagnes?* Are there cows in the mountains?'
'*Oui, il y a des vaches dans les montagnes.*'
His face lit up like a child's.
'*Comme ici?* Like here?'
'*Oui, comme ici.*'

We climbed the wooden staircase. I found the taps with a match and began to run a bath. Candlelight, and rising steam, Kiki and I washed together. We crawled under the covers of our mattress on the floor. Held each other tighter than we had held each other before. Perhaps it was me that held her and she that let it happen. Silently, we knew that this could be the last night we might ever spend together. I tried to re-see all of her features. The delicate shape of her lips. The feeling of her jaw within my hands. Her legs with mine. She forced me down and rose on top, her hair draped in the dimness and her amber stones shining. We were together, as if in the waves of the sea.

It was nine o'clock the next morning. We drove fast towards the Spanish border, Col du Portalet. We were late.

The flat open basin of the valley was an archipelago of villages and towns, moving from pasture to forest. The land around us blue and cool. And then heavy oak forests dwindled and only brown grass surrounded the road. Low rolling plains reclaimed the land. Flocks of sheep lingered eagerly in pens, clustered like fallen cairns upon the rugged stretch.

The car came to a halt two miles before the border and we walked on foot to the track of Col du Portalet. Earth ways notched the tan and pale green land, sketching the belly of the valley bowl, threading up, over the top. The shapes of stout horses, button-like sheep, rose-gold cows with bells around necks. We came across a shepherd's hut.

'*Joachim? Connaissez-vous Joachim?*'

The shepherd gestured north.

Eventually there were two bodies amongst a flock of sheep, crowded in a pen. The sun beat to the east, the shapes of the people were bent, as if digging at the ground with their hands. The whines and bleats of the sheep chased through the air. One of the bodies bolted upright amongst the flocked crowd and then waved. It was Joachim.

He took us away from the sheep to see the horses. He had a wooden staff in his right hand. His dark beard and hair were curly and sweat sat upon his brow and dripped down his temples. We followed him and found his herd standing together on a ridge in the distance, within a canvas of blue sky. The grass was greener there.

Their heads swayed, their warm bodies latent in the morning sun. Cattle ambled down the hill towards us and mingled with these bathing animals, seeking the damper shelf of grassland.

'There is no stress for these horses,' said Joachim, running his hand and forearm down necks and across backs as I remembered Eugene doing in Ossès. 'As it is with a human, if survival is the only concern, they grow natural. They are not afraid of humans, or anything that is crazy or strange.'

'Except the tourists – don't they scare them?'

'The sound of the motorbikes is like hell... but they get used to it.'

He led us up a gorge that burrowed into the middle of the hill. At the top, standing upon the rim of the bowl, a navy and green plain stretched below like a rug, a wide flowing stream curving through it. Cows lay down upon the saccharine banks. Hill faces guarded from all sides, the plateau held together by hands made of mountains.

'This is called the Anéou Circle.' Joachim pointed down to the arcadia with his staff.

A shape crossed the disc of the sun, a sudden shadow cast upon the land. And then another. We looked up. Vultures, at least ten of them, flying towards us. Raspy calls rang louder as they soared over our heads, down into paradise.

'Something is dead,' he uttered.

We walked together in the direction of their flight. More vultures speckling the blaze of light upon grass and rock, and we were all moving together in a calling, vulture and man.

A wake of twenty circled a space that lay ahead, hidden somewhat in the shade of the western hill side. We approached. The unmistakable pang of rotting flesh cut through the air.

I jumped up onto a rock. Twenty metres ahead I saw the body of a dead horse. A mare, lying on its side. Grey tongue hanging out from its open mouth. A relentless gang of a dozen vultures ripping the flesh to pieces. They fought for their meat; their black wings rose up and down in warning and anger. Hooked beaks plunged into the belly that had ballooned and exploded days before. The mare had no eyes, only empty holes.

I glanced beyond the sight of the rotting animal. Over a hundred vultures, spun-out above, waiting their turn.

Joachim said they will scavenge and fight like this for up to three days. They will then leave, returning once the rest of the mare has begun to decompose. The remaining flesh easier to tear.

'The horse belongs to another farmer. It's a meat horse. These ones are usually sold to Italy... or Switzerland. But they are not worth as much as the foals.'

'The foals?'

'Since whaling has been banned, a new luxury has emerged in Japan: Pyrenean foals. The young horses are fattened up and then taken from these hills. They are flown east, alive, before being slaughtered on arrival. They are then served as sushi.'

Kiki said goodbye to Joachim, and we drove away from Col du Portalet, back down the valley. She collected her things from the house. We drove on to André and the horses.

We saw them from afar. Ducked under the electric tape and went into their dishevelled home. They were eating in the long grass and they were together. They ambled over to us, lazy. Kiki took Istia's bowing face in her hands and kissed her nose and stroked the space between her eyes. She then put her bare arms around her horse's neck. Sasha stood close.

The two of us then meandered down the track that led to the pastures below. We held each other. One day I will ride with you again, just like we said we would. Beyond Finisterre.

She slipped out of my grasp and I watched her get into the car. She brought her hand to her chest, holding tight the malachite necklace, and then, inharmonious, the car pulled away. A fog left behind. The car turned left at the tarmac road and I watched as she drove out of sight, her hand out the window, balancing in the wind. Back through the places we had ridden from, back to everything that she now had to face.

We made no plans to see each other. We made no plans beyond keeping the horses together.

I travelled on the tyre marks of her car and then turned right at the road, back to Louvie-Juzon. The sun was hot and I couldn't think about doing anything other than walking. Joachim's house was empty. A temperate breeze blowed through from the open and broken windows. On the kitchen table I found a book from Kiki, *The Letters of Vincent van Gogh*. The last book Siu ever read. Kiki had turned down a page with these words written,

> If ever you fall in love, do so without reservation, or rather, if you should fall in love, simply give no thought to any reservation.

I read until I slept.

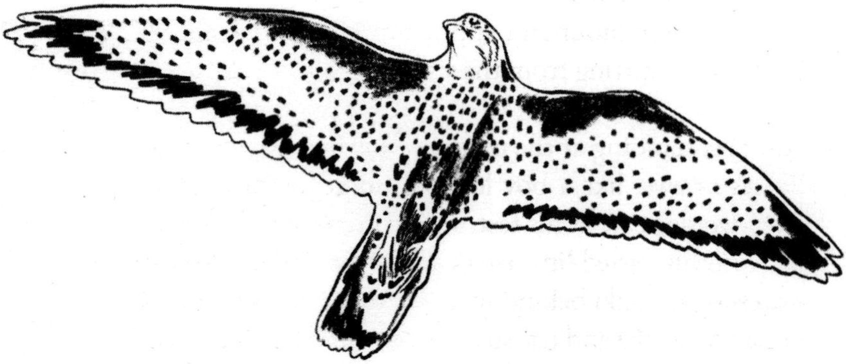

26 July –
Louvie-Juzon –

The pillow next to me still holds the shape of Kiki's head. I am alone on the mattress on the floor. This is the first morning.

An amethyst sunlight finds its way through the cracks in the ceilings. I walk barefoot upon the floorboards. To the west, the blue mountain appears morose above the village. Later I hear stirring from the street.

André is standing at the corner of his house, witnessing the horses in awe, like a boy looking up at mythical creatures. The two dogs are at his feet, an unfiltered cigarette propped between his parted lips. Istia's eyes seem darker today. She is searching for Kiki behind me, near me, somewhere she can't see, and I stroke and reassure her that it's all going to be OK. I try not to think of anything beyond the texture of her neck and mane underneath my right hand. Sasha looks tired. He lets out a deep sigh and I feel his head heavy above me as I hug his neck.

I follow André to the wall that overlooks the valley. A peregrine flies across our view and is lost in the nebulous shapes of trees upon the other side. There are moments when this land is like Scotland. But then, trembling within the still core of all of this space, there seems another province; the lurid colours of the earth, the brasher torrents of water, the lithe, knowing way that the birds fly, bored, as if they are just paying a visit from a secret, incarnate place. If I close my eyes this valley will continue. Nothing will stop. For these past months, I have been walking along a slow-breathing body. I only realise this now. Covering so much land I have seen so little. André invites me inside.

As it is with Joachim's kitchen, there are white-and-red linoleum tiles on the floor. A large black pot is hung above a waning fire like a cauldron. André slumps down upon a wooden chair and asks me again if there are mountains in Scotland and if, in those mountains, there are cows. I reassure him that there are. He pours two glasses of rosé from a plastic container and we listen to the sound of the fire. Somewhere in the room a clock is ticking. It gets late. As I get up to go André looks up from underneath his beret, concerned. '*À demain?*' he asks. I nod. '*Demain.*'

I decide to find a new path back to the village. I close André's door and head down to a track that leads from the field below the horses into a glade of rich grass. There are trees roaming here in solitude, wooden, crooked people lost in a maze; some have been felled, some remain, leaning awkwardly upon themselves. A flaming white stalk lifts off, shaking the dry branches. Along the new way I move. Chestnut trees gather and reach for each other, forming an embrace that takes me in and out of daylight. The track becomes ignited by ivy, Irish shamrock and wood sorrel that glow on the stone wall. I take care to travel slowly, altering the pace of my steps so that I notice how the ground actually feels on the balls of my feet. Strangely, I have not yet felt empty or alone since Kiki's departure, only a new closeness to where I am.

At the back of Joachim's house I discover an entrance to an overgrown vegetable garden, and amongst the velvety green beans I watch nine ducklings following their mother in a train that crosses their little jungle. Their whole existence revolves around this garden. I lie upon the mattress and my eyes follow the flame of the burning candle.

There are peaches, early raspberries, ceramics and enormous courgettes in the square. It's market day. I move on, back to André's farm, slowly now along the new shamrock way. Sasha and Istia nicker and trot towards me. Their bodies press against my shoulders, asking things but wanting for little. Just curious, perhaps, about what happens now. I don't know either. But we are here, together. For the first time in almost four months there is no further place that we are headed. This field, my path in green, is now the world. I am comforted in the knowledge that they are growing closer to each other by the day. Soon I will become useless to them – the way it is meant to be. Just like the valley. In reality, I mean nothing to the force of their nature, nor does their nature necessitate a human eye or hand to reveal its presence. While time makes them grow and diminish in stature, there is a deep, intransigent spirit that seems to come before and after their beings. By spending hours in the presence of these animals, I seem to change, catching glimpses of what lies within them, beyond them. The mystery.

I set about to extend their wilderness. This way they will have enough grass to keep them full until the autumn transhumance, when Joachim plans to introduce them to his own herd in the winter pastures. I use a scythe to flatten the brambles. My arms and legs are cut all over. Joachim and Morgan come down from Col du Portalet to help. Morgan's body is the colour of walnut from the sun. She fills her cupped hands with raspberries until they overflow. She then rolls up her torn t-shirt to use instead. Her sunburned hair has streaks of blonde and falls over her strong shoulders. She has a primal kind of beauty, androgenous. A temptation for a god. She leaves with raspberry juice all over her hands, her navel, forearms and around her lips. The berry stains and the blood from the cuts make more sense upon her skin than the clothes that cling to her.

The rain pours down and thuds upon the concrete village. The walls of Joachim's house are going to burst from the pressure. I'll be lifted from these foundations and taken away upon a new forming sea. I imagine the pale stretches of Col du Portalet will be trembling. The ridge lines reshaping. I sleep soundly, covered by everything, accompanied by falling water. My last thought is the face of Kiki and seeing her body at the edge of a river.

Light wakes me from through the glassless windows. I look down at the square and expect to see floods and driftwood, but only darkened patches upon the asphalt show any signs of what occurred overnight. Walking along the path, the smell of trees is sweet and muddy. New patterns are revealed. An American basswood tree has begun shedding its leaves. I wonder how many leaves fell in the storm. Petals are emerging, fermenting in colour and steam. The ground glimmers more brightly, blinks of burning magnesium. I discover a wildflower that joins the tundra: hemp-agrimony. It's a fine, wild angelica that grows high with a blushing clustered head, crowning like an oak tree. The long pale meadowsweet is the highest of them all.

My body slows and I am forced to stop. I sit down on the wall, and I start to weep. I cry. Big, heavy tears. I can't control them. The storm and the rain in the night was a duvet over me. Holding me so tight. It doesn't make sense, but I feel so terrifyingly invisible. And free. As if I too am being soaked to the core, a blade of grass smothered in green life. Everything appears reinvented. I never saw this when I was with Kiki, when we were moving. This is all for the first time. Now that the journey is over.

I eat and sleep silently, heavily. I am living amongst breathing things made of colour, so close to them now that this valley is unrecognisable to when Sasha and I first passed through. A veil has been lifted. I need this green way to hold me still, to keep me buoyant. I don't want to ever leave this state. Kiki is gone and the memory of her head no longer shapes the pillow next to me on the mattress. I am left now with only a path of the valley, the ceiling of an ever-changing sky. A room of the moments in between.

André stands at the wall of roses. We speak about the rain and of the temperament of the mountain cows and of Istia and Sasha. Both of them are getting fatter by the day and their coats are bronzing and soft. It seems they know we won't be moving on. They appear at home. The sky darkens. The clouds move as they did upon the summit of Mont Férion, encasing us on Siu's birthday, and I stand and I watch closely. A shimmering vane of lilac comes and goes. André turns to me and asks if I saw lightning last night and if I heard the thunderclaps. The clouds heave a little, the heart rate of the valley increasing. I tell André how formidable the land and the trees are here, and he inhales his cigarette and then looks at me, anxiously. He asks me if there are mountains in Scotland. Once more I assure him that there are mountains. He asks me if there are cows in those mountains. There are, I answer. I have *seen* cows in those mountains. His wispy eyebrows rise up underneath his beret and he grins like a cat.

We sit in his kitchen for some time with the fireplace and the red-and-white linoleum floor. I can only imagine the winters here, the cold. I would love to be here to feel that cold. With glasses of Ricard, we watch the driving rain through the window frames as if it is only us who can see it. The fire rejects a glowing piece of bark. André waves his hand in dismissal and we watch it smoulder on the floor. I could sit here forever. I trust this man I don't know. I trust Joachim and the things of this valley. I think of the fire that I wrote by at Castello del Calcione, almost four months ago. And then I recall Naples. Ciro in the warm-lit workshop, and the prince. I don't think I will ever see him again. I am now with the shepherds.

The rain stops and I put down my glass and go to find the horses. They nicker and amble over to me. Now ready to be released into their extended wilderness, I disconnect the electric wire and travel with them to show that it's safe. Istia puts her nose to the ground and inhales the scents of this new space. Her hooves move, tentatively, daringly, and her legs then lead her beyond the place where the wire once was. Sasha follows and then, with a jolt, the pair run together into the untrodden. They pause and tear at the grass before raising their heads and turning back to look at me, noticing I have not followed. I go to them. I stand with them, holding their faces as they bow their heads. Sasha puts his nose to my chest.

Moss lights up the stone wall of the path like a trail of glow worms. There are rooks, soaring high above dripping trees.

Afterword

April 2024
Fife, Scotland

Dear Lu,
 I forgot to say goodbye to the horses but made sure that they were fed this morning. They are getting a mixture of feed at the moment; alfalfa, conditioning cubes, biotin and vitamin supplements, some linseed oil and a little pinch of salt. It seems like they are slowly regaining their weight. They have done well, surviving their second winter out in the fields, first in the Pyrenees and now in Scotland.
 Your mum gave me a kiss and said I love you as she dropped me off at the train station. I'm more tired than I want to be. There was wine last night, and there were cigarettes. We got talking about you, as we always do at some point. Apparently, you told her that I taught you to be more present. More 'in the moment.' She said it happened in a field somewhere in France, and I knew the day.
 It was the day of Arles, where Sasha climbed the stone steps towards the amphitheatre like a mountain goat. Where we sat down for a coffee and a croissant and an orange juice, the horses tied up in front of us overlooking the Roman theatre, when you turned your piercing blue eyes to me and asked me if I ever felt that, when we set off every day, we entered some different world, a world of our own. The four of us,

you, me, Sasha, Istia. A world that no one else was able to enter.

But that was not the moment your mother was talking about. It was after that, after Arles, after the poppy fields. We were cantering through a rough, wild patch of land, with high grasses growing on either side of the sandy track. When we saw an oak tree we stopped to have lunch. I remember that it had become a daily sport to find the best lunch spot. We let the horses roam free and fell back in the tall grass.

We couldn't see each other. You started: 'Isn't it a shame that one can only really value these moments much later, when they have already gone by? I know that in two years' time I will think of this moment and miss it.'

It was typical of you to say and it made me sad. I made an attempt: 'What about these clouds, the blue, what do you see? What about those dog-like horses, free and loyal, what about this late-afternoon sun on your skin, what about this person, this new friend next to you? Look, look, look around you, inside you, above you.' Later, when we got up, we embraced and it electrified me.

The pastures glide by as the train rushes down the country. I will resume the horses' training as soon as I get back to Scotland, preparing them for the upcoming ride across the Highlands. It's a short route, about a hundred miles in six days, so we can take it slow. It'll be our second ride in Scotland, this time raising funds for two local suicide prevention charities.

You are down in Oxford, where I am coming to see you, coming to distract you from your master's in Creative Writing. I will then move on to Amsterdam, *for my sister's birthday on 26 April and our first family therapy session the day after. I will undergo it all, grieve just like we do every day.*

It will make little difference that there is another anniversary. I will just sit quietly and wait. I will wait until we get back to the horses, call the farrier, groom the tack, top up the hay, look up to the sky, look out for the next field, fall back into the tall grass.

Yours,
Kiki x

Acknowledgements

Some names of individuals in this book were changed for their privacy.

There are certain people who helped me when this was all still something in my head. Philipa Torlonia. Thank you for your vision, your time and your quixotic heart. You lit the fire that started it all. Peter Crisp. You shaped the genesis of this undertaking with kindness and care. Apologies for any moments of madness. Thank you. Ita Marzotto. Without your expertise and generosity, Sasha and I would have been unable to even begin. I am indebted to you.

This journey would not have been possible without the hundreds of strangers that I met along the way. After the first step was made, we were in your hands. Food, hay, water, advice, medicine, some wine, a hug. I am fortunate enough to say that many of these people are now friends. To Leila and Serena: Liguria would have been unpassable without your dream. I miss you both very much. Joachim and Morgan, you helped when Kiki, the horses and I needed it most. Thank you both. I have no idea what we would have done without you both. Probably ridden on into the sea.

Gwan and Bernadette. Your support before, during and after is a constant reassurance. The strength of your family makes me know more about life.

To the three people that make up the herd. Raffi. Your warm smile, calming eyes and deep hugs seem to cure everything. Your presence made me and many feel calm when it really mattered. Mariella, I am lucky to have you as my sister, and feel sorry for you for having me as your brother. Being related to you is worth living for. And Kiki. Thank you for teaching me how to see. And how to ride. I am always with you. Wherever you are.

Back home, I would like to thank Hannah MacDonald for taking me through this process so patiently and Molly Beardall for your beautiful illustrations. Thank you Caroline Duncan for being so kind and for putting up with me as your lodger (I still owe you £150). To Kirsty Nye and all the horses of Ross Nye Stables – thank you for providing me with a job when I first came to London. This is all your fault! To my parents – you have never doubted and never curbed, you have only given, listened and loved. Wherever I am, this makes me feel held. And finally, Sasha. Thank you for trusting me. Together, with Mariella, Serena, Leila and the spirit of the Ligurian people, you have created the first conclusive horse trail across the Ligurian Alps in recorded history. Scotland may not be quite as sunny as Italy but the grass is certainly green. What you and Istia are now doing for charity is worth the midges and the bogs, I promise. Besides, it could be worse – you could be living out your days riding in circles, sleeping in a wooden box.

Before setting off, I dedicated this journey to a charity that combats the psychological traumas experienced by Ukrainian refugees. I was determined that this enterprise was going to do some good somewhere. Kiki chose a Dutch organisation that destigmatises neurological divergencies. All funds raised went directly to both causes. Thank you to all of those who donated and supported.

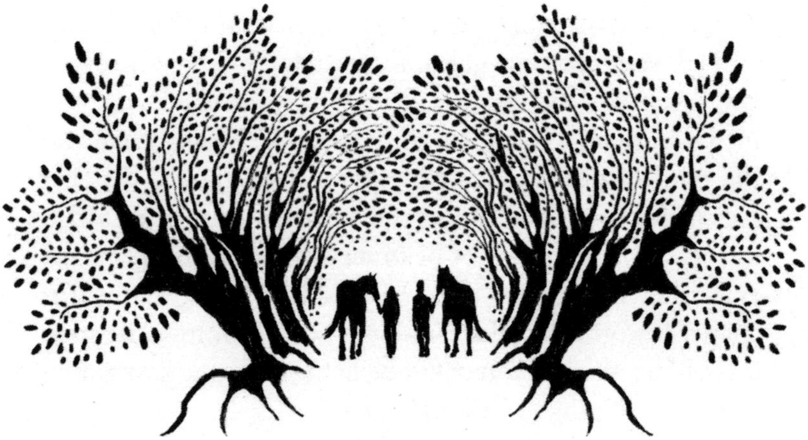